Dreams
The Theatre of the Soul

Dreams:
The Theatre of the Soul

Through contemplating our dreams, we can learn much about ourselves.

Joan Lougheed

*We are such stuff as dreams are made on,
and our little life is rounded with a sleep.*

William Shakespeare
The Tempest

*To Dennis,
Follow your dream...
Every Blessing
Joan*

Dreams:
The Theatre of the Soul

Published by Lochan Publications
15 Lochan Avenue, Dunoon, Scotland PA23 8HT

Copyright © Joan Lougheed 2013

ISBN: 978-0-9926731-0-9

Printed in Scotland by: E & R Inglis Ltd
84 John Street, Dunoon, Argyll PA23 7NS

The author asserts the moral right under the Copyright, Designs and Patents Act 1988 to be identified as the author of this work.
All rights reserved. No part of this publication may be reproduced, stored in a retrieval system or transmitted in any form or by any means without the prior consent of the author, nor be otherwise circulated in any form of binding or cover other than that which is published and without a similar condition being imposed on the subsequent purchaser.

To Eric –
Who believes in me, has encouraged and supported me throughout.

Thanks to all who have inspired me and encouraged me to keep dreaming. Especially to colleagues whose inspiration motivated me to research and write this book: Michael Openshaw, Phillip Bauser, Colin Andrews.
I rejoice as I remember all those (too numerous to mention individually) who enthusiastically supported my Dreams Study Groups, Workshops and Seminars and helped make them exciting and meaningful.
I am truly grateful for the encouragement of friends in the Erskine Writers Group.

Front cover picture: "Landscape with the Dream of Jacob" – Michael Leopold Lucas Willmann 1630-1706

Table of Contents

Preface: Dreams 1

1. The Theatre of the Soul 5

2. The Spiritual Dimension of Dreams 13
   The Three Facets of Our Humanity
   The Spiritual Influence on our Physical Being
   The Spiritual Influence on our Psyche

3. A Scientific Perspective on Dreams 23
   Clinical Studies on Sleep and Dreaming
   A Psychological Perspective on Dreams
   Views on the Function and Purpose of Sleep
   Psychological & Spiritual Connection in the
   Supra-conscious

4. Different Types of Dreams 35
   Common Dreams
   Nightmares
   Transgression Dreams
   Transcendent Dreams
   Wish Fulfilment Dreams
   Confirming Dreams
   Warning Dreams
   Precognitive Dreams
   Psychic Dreams
   Prophetic Dreams
   Premonition Dreams
   Recurring Dreams
   Lucid Dreaming
   Waking Dreams
   Visions
   Visions in Meditation
   Déjà-vu

5. Scripture References to Dreams and Dreamers ...53

6. Dream Recall 83
   Remembering Dreams
   Recording Your Dreams
   Reflecting on the Dream
      The Atmosphere of the Dream
      Emotions in the Dream
      Common Feelings in Dreams
      Feelings on Waking
   Examples of Completed Dream Worksheets
      Jacob's First Dream Worksheet
      Jacobs Later Dream Worksheet
      Pharaoh's Dream Worksheet
      Claudia Procla's Dream Worksheet

7. Philosophy of Dream Interpretation 109
   The Mood
   The Setting
   The Scenery
      Objects
   Dreams and the Five Senses
   Actions in Dreams
   Sexual Acts in Your Dreams
   Questioning your Dreams

8. Colours, Gems and Metals 123
   Diagram of the Endocrine System
   Gems
   Metals

9. Numbers in Dreams 141

10. Dream Characters 153
    Our Multiple Identities in the Theatre of the Soul
    Our Many Selves in the Good Samaritan Parable
    Common Dream Characters
    Personality
    Self and Shadow Self
    Family Members
    Archetypes
    Undesirable Characters
    Clothing and the Persona
    Occupations

11. My World 165
    Buildings in Dreams
    The Great Outdoors
    Vehicles in Dreams

12. Animal Life & The Four Basic Elements...........173
    Terrestrial Animals
    Fish and Aquatic Creatures
    Birds
    Insects
    The Four Basic Elements
        Air
        Water
        Earth
        Fire

13. Emotional Healing through Meditation and Lucid Dreams 185
    Meditation Exercises

Exercise 1 – The Counsellor
Exercise 2 – The Picture Gallery
Exercise 3 – The Staircase
Exercise 4 – A Walk with God
Picturing Jesus
Psalm 139

14. Common Dream Symbols..................................201

Appendix: Various Dream Worksheets...................325

Bibliography..337

Illustrations:

Front cover: "Landscape with the Dream of Jacob" – Michael Leopold Lucas Willmann (1630-1706)

Veiled Windows of the Soul..8

Enlightened Windows of the Soul 10

The Triune God and Our Human Tri-unity...............19

The Human Brain..26

The Human Mind or Psyche 28

Jacob's Dream 96

Plan of the Tabernacle...125

Diagram of the Endocrine System 133

Gemstones in the Breast Plate of the High Priest ..136

Zodiac Signs and associate Gemstone Foundations of the Heavenly Jerusalem engraved with the Apostles names..137

Picturing Jesus ....196 and 197

Dreams

☯

Here we all are, by day;
by night we are hurled by dreams,
each one into a several world.

Robert Herrick (1591-1674)

Preface: Dreams

The day has ended – at long last! It's finally time to begin to unwind. Now I need to escape the stresses of this hectic day. The endless demands and pressures can wait for tomorrow when a new day dawns, then I can rise refreshed and invigorated to think more clearly about how to tackle that project. I'm not ready to face tomorrow – not yet. For now I simply want to forget about today. I need to lay it aside and make my getaway from the hustle and bustle of the world and the people who lock me into their expectations.

It is a world that has shaped and moulded me, thrusting me into my present circumstances in time and space. I am who I am, what I am, where I am – right now. There is no escape… But thank God, there is – if only for a brief respite!

I'm more than ready for that blessed retreat into oblivion. I slip into my cosy capsule of escapism. The lights are dimmed, the hurly-burly of the busy day is stilled and peace descends.

The curtain rises smoothly, silently. The stage is set. Subdued lighting picks our hazy shapes, indistinguishable forms creating an atmosphere of expectation. The cast is waiting in the wings, each character eager to make their own dramatic appearance to entertain, challenge, divert or stretch the imagination.

The plot unfolds. Sometimes it makes sense, and then again it bewilders, frustrates, angers…. It doesn't matter. This is the drama of the subconscious mind, the theatre of the soul. Anything can happen. Let the players have their say, do their best – or worst. Each character takes their turn and plays their part to perfection – free to express themselves as they will, for they are not permitted to do so in the confines of the ordered world in which we live.

Eight short hours (or six, or ten) speed by as though they were condensed into just one. There are short intervals between every presentation, but I don't notice them. As I watch each performance the added delight is that I, the audience of one am invited to participate. No, I'm not invited, I simply take centre stage and play my part. I'm given no scripts nor am I expected to attend rehearsals. The props and costumes appear with no need for fittings, dressing rooms or dressers – nor calls to come onstage. I simply slip into my role as the drama unfolds.

One performance is followed by another... and another... and another – all unconnected. It all makes perfect sense – but then it doesn't, and that's the whole point. That's the delight of this drama.

I'm not left wondering what's to happen next. In the theatre of the soul I don't need sense or logic or order – that I get enough of in the prison of my days where I am constantly observed, judged and categorised.

Too soon – too soon, the curtain falls, the lights go up and I must arise to a new day in the world of ticking clocks and calendars, rushing traffic and noise, diaries and appointments, telephones and endless clamourous demands on time and energy.

Thank God for sleep and dreams – the diversions in the theatre of the soul. I may not fully understand – but...*by God I needed that!*

* * *

We are the music makers,
We are the dreamers of dreams,
Wandering by lone sea-breakers,
And sitting by desolate streams –
World losers and world forsakers,
On whom the pale moon gleams:
We are the movers and the shakers
Of the world forever, it seems.

For each age is a dream that is dying,
Or one that is coming to birth.

Arthur O'Shaugnessy 1844-1881

1. The Theatre of the Soul

We all enjoy the recreation of the theatre, cinema or TV drama. We temporarily lay aside whatever has previously occupied our thoughts and activities to relax and be entertained. Relaxed, we welcome the suspension of disbelief for the sake of the diversion from the world of order and reason that taxes our physical and mental energies. Absorbed in the drama played out before us, we slip into the scene and identify with the characters. We are there, caught up in the drama, feeling the atmosphere of the setting and our feelings are given free reign because we know that it's safe. The inner parents (our will and our intellect) give the inner child (our emotions) freedom to play.

When the performance is over, our spirits lifted, we wipe our eyes, look to our companions and nod in agreement – that was good. We needed that break from reality. We are free to express our emotions because the actors were not us, nor were they really suffering or injured, only playing it out for our amusement. We can laugh at the ridiculous comic; weep on behalf of the suffering child; vent our anger towards the brute… or be the monster, for we know that when the lights go up we will not be held accountable. It was only fantasy.

On reflection we discuss the play with others. If they were not there, we will tell them about it. If they were, we will share our opinions – what we thought of the characters, their performance, their roles, the plot and whether or not we would like to see it again. We may not agree on the merits of the performance, but we certainly all agree that all of us need entertainment for recreation in our lives.

Dreams played out in the theatre of the soul are more than entertainment; they are, through recreation, a re-creation. We need to take a break from mental activity for our dreams to process what we have assimilated throughout the day.

Through dream-work we can learn a lot about ourselves – the hidden self; the shadow side; the dark corners of our soul. There is much within us that is hidden from us, but known to others, just as there is much within us that is known to us alone unless we choose to share with others those secrets of our inner life. Dreams give us a new perspective on ourselves – revealing not only what is hidden from us but also what none but our Creator knows.

Dreams are like windows into the soul. They can remain veiled, concealing the mysteries within, or they can be opened and illuminated, revealing the treasures of our innermost being.

Veiled Windows of the Soul[1]

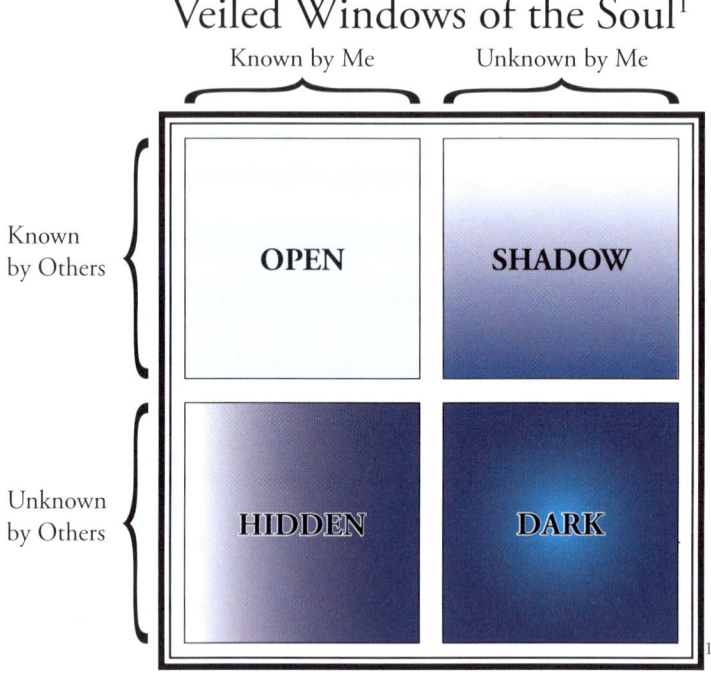

That which is openly known about us – known to us and to others, even through a casual encounter, is our general outward appearance – gender, race, age category, style of dress revelling occupation or status.

That which is known to others and unknown to us about ourselves could be certain mannerisms that we are unaware of – whether or not we snore or talk in our sleep; forgotten incidents in our life; facts that only our parents, relatives or older siblings know about us. Unless they choose to bring

1 Inspired by Johari's Window Model

to light these pieces of information, they will remain in the shadows. Through dream interpretation we can bring out of the shadows the forgotten, or shadow self.

There are things about us that we know and no one else knows because we choose to keep hidden our thoughts, feelings, fantasies, secret hopes and aspirations, or actions for which we are ashamed or fear reprisal. They will remain hidden unless we choose to reveal those secrets to another. Some hidden secrets can be so deeply buried in the gloom that they fester beneath the surface causing decay and destruction. Not all secrets are damaging, but there are some potentially destructive elements that can lead to disaster if left to grow in the gloom – like anger, bitterness, jealousy, prejudice, lust, greed....Dreamwork can bring these issues to the surface where we can deal with them and bring them into the healing light.

We all have dark corners in our soul that are known to no one – not known to us or to our closest companion. These are the things that are known only to our Creator – like the purpose for which we were created, our destiny, our undiscovered talents or potential. Working with dreams can make clear that which is by nature in the darkness of our being. In our dreams we can enter into the dark recesses of our soul, and through analysing our dreams we are able to explore the workings of our innermost being.

In the chapter on Biblical references to dreams and the interpretation of God's message to the dreamer, we will see the spiritual dimension and depths of spiritual significance in dreams.

When we analyse our dreams we are exposing our soul to the light of knowledge with a new understanding. What was openly known becomes much brighter; what was in shadow becomes light; what was hidden is revealed and the mystery of the dark unknown is made clear. This happens in dialogue with your dreams and is even more helpful when you share dreams in a Dreams Study Group or with a like-minded companion.

Enlightened Windows of the Soul

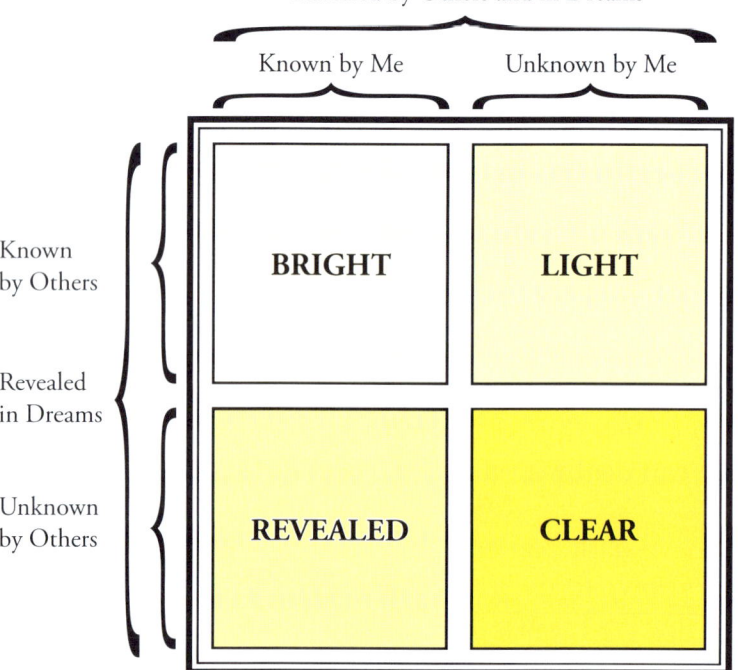

Why is it that so many people don't take dreams seriously? Some folk are adamant that they do not dream. It is a proven fact that all of us dream several times each night. Others will say that they had a strange dream last night and when asked what it was their eyes glaze over or a look of vulnerability overshadows their face and they reply, too quickly, that they cannot remember. Is it that they suddenly realise that their dream was so weird that they may be thought to be deranged, or is it that they know that dreams reveal the secrets of the subconscious mind and they are not ready to be psychoanalysed right here and now? Perhaps it is a little of both. Dreams are weird. Dreams do bring to the surface our hidden, secret inner self – and that is the joy of dreaming.

When we learn to love our dreams we can mull them over and watch as our inner being is exposed and brought into the light of a new understanding. When we learn how to work with our dreams and interpret them correctly, we discover the delight of a new understanding of who we are, how we function and where we are going – and that is exciting. It is like nurturing a scraggy little plant and watching it blossom into an exotic orchid.

There is no such thing as a bad dream, only a dream that is neglected and left to die without having fulfilled its purpose in your life.

*...chief of all Thy wondrous works,
Supreme of all Thy plan,
Thou hast put an upward reach
Into the heart of man.*

Harry Kemp (1883-1960)

2. The Spiritual Dimension of Dreams

Humans are spiritual beings created to have fellowship with their Creator. Within the core of our being there is a longing for spirituality, whether or not it is acknowledged. We yearn to know from where we came and to where we are going. We search for meaning and purpose, to know our destiny and realise our full potential.

Knowing our roots gives us a sense of belonging and looking to the future motivates and gives us purpose. We have a fundamental need to make sense of life, death and the assurance of an after-life. Eternity is within us. In fellowship with God, our core hunger is satisfied. God reaches out to us and guides us to accomplish God's[2] purpose in and through us to fulfilment.

There is evidence that from the beginning of time human beings have had an awareness of the existence of the spiritual realm. We know that Neanderthal man buried their dead with special reverence. Archaeological sites of later prehistoric cultures reveal evidence of religious rituals, sacrificial offerings, altars and tombs. Burial rites were complex and elaborate, often including offerings of provisions for the after-life.

Primitive peoples have an intense awareness of the spiritual realm, of a Supreme Being who created and sustains life, and a passionate desire to be in touch with, and to please the Almighty God.

From earliest times people have believed that dreams, visions, prophetic messages and a personal encounter with the supernatural were the means by which God communicates with us.

Native Americans would fast and pray so as to see visions and receive divine guidance through their dreams. They would then share their insights with the rest of the tribe who would

---

[2] Throughout I prefer not to use 'His' or 'He' in reference to God, for God is neither male nor female but complete and balanced in both masculine and feminine qualities. We can experience God as both or either Father/Mother.

receive the messages with awe.

Ancient Greeks believed that dreams gave warning of illness and brought healing. They believed too that dreams offered divine guidance and inspiration.

Judaism has a traditional ceremony where the rabbi interprets the disturbing dreams and in interpreting dreams he transforms the negative power to bring a positive beneficial meaning of the dream for the dreamer's guidance.

With advances in science and technology, many people tend now to feel that the world has come of age. They no longer want to be controlled or to be answerable to some mysterious Higher Authority that they cannot analyse. They want to manage their own lives and destiny. In general, many educated people no longer believe in the supernatural or see any need to put their trust in someone or something invisible, intangible and incomprehensible. If something cannot be proved scientifically the rational thinker mistrusts it or dismisses it as myth or fantasy.

Visions are then viewed as the mind playing tricks or the result of a mental disturbance, so visions are ignored or not admitted to by the visionary for fear of ridicule or being suspected of mental illness. Dreams are also seen by many as nothing more than the mind relaxed and at play during sleep.

The truth is that God is known by faith alone. As we choose to believe, then God reveals. As we persevere in seeking to know and do God's will, so understanding grows. When we have no desire to be in touch with God our spiritual senses are dulled, we stop listening or looking for signs and cease to recognise God communicating with us.

That is what happened to the Israelites when God told Moses to gather all Israel at the foot of Mount Sinai so that God could speak with them. Moses gathered the people and told them to prepare to meet God face to face. They came in great anticipation, but when the lightning flashed and the thunder rolled and the trumpet sounded they were so terrified that they told Moses that if he spoke to them they would listen, but not to let God speak to them again.[3] They did not want to have another such encounter with God. All that God had offered them was the Ten Commandments and a personal relationship. They rejected the relationship, so God spoke with Moses, as they had requested, and gave him the hundreds of commands, rules and regulations of the rest of Exodus, Leviticus, Numbers and Deuteronomy that followed that encounter – a heavy burden as an alternative to the joyous relationship that God wanted, whereby God would give gentle guidance by God's Spirit.

Many believers today have continued to dull their senses because now we have the Bible and theological aids. They have become dependent on the professionals to give them a word from God. This is so much easier. They can then choose to hear and respond or ignore what is uncomfortable or challenging. God must be listened to and obeyed, but a human being – even a theologian, bishop, priest, minister or pastor can be ignored. So they tune God in and out at will and wonder why so few have visions, signs and wonders in this day and age, and many of those who do, choose to keep quiet about it.

Dreams are one way in which we can again connect with the spiritual realm and hear God speak to us. It is the easiest way to received God's guidance because dreaming is common to everyone. The mind in our dream state is open to the Spirit of God and God can break through the layers of rationality: barriers that modern humans have erected.

The more we practice dream interpretation the more sensitive we become to God's guidance in our waking lives. For through the spiritual discipline of spiritual listening we progressively re-open those blocked channels of communication between us and God.

---

3 Exodus 19:10 – 20:19

The Three Facets of Our Humanity

Of all world religions, Christianity alone recognizes the triune God – Father, Son and Holy Spirit. Even then, many Christians struggle to understand the concept of one God in three Persons. It may be easier to comprehend if we think of God in relation to what we do understand – ourselves. We view ourselves as one being, yet we have three components – body, mind and spirit.

Created in the image of God, humans reflect the tri-unity of spirit, soul and body but the three are so closely connected that we function as one and undivided. Our body is confined in time and space to the physical realm, functioning by the harmonious performance of our bodily organs and governed by the five physical senses of sight, hearing, smell, taste and touch. But our physical body is so closely connected to our mind that the body reacts immediately to mental stimuli. Our thoughts can cause us to smile, weep, blush, chuckle, tremble…

It is even more difficult to distinguish between soul and spirit. Throughout the Bible, the word soul appears to be synonymous with the mind and life of a person. The Oxford English Dictionary defines soul as 'the principle of life and animate existence; an entity distinct from the physical body of a person, living on after the body dies; having moral, intellectual and emotional energy'. I therefore describe the soul as the essence of our being – governed by our will, intellect and emotions – the components of our mind, with inherent identity, remembered stimuli and constantly reacting to our environment.

The soul is that part of us which is uniquely individualistic. Identical twins share the same physical identity through their identical gene structures, but each has a uniquely individual soul. The diagram below serves to clarify the Tinity of God and our human tri-unity:

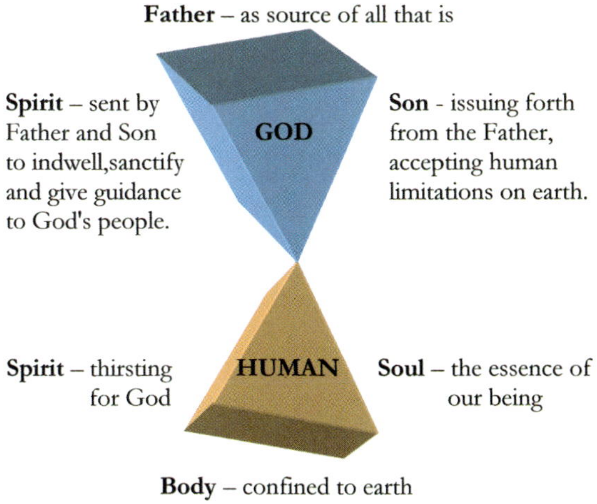

Father – as source of all that is

Spirit – sent by Father and Son to indwell, sanctify and give guidance to God's people.

GOD

Son - issuing forth from the Father, accepting human limitations on earth.

Spirit – thirsting for God

HUMAN

Soul – the essence of our being

Body – confined to earth

The human soul (or mind) also displays triunity in essence:

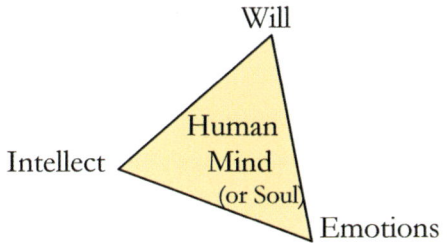

Will

Intellect — Human Mind (or Soul)

Emotions

Spirit, breath, wind and air are the same word in Hebrew 'Ruach' and in Greek 'Pneuma'. In the scriptures spirit is used for the Holy Spirit of God, angels and demons – spiritual beings in the spirit realm and for the renewed human spirit of the person who has received spiritual life as a gift from God. Our spirit is therefore that part of us which relates to the spirit realm having received life by God's Spirit. The spirit functions apart from the five physical senses by a sixth sense of intuition, and complementing the five physical senses. Seeing visions, hearing God speak to us, sensing a smell or taste that another cannot detect, and feeling a touch from God. All come to us through our newly awakened spiritual senses but unconnected to our five physical senses.

Let us then look at the purpose of dreams relating to those three facets of our being.

The Spiritual Influence on our Physical Being

The body is the physical, visible, tangible, audible, animate home of our soul, in touch with and relating to the material world. The five senses of sight, hearing, smell, taste and touch by which we relate to our surroundings are governed by the bodily organs – eyes, ears, nose, tongue and skin. In sleep our body and organs are at rest and relaxed and the level of the growth enzyme increases.

Stimulated, it facilitates healing in the body. Similar enzymes repair nerves, promoting mental stimulation for intellectual growth and emotional well being. There is a theory that this mental stimulation causes hallucinations which are our dreams.

It is during this rest period that the natural healing processes can function without distractions. In some mysterious way, dreaming is vital to the healing and restoration process. Experiments conducted in dream laboratories show that those people who were prevented from dreaming, though given sufficient sleep, experience stress and a decline in their physical condition. Dreaming is essential to our physical health and well-being. Everyone dreams – we need to dream as much, if not more than we need sleep.

Dreams often give warnings of sickness or physical disease. Accounts of this have been acknowledged by many who have acted on those dream warnings. When ignored, these warnings have persisted until the disease has manifested itself physically. Acknowledging the close connection between body and mind, it should not be surprising that as dreams come to our bodies so illness can manifest in our dreams. (For more details see 'Warning Dreams' in Chapter 4 – Different Types of Dreams)

The Spiritual Influence on our Psyche

This aspect is pretty much covered in the next chapter on Science and Dreaming but it needs to be noted that human beings are created in the image of God[4]. God continuously

---

4 Genesis 1:27

comes to us, communicating that presence in an infinite variety of ways; desiring for us to enjoy a personal relationship with God. When our minds are distracted in our waking state through the pressures of life, commitments and preoccupation with worldly pursuits, we fail to hear the still small voice of God. In sleep the mind is disengaged from the worldly diversions of our waking life so God is able to communicate with us in the spiritual language of symbols and images.

This is where dream work is important. Through analysing our dreams we can gain an understanding of the mystery of our innermost self, our God-given potential and purpose in this life. In sleep we make sense of the nonsense of our waking lives.

And what place is there in me
Into which my God can come,
Even He who made heaven and earth?
Is there anything in me, O my God,
That can contain Thee?...
Or should I not rather say,
That I could not exist
Unless I were in Thee,
From whom are all things,
By whom are all things,
In whom are all things?

Augustine (353-430) 'Confessions'

3. A Scientific Perspective on Dreams
Clinical Studies on Sleep and Dreaming

In 1875 Richard Caton, a British scientist from Liverpool discovered that the brain is active, even in its neutral state of sleep.

From there Hans Berger, a German neuro-psychiatrist continued research into brain activity during sleep. He first recognised the alpha rhythms that indicated a state of relaxation during meditation and in sleep. He recorded the first electroencephalograms (EEG) of sleep in the early 20th century.

More research was conducted at Harvard University in the 1930's using Berger's findings. By the 1940's, sleep was viewed with deep interest by scientists, but dream studies from a physiological perspective did not really begin until the 1950's.

In one of his experiments, a graduate student at the University of Chicago attached electrodes to his son's head and observed stronger brain activity coinciding with rapid eye movement, thereafter it has been referred to as REM sleep. This is not the eyes following the scene enacted in our mind while dreaming, as it has been observed in dream-laboratories that people blind from birth also display rapid eye movement while dreaming. REM was therefore linked with dreaming and one large puzzle was now solved in the sleep laboratory.

Neuroscientists have discovered that sleep helps to reinforce the memory by rearranging neurons in the cortex of the brain. One subject noted that when he studied for examinations last thing at night, then slept on it, the material he had studied could be recalled more easily on waking in the morning and for the examination later that day, than if he crammed in the morning prior to writing the examination and without having slept on it.

For scientists, dreams have now become a respectable subject for clinical studies. They are not simply the haphazard firing of disorderly neurons in some kind of random 'epilepsy' as some have proposed, but vitally important mental processes which are beyond our conscious control.

Dreams from a Physiological Perspective

In scientific studies, sleep was found to be a state of chemical regeneration in the brain and dreams were described as a series of involuntary images played out in the arena of our subconscious minds during sleep.

Neurologists described dreams from a purely physiological point of view as responses to natural neurological processes. Though they have attempted to locate the area of the brain that is responsible for producing dream imagery, the exact location of the dream centre of the brain has not been established. It has however been observed that patients with damage to the parietal lobe of the brain cease from dreaming.

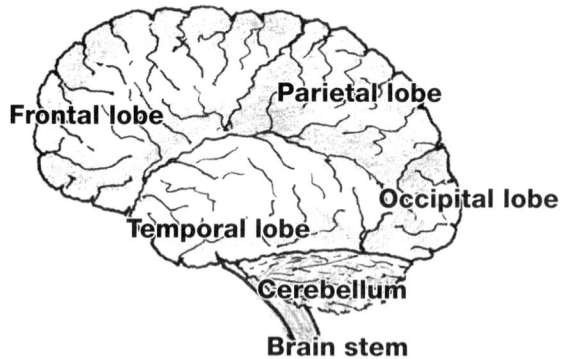

The Human Brain

Through scientistific recordings of brain waves, eye movement and muscle tension during sleep, a psycho-physiological approach to dream research was established and four phases of sleep have been noted.

The first phase lasts only a few minutes when strange imagery is experienced and sometimes muscle twitching or the experience of falling occurs as muscles relax. This phase leads us into sleep.

The second phase pulls us into a deeper sleep and the relaxation of our muscles with little eye movement. It is possible for dreams to occur in this stage, but dreams are shallower than in the following stage.

In phase three, brain waves are accentuated; eye movement and muscle activity is increased. It is in this phase that walking or talking occurs if the sleeper has the tendency to sleep walk or talk.

Phase four is the deepest level of sleep and once again the muscles relax and little or no eye movement occurs. If the sleeper is awakened at this stage it is unlikely that the dream of stage three will be recalled.

This four-phase cycle lasts approximately ninety minutes after which the phases are reversed. It has also been noted that the four phases get closer together and the dream phase gets longer. This is good news for those wanting to work with their dreams, as more dream-time occurs in the morning before waking. Therefore, dreamers interested in cultivating their dream life may want to plan one or two days per week to sleep late or to take periodic dream retreats.

Psychological Perspective on Dreams
Views on the Function and Purpose of Dreams

Many theories have been put forward by the various branches of science – biologists, neurologists, psychologists, philosophers and parapsychologists – as to the functions of sleep and the purpose of dreams.

Antti Revonsuo, a Finnish philosopher, spent a decade observing and recording the content of dreams, illustrating the patterns of threats in the dreams of children, traumatized patients and nightmare sufferers, comparing them with present day hunter-gatherers of various cultures. It is not surprising to note that it has been found that people traumatised by war, abuse, natural disaster and loss have more threat-related dreams.

Revonsuo believed that the purpose of dreams is to

reproduce threatening events so as to practice dealing with or avoiding similar threats. It is not clear whether or not we need to remember the dream to know how to deal with the hazard. He suggested that perhaps simply dreaming it programmed the mind to deal with the danger.

There are widely-accepted observations that most dreams that are remembered are stressful ones – filled with dramatic conflicts and negative emotions.

Psychologists generally tend to take the view that dreams are the activities within the psyche, related to our waking experiences and stored in our subconscious mind. The rich imagery of dreams and their possible relevance for our waking life have had psychoanalysts studying and theorising about the significance of dreams for centuries. Dream therapists and their patients have discussed their dreams in order to bring new insights into the workings of the subconscious mind and the healing of emotions through a clearer understanding of their patient's dreams.

Various psychoanalysts describe five levels of sensory perception in the human mind: conscious, preconscious, subliminal, collective unconscious and supra-conscious.

The Human Mind or Psyche

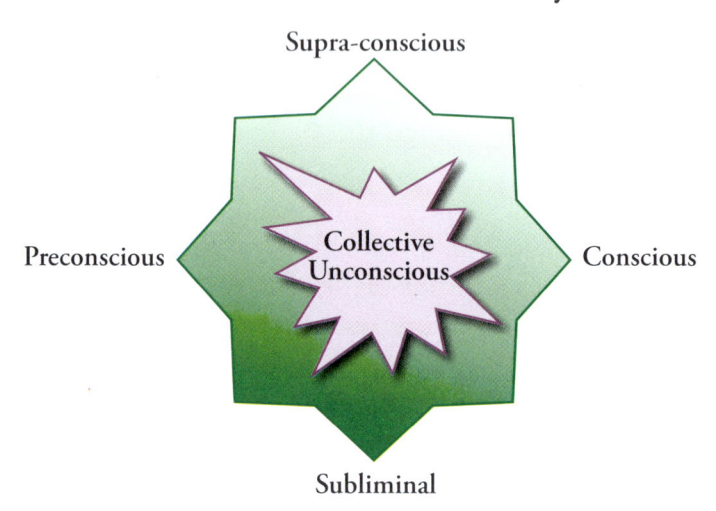

Supra-conscious

Preconscious

Collective Unconscious

Conscious

Subliminal

The conscious mind interacts with the world around us during waking hours. We process through our senses of sight, hearing, touch, smell and taste what we encounter through the day.

The preconscious mind is the memory-bank where information is stored for possible use in the future. These are memories that we are not actively engaged with in our conscious mind but they can easily be recalled at will at any time.

Sigmund Freud describes the subliminal level in the psyche as that which lies below the threshold of consciousness. Stimuli of a low intensity produce a discrete sensation on the conscious mind, not strong enough to be noticed yet intense enough to influence the mental processes or the behaviour of the individual. An excellent example of subliminal stimuli is the reaction to pheromones, which are chemicals released by the body into the atmosphere. They cause a specific reaction in members of the same species even though they are not consciously registered by the five senses.

The subliminal technique is frequently used in advertising – some examples are: The smell of popcorn wafting through a cinema luring patrons to purchase popcorn; in picture advertising, the body language and direction of gaze of the models draw our eye to what the advertiser wants us to see; music is often used to relax, stimulate, excite, lift our spirits or even accelerate the heart rate.

The collective unconscious, according to the Swiss psychiatrist, Carl Jung, is a shared pool of memories or thought patterns that comes to us from the shared experiences of our ancestors and is common to the whole human race. It is an immense depository of ancient wisdom, which coexists with our store of individual experiences of personal unconscious material. He states that primal experiences are represented by symbolic images, archetypes or personifications and are common to all cultures. These symbols often appear in our dreams.

Most psychologists agree that dreams reveal our past traumas and correspond to our present conflicts. Dreams, they say, present a way of working with the turmoil of living. There is also a widely held evolutionary theory that the means of managing danger is passed on from generation to generation in our genes and is stored in the collective unconscious.

The supra-conscious awareness originates as impulses from a higher intelligence. We can say that it is the part of our psyche that is in tune with the infinite, omnipotent and omniscient God, our Creator.

Psychological and Spiritual Connection in the Supra-conscious

According to one unspecified source, 'The supra-conscious, when stimulated through the supernatural spiritual influence, manifests the following nine properties:

1. It has complete control over our physical condition and bodily functions.
2. It has the power to alter the natural course of events.
3. It is always willing to be controlled by the power of suggestion from its source.
4. It is capable of independent reasoning by the process of induction.
5. It has the ability to deduce perfect practical conclusions from a given principle.
6. It is inspired with perceptions of the laws of nature and intuitive knowledge of laws governing the spiritual realm.
7. It communicates by means other than the normal channels of the five senses.
8. It has the ability to determine in advance the outcome of events.
9. It is gifted with perfect memory.

It is interesting to note that corresponding to the nine recognised properties of the supra-conscious listed above, we see the nine God-given Spiritual gifts as listed in the Bible by the apostle Paul in 1 Corinthians 12:1-11.

1. Healing is the special ability to cure physical disorders and restore prefect bodily functions without medical intervention. (Acts 3:1-8)
2. Miracles are performances of powerful acts that have altered the ordinary course of events and appear contrary to the laws of nature. (Acts 9:36-41)
3. Faith is the ability to visualize what God wants to happen and a certainty that God is going to do it even when there is no concrete evidence (Hebrews 11:1ff)
4. Wisdom is the reception of insights into how given knowledge may best be applied to specific needs (1 Corinthians 2:6-16)
5. Knowledge is the supernatural revelation of facts, past, present or future, which are not learned through the efforts of the natural mind. (Luke 2:25-35)
6. Discernment is the ability to distinguish between truth and error and to know whether an act or utterance is from God or not. (Acts 5:1-4)
7. Speaking in tongues is the ability to speak a language that has not been learned (1 Corinthians 14:2). There are three ways in which 'tongues' may be manifest: The first is for private devotional prayer when the person praying does not know what to pray for or about (Romans 8:26). The second is used in public to bring a message from God to foreigners (Acts 2:4-11). The third way is in public worship to bring a message from God bypassing the intellect of the speaker (Isaiah 28:11). This third manifestation needs to be interpreted by someone in that gathering and in a language understood by the gathered people (1 Corinthians 14:27).
8. Prophesy is the ability to proclaim and apply God's truth so that believers may be encouraged, edified or consoled and unbelievers are convinced. (Acts 27:9-10, :18-26, :39 – 28:1)
9. Perfect memory is not listed here as one of the gifts of the Spirit, however it is a means by which the Bible

writers accurately recalled and recorded events that they had experienced decades before. The apostle John, for example, who was the youngest of the twelve disciples of Jesus, wrote the Gospel according to John at least sixty years after the events that he had witnessed. Likewise, all of the disciples most of the time, did not know what Jesus meant when he spoke of the mysteries of heaven, yet, after Pentecost and the outpouring of the Holy Spirit, they were able to recall events and understand the meaning of Jesus words. We will see later how forgotten dreams may be recalled.

It must be noted that all of the above Spiritual gifts are exactly that – gifts from God given to us to serve God's purposes, not our natural talents or abilities nor learned or earned. (See Acts 8:14-24)

It may surprise some that psychologists, dream analysts, therapists and counsellors differ in their analysis and construal of common dream experiences. Flying dreams are one example of how individuals differ in their interpretation of dreams.

Some dream counsellors believe that flying in our dreams is an out-of-body experience, and that the spirit goes to places on the physical and spiritual plane.

Edgar Cayce thought that the psyche travels within the soul in flying dreams and this is a precursor to lucid dreaming.

Carl Jung's idea was that in a flying dream we are expressing our desire to break free of difficulties and restrictions. We have a desire to be free and rise above all limitations!

Alfred Adler thought that to dream of flying reveals the desire to dominate and be superior over and above others.

Sigmund Freud, focusing on the libido, considered flying dreams a sexual expression.

Morton Kelsey's view was that there is no such thing as a bad dream, with one exception – Flying! To dream we are flying is a wish to be detached from reality.

As you begin to work with your dreams, you will learn to interpret you own dreams more accurately than anyone else can, as they are your personal dreams coming out of the privacy of your own mind or psyche, related to your unique experiences and exclusive world view.

To you before the end of day,
Creator of the world we pray:
In love unfailing hear my prayer,
Enfold me in your watchful care.

Keep all disturbing dreams away,
And hold the evil foe at bay;
Repose untroubled let me find
For soul and body, heart and mind.

Almighty Father, this accord
Through Jesus Christ, your Son, our Lord,
Who reins with you eternally
In your blessed Spirit's unity.

Anonymous (before the 11th Century)

4. Different Types of Dreams

Some dreams can be categorised quite easily on waking, like nightmares and transgression dreams, but for most dreams we are only able to determine what type of dream it was by examining and reflecting on it. One always needs to begin the analysis by assuming that it is a common dream, for most dreams fall into that category. Every dream is significant and none should be discarded as simply nonsense or a rehash of the previous day's events, for we can always learn something from every dream.

All of the examples given below were the experiences shared within dreams discussion groups and are shared here with the permission of the individual concerned, or if that person was not available to give their consent, the name and sometimes the gender has been changed to avoid identification and embarrassment.

Common Dreams

Most of our dreams fall into this category. These are ordinary dreams loaded with the issues we face in our daily lives. They usually relate to the events of the previous day. In the dream we review and revise the event, with missing elements filled in and sometimes improved upon or with a simpler way of handling the issue. In the dream you may relive a stressful encounter with an opponent, this time giving the appropriate responses that defuses the tension.

In sleep we sort out the muddle of the day's events and file them into the appropriate sections of our psyche: 'That event needs to be amended, revised or reworked when I get the chance'... 'This needs to be discarded as irrelevant, or as having been dealt with'... 'That event I would rather hide and forget about, or deny it happened because I do not ever want to face it again' (It will probably come back to haunt you as a nightmare or recurring dream unless you deal with it: see Nightmares and Recurring Dreams below) or 'I didn't realise that this incident was playing on my mind – keep it up front to be dealt with in the morning.'

In our dreaming the subconscious takes control, information is sifted, confusion is eradicated and order restored.

Dreaming of the problem that we wrestled with through the day will usually result in us finding the solution in our dream, or if not, we wake knowing how to handle it. Have you ever said of an insoluble problem, 'I'll sleep on it'? It could be that dreams solve the problems by drawing the mind away from 'common sense' solution to some preconscious logic.

Dreaming that I am sorting through and clearing or not able to clear a mountain of paperwork on my desk is a common dream. This is simply the result of having gone to bed anxious about a mountainous job that needs to be tackled.

Physical sensations can be brought into the dream. Dreaming of being shackled and unable to walk could be caused by a foot getting tangled in the bedclothes. The bedside clock-radio switching on to a music programme may come into the dream as attending a concert performance. A dream of wanting to urinate and being unable to find a toilet is the result of a full bladder. Or it may happen that dreaming relief at finding a toilet, wakes a person to discover a wet bed.

Common dreams need to be analysed by thinking back to the previous day or past few days and seeing the links between dream symbols and activities. Simply doing this helps to slot them into the appropriate category.

Nightmares

These are anxiety dreams which are very common among young children. The great big world is a frightening place when one is very small and does not know what is lurking in the dark corners. The fears of our waking world come out in our sleeping state to terrorize us in our dreams. Nightmares can also be the result of stress, unresolved emotional issues or can follow a traumatic experience or occur during illness or while on medication or drugs.

Some people have frequent nightmares that appear to be unrelated to their waking experiences in life. These could be caused by frightening experiences long forgotten but returned to haunt us. Freud suggested that bad dreams help the mind to learn how to deal with the emotions that come from distressing experiences.

A common nightmare is of being chased by something we fear only to find that we are rooted to the ground, unable to run. We try to scream but no sound will come out. We awake in a cold sweat, relieved that it was only a dream. What we need to do is to make up our mind to face the fearful thing the next time it threatens us in a dream.

My sister, Clair, told me once of a lion that often chased her in a nightmare. I suggested that she turn and face the lion next time. She was a little sceptical saying that it might attack her. 'So what,' I replied, 'it's only a dream lion, it's not real.'

The following morning she phoned me in great excitement, saying, 'Guess what, I dreamed of the lion chasing me again last night and I did as you suggested. As I turned and faced him, he lay down and rolled over so I stroked his tummy. It was wonderful!'

There was a time when I had recurring dreams of needing to go down to the cellar under my house to fetch something. (At that time I had never lived in a house with a cellar.) As I approached the cellar I knew that there was something terrifying lurking there. It could possibly be vampire bats, devils, evil spirits or some other diabolical creature ready to spring out and attack me.

I'd awake from the nightmare stricken with fear, and breathe a sigh of relief that it was only a dream. I could not think what it was that was causing these nightmares. I shared this with a colleague of mine who was also interested in dream analysis. He suggested that I needed to go into the cellar and confront the 'demons'. I told him that I simply could not bring myself to do that. 'Take someone in with you,' he suggested. It crossed my mind to ask him to accompany me, but how could I do that? Was I to ask him to come to bed with me? I smiled at the thought and realised that even if I could do that, it would not solve the problem. There was no guarantee that he would have the same dream or even be in my dream when I had it again.

That night I went to bed thinking about Mike's suggestion and had a bright idea. I asked Jesus to come with me into the cellar the next time I had the dream. I dreamed again that night of needing to fetch something from the cellar. I was not aware of anyone with me. I hesitated for a moment, then simply opened the door and went in. In the darkness dozens of horrid little creatures fled screeching in terror, trembling with fear and made their escape out through cracks in the walls, or some other fissures. I knew that they were now gone forever. I awoke with a tremendous sense of wonder and victory. That happened over twenty years ago and I have never since had another cellar dream.

A week later I was reading my set Bible passages for the day and one of them happened to be Psalm 91 and there, in verse 9, was my answer to the mystery – 'Because you have made the Lord your refuge, the Most High your dwelling place, no evil shall befall you, no scourge come near your tent.'

There are hundreds of promises in the Bible and every one of them is conditional. Psalm 91 is a perfect example of that. When we live in God and God in us, God is with us at all times, even in our sleeping and dream state. We need not fear the terror of the night (Ps 91:5)… and verse 15 – 'When they call to me I will answer them; I will be with them in trouble, I will rescue them and honour them.'

There is no such thing as a bad dream, only a dream that is allowed to reinforce our fears to give them a hold on us, which can take control of our waking life, limiting us from reaching out into the unknown. Extending ourselves is the only way of discovering our hidden potential.

Transgression Dreams

Obscene, obnoxious or immoral acts in dreams reveal our shadow, or hidden lower self. Things that we would not perform in public or admit to in our waking life or perhaps even be aware that such thoughts were in us, occasionally come into our dreams. The monster within escapes, and set free, it emerges in our dreams, for it could not or would not come out when we are awake and in control of thoughts and actions. Being naked in public is not a transgression dream but a common dream coming at a time when we feel vulnerable. With a transgression dream, one wakes not only relieved that it was only a dream but horrified at having had such a dream.

After a discussion on transgression dreams Gerald confessed to the group that he had dreamed that he had urinated around the organ in his church. He was horrified by the dream as he is a deeply devoted Christian and the organist in that church. This dream was not the result of discomfort through a full bladder. In analysing the dream we realised that he had, in his dream, been marking his territory as the following week a visiting Worship Team would be coming to the church bringing their musicians.

It is common for someone who is trying to curb an addiction – like a smoker, alcoholic or drug addict coming off dependence – to dream of indulging in their habit. Viewing the dream positively has the effect of facilitating the cure.

Megan confessed to the Dreams Study Group that she had been a bit of a nymphette in her youth. After her Christian conversion she was a changed person, but she began to occasionally dream of sexual encounters with known or unknown men, but always awoke horrified before the act was completed. She would feel guilty, ashamed, sexually frustrated and relieved that it was only a dream. After one such dream she decided that as she was not in control of her thoughts and it was only a dream she was not sinning, so why not just enjoy the encounter? The next time she had a similar dream she carried on to completion, reached a climax – and awoke feeling blessed. (See: Sexual Acts in Dreams in Chapter 7 – Philosophy of Dream Interpretation)

Transcendent Dreams

These are dreams which reveal our hidden potential for fulfilling our purpose in life. We are all limited by others, society, circumstances or that which our ethnicity places upon us. By working with our dreams we gain a far greater view of self and possibilities, which can give us the incentive to realise our dormant strengths.

The most exciting dreams I've ever had were what I call my Mansions Dreams. I called them that because over a period of three or four years, while I was studying for my theology degree and in my years as a probationer minister I had what were not so much recurring dreams, but dreams of numerous different dwellings. None were of homes that I shared with my husband and children, nor were they houses I had lived in with my parents and siblings. Each of the dwellings in my dreams were mine and mine alone, shared with no other and provided for me by some magnanimous benefactor.

Each dream was different and each home in that dream was different, but there were common elements. Every house was enormous. In one dream it was a castle; in another it was a palace; a large Edwardian house; a Tudor mansion; a grand Victorian home; a stately home in the country; a manor house; or an ultra-modern dwelling …

The other common factor was that all of them were accessed across water – either on an island, or surrounded by a moat or I needed to cross a river or a stream to get to it. I thought of it as a precognitive dream – a promise of the scale of my mansion in Paradise. This was reinforced in my mind by the mansion being reached by crossing water – one image of death being crossing the River Styx. (See: Water in Chapter 12 – under The Four Basic Elements.) It reminded me of Jesus' words of comfort to his disciples before his death: 'Do not let your hearts be troubled. Believe in God, believe also in me. In my Father's house are many mansions. If it were not so would I have told you that I go to prepare a place for you? And if I go to prepare a place for you I will come again and take you to myself, that where I am going you may be also.' (John 14:1-3)

The most exciting part of each dream was exploring my mansion. I'd walk through the great entrance-hall, totally awed at the opulence and beauty. I'd open doors and discover luxurious rooms decorated lavishly. I'd gasp at the many surprises behind the various doors – a library with leather bound books on shelves around the four walls; a conservatory filled with tropical plants; dozens of bedrooms each with different types of beds...

When I relayed my dreams to my mentor his response was that I was studying and expanding my mind, learning about the vast undiscovered potential within my soul and realising my capabilities. And indeed it was so. My studies completed, my degree obtained and ordained as a minister, I no longer had my mansion dreams but had certainly discovered strengths, abilities and gifts that surprised me.

Wish Fulfilment Dreams

These dreams are simply our desires being acted out in our subconscious state in the theatre of the soul. It is what we wish would be true in our waking life.

Barbara was perfectly reconciled to the fact that she was infertile. She and her husband had adopted two lovely children, her family was complete and she was very happy and fulfilled as a wife and mother. She told me however, that she often dreamed of giving birth. Sometimes the baby was premature, very small and frail, but with nurture and love it survived and grew strong. On other occasions the baby was chubby strong and looked more like a three-month-old child. Mostly, the babies that she gave birth to in her dreams were the children that they had adopted.

Freud's hypothesis was that all dreams are wish fulfilment dreams. But then he also suggested that all dreams had sexual connotations; especially since his theory of the Oedipus complex states that all men have an unconscious disposition to maternal incest and patricide and women to paternal incest and matricide, which affects their dreams.

Confirming Dreams

These may come at a time of indecision when we need to decide on a course of action. In your dream you make a choice, which is clearly the right one. You awake with a feeling of inner peace and know instinctively that the dream revealed the decision that needs to be made.

Warning Dreams

These are the opposite of confirming dreams. You enter into the situation and the negative outcome warns you of the danger of the action or the scenario to be avoided. You awake feeling relieved that it was only a dream.

Another type of warning dream notifies of impending illness or disease. It is important to know what to look for in warnings of illness as one can become paranoid after reading that dreams can give warning of disease, but when you record dreams in a dream journal you will note repetition and/or nightmares that signify they are screaming for attention. Becoming familiar with dream symbols will give an indication of where to look. For example, animals tearing at specific organs may indicate a malfunctioning.

Chris told the group that at one time he had recurring dreams of his car breaking down on a track. He would wake feeling troubled but not knowing why that should bother him. He was puzzled by it so he drew the dream as best he could. He noted that the shape of the track was always the same. It was kidney shaped. Could this be a warning? He made an appointment with his doctor and asked him to check his kidney functions. It was found that it would be a matter of weeks before he would experience acute renal failure.

Precognitive Dreams

This dream predicts an event before it happens. There are many people who are convinced that they have had precognitive dreams, and gamblers who lay bets on the basis of their dream of the night before.

Jennifer told me the story of how she met her husband. She had been told that if she put a slice of wedding cake under her pillow for three successive nights, she would dream of her future husband. She did this and on the third night she dreamed of a man she had never met. A week later she went to a party and to her surprise, she immediately recognised among the guests the stranger she had dreamed of.

She noticed that he muttered something to his friend then came across the room and asked her for a dance. They danced all night. A month later he proposed to her. Before the year was out they were married. It was not until after they were married that she told him of the dream. He then informed her that when she entered the room that evening, he had said to his friend, 'There's my future wife.' She told me that theirs was a marriage made in heaven.

Psychic Dreams

Clairvoyant, Telepathic or extra-sensory perception dreams are those spontaneous perceptions across space and time of which you could have no rational knowledge. Another example is: two people closely connected dreaming the same dream.

While on holiday one year, my daughter Cindy, her friend Faye and I shared a room. One morning I awoke to hear Cindy and Faye in conversation, but when I spoke to them neither responded for they were still both fast asleep. When they awoke I asked them what they had been dreaming. To my surprise they had both been dreaming a similar dream and discussing their plans for the day. They laughed when I told them what they had said because they had not made any such plans the day before.

Prophetic Dreams

This type of dream, often encoded, foretells an event which will take place in the near or distant future. The message is only understood in time through ongoing dream analysis work. Several of the dreams recorded in the Bible are prophetic dreams. Note especially the dreams of Joseph and the dreams of Pharaoh's cup-bearer and baker who were imprisoned with Joseph; also Pharaoh's dream of the seven lean cows eating the seven fat cows, and the seven withered grain stalks swallowing the seven plump stalks. All were prophetic dreams interpreted by Joseph and fulfilled in his lifetime.

The only way to recognise a prophetic dream is to record your dreams regularly. It is a worthwhile discipline to keep a journal in which to record dreams, events, concerns, blessings, thoughts and prayers. Then to read through the entries, perhaps at the end of six months or a year. You may be amazed to see a pattern running through those experiences; answers to prayers; strange dreams making sense – evidence of God's hand guiding and directing you. Even sporadic journalling will prove valuable.

Premonition Dreams

The vast majority of premonition dreams will occur the night before an event. They are usually more down to earth than common dreams; however, they can also be cloaked in deep symbolism. Premonition dreams are almost always deeply personal, such as a major change in one's circumstances or the death of a loved one. These dreams tend to lack 'padding' and one awakes simply knowing that it is a premonition or short-term prophetic dream.

It is common for a person who has had a premonition dream fulfilled to interpret other dreams that follow as also being prophetic. Prophetic and premonition dreams are rare and what are mistaken for a spate of premonition dreams are probably common dreams reviewing events that play on our minds and dominate our waking thoughts. All dreams should first be viewed as common dreams before re-categorising them as anything else.

The person who cancels a flight because they have dreamed of a plane crash could in fact have dreamed the crash out of a fear of flying playing on their mind before sleep, or dreaming of the death of a spouse could be the result of watching a murder story on TV before going to bed.

Recurring Dreams

These dreams in particular need to be taken seriously for there is something that needs to be dealt with or some aspect of life that is being worked on. These dreams will continue until that which needs to be dealt with is resolved or comes to completion. If one wakes with a feeling of anxiety it is usually a strong indication that there is some unresolved issue that needs attention.

Morton had a recurring dream that his childhood home was on fire. Each time he dreamed the dream, he would try desperately to put out the fire. He would always meet with frustration. Either the hose was too short to reach the house or the bucket too heavy to lift or the water spilled out before he reached the house or he couldn't find a tap or when he found the tap he could not open it or if he did no water would come out... He would wake each time in distress. Sharing the dream with a dream analyst, he was told to just let the house burn down.

The following night he dreamed again of his childhood home on fire and he stood by and watched it burn to the ground. He awoke with a sense of peace and closure. He never had the dream again. Was there something in his childhood that had to be purged or laid to rest?

Lucid Dreaming

A lucid dream is one in which you are dreaming yet aware that you are not asleep. It is not day-dreaming but images played out on the subconscious level, even though you are awake. When this happens it is usually in the semi-conscious state just prior to dropping off to sleep or in the period between sleep and being fully awake.

Having come out of sleep the dream continues to unfold without you directing it in any way. You can control the characters and environment if you wish to, but it is far better to allow it to play out before you as the dream wills it.

Waking Dreams

Waking dreams are different from daydreaming. It is similar to lucid dreaming but you are fully awake and conscious, aware that the scene unfolding in your mind is being enacted on the supra-conscious level.

I have experienced this only once. When I awoke one morning, the demands of the day crowded the dream out. It was totally forgotten, as so often happen, but I had the intense feeling that it had been a truly significant dream. Later that morning, when I had space to be quiet and reflective, I prayed that God would reveal to me the lost dream and what was significant about it. All at once the dream began to unfold in the theatre of my mind, exactly as it had played out in my sleep. I was delighted and able to record every nuance of it accurately.

Visions

The Bible sometimes links dreams and visions, as in Job 20:8 'They will fly away like a dream, and not be found; they will be chased away like a vision of the night.' Some concordances add 'see Vision' after listings of dream references. The Oxford English Dictionary defines vision 'something seen other than by normal sight; supernaturally presented to the mind in sleep or in an abnormal state...'

Vision is also described in a secular sense as having

imagination; or being able to see with the mind's eye what is being planned, but this is not what we are referring to here.

There are then two ways in which we can see visions in the spiritual sense – one is in sleep as a type of dream, the other is in a fully waking state as a revelation of the invisible spiritual realm.

Visions are given by God to reveal to us a reality in the spirit realm. Coming to us in sleep the vision would be a revelation of some aspect of heaven. Someone who has died could come to us in a dream. Seeing Jesus, an angel or someone close to us who has departed this life coming to us in a dream, with a message, could be a vision.

I have often dreamed of deceased relatives, but I wouldn't classify them as visions but under the category of common dreams.

What I would classify as a visionary dream was what Emma told me once. Her late husband came to her in a dream one night shortly after he had departed this life and told her where to find the papers she had been looking for. The next morning she looked in that unlikely place and found them there.

Iain, at the age of three, surprised his mother, Carol, one morning. He had looked up into the corner of the room and begun chuckling with delight and calling out, 'Angels – beautiful angels. They are love – pure love.'

Julie, sitting at her sister's deathbed saw what she described as the most beautiful angel. He was clothed in the finest fabric and his cloak was embroidered with gold thread and covered with real jewels. As she looked at him he held his forefinger to his lips indicating to her that she was not to reveal his presence to her sister, who was at the time awake and conscious. Julie kept her silence. Her sister passed away peacefully that night.

Visions in Meditation

God speaks too through visions that come to us during meditation. As Christians we are taught to pray, to study the scriptures and practice spiritual discipline, but meditation is sadly neglected by many today. I have heard some Christians warn that it involves emptying the mind and is dangerous, because emptying the mind gives evil powers room to enter. This is not so for the person who is indwelt and covered by the Spirit of God is protected.

The neglect of the discipline of meditation is due to several misconceptions. The first misunderstanding is that it is associated with Eastern religious practice, which attempts to empty the mind. Meditation practiced in Bible times and by Christians today is quite different; it is an attempt to fill the mind, or to know God's mind.[5]

A second reason for avoiding the discipline is our busy lifestyle. Our days are so filled with busy-ness, crowds and noise that inactivity, solitude and silence make us uneasy. We want to be in constant contact with friends and fill our time with noise and activity.

Another reason for not building meditation into our devotional time is that we have not been persuaded to practice it. We are urged to gather for worship, make time for daily prayer and scripture reading, but not guided into a contemplative lifestyle.

It is clear from biblical accounts that the discipline was certainly known and practiced by the patriarchs, prophets and writers of the scriptures, and has been part of devotional life down through the ages. Meditation is simply listening to God. It takes time to tune out the clamour of the world around us and be still enough to hear God speak. Moses spent six days in silence and solitude before he heard God speak.[6] It takes determination, persistence and patience.

There are basically five forms of meditation:
1. Scripture Mediation[7] – is internalising and personalising the passage of scripture. Dietrich Bonhoeffer recommended spending a week on a given text; Richard Foster suggests spending that time on one character; or on a phrase; or even on one word. St. Ignatius of Loyola encouraged the

---

5 1 Corinthians 2:7,9-10
6 Exodus 24:15-16
7 Joshua 1:8 Psalm 119:15, 97-99

practise of using the 5 senses. Enter into the scene and in your imagination 'see' the scene; 'hear' the sounds; 'feel', 'touch', 'smell' and get the 'taste' of whatever is there.

2. Centring Down[8] – This method is practised by the Quakers. It is a time to be still and enter into a re-creating silence to allow the busy mind to be stilled. In the silence one lets go of concerns; anything that busies the mind, releasing it to God. Then into the silence and emptiness of the inner-being, receiving the healing peace, love, joy, tranquillity, or whatever God is offering in place of what was released.

3. Contemplative Meditation[9] – The great mystics called it, 'the discovery of God in God's little creatures'. It is not pantheism but opening the mind for the Great Creator of the Universe to show us something of God's glory in creation. Study a sunset; the sea; the sky; the hills; a tree a leaf a petal; a drop of water…listen to birdsong; rippling brook… taste the nectar of a honeysuckle… smell a leaf, the soil, grass and flowers… feel the bark of a tree, the fur of a cat, the texture of skin.

4. Meditation on Current Events[10] – seeking to understand their significance. Prophetic insight is needed to discern where these events lead. This is where keeping a journal is enlightening, when reflecting back on past events and outcomes reveal that seemingly meaningless events in our life had purpose for our ultimate growth.

5. Meditation on our Dreams – which is the focus of this book. But I encourage the practice of all these disciplines for a broader understanding.

To begin meditation one needs to set aside a regular quiet time for contemplation. Choose a quiet place to get comfortable, but not so comfortable as to risk falling asleep. Begin with prayer, asking God to fill every corner of your being with God's Holy Spirit as you open your mind to God's influence and guidance and your senses to perceiving God's

---

8 Psalm 63:1-8
9 Psalm 19:1-6, Psalm 143:5
10 Psalm 73:15-17

word to you. Then gaze upon a picture, an icon, a scene and allow it to speak to you. It may take some time or several sessions where nothing comes, but have patience.

When the vision unfolds simply follow and enjoy as you would a dream. Then thank God, record it, and seek to understand its meaning for you.

Déjà-vu

Déjà-vu means 'already seen'. It is sensing that you have previously been where you are standing, experienced an event, had a conversation and forgotten about it until now, but you cannot remember where or when it was. Could it have been in another life? Or could it be a forgotten predictive dream, the recall triggered by the waking experience of it? God knows.

*'Call unto me and I will answer you
and show you great and hidden things
that you know nothing of,' says the Lord.*

Jeremiah 33:3

5. Scripture References to Dreams and Dreamers

Most people with a fair knowledge of the Scriptures and Bible stories, if asked about dreams and dreamers referred to in the Bible, would respond by saying that Joseph, Pharaoh and perhaps Mary's husband Joseph were the dreamers of the Bible. As we can see from the list below, the dream references recorded in the scriptures are extensive. When we study these references and the interpretations of those dreams, and observe the outcome for the dreamers who acted upon their dreams, we realise that the dreams were indeed messages from God.

God is eternally unchanging – the same, yesterday, today and forever; and God continues to communicate with humans as God always has. Why then should we not believe that God still speaks to us through our dreams today and guides us through our dreams to fulfil our potential or our mission – as God intended?

Here are over forty Biblical references to dreams or visions in the night as messages from God. Some of the better known ones we can analyse and interpret as we could our own dreams.

We dream in pictures; Jesus taught mainly using parables and pictorial language in his messages. The Bible is rich in symbolism, for symbols are a universally understood language. We do not all speak the same language, but we all see and read pictures without difficulty. We simply need to understand the culture of the day to interpret the dreams recorded in the Bible.

1. Genesis 20:3-12 – Abimelech is Warned by God in a Dream

God appeared to King Abimelech in a dream, warning him that he could die because he has taken Sarah, Abraham's wife. Abimelech pleads his innocence because, first of all, he had not yet touched her, and secondly, he had been led to believe, by Abraham, that Sarah was Abraham's sister.

Abraham had not lied to Abimelech as Sarah was his half-sister, daughter of Abraham's father but not his mother.

God informed Abimelech in the dream that God knew that he had not touched Sarah for God had prevented this from happening because Abraham, being chosen by God, was under God's protection. This shows us that God's protection of God's covenant people will not fail.

What type of dream would you say this was? I would say that it is first a Common Dream: Abimelech had that day taken Sarah and was planning to make her his wife. His mind was on his new acquisition as he went to sleep that night so it was logical for him to dream of her. It was also a Prophetic Dream: God appeared to him in the dream, informing him of something that he had previously not known. Thirdly, it was a Warning Dream. Abimelech awoke feeling troubled and knew that he needed to put things right.

Abimelech acted in response to the dream and restored Sarah to Abraham. We are not told that Abimelech asked for prayer and it is not known if Abraham, through the gift of prophesy knew to pray for Abimelech, but he did and as a result Abimelech's life was spared and his wife and female slaves were healed of their infertility.

2. Genesis 28:12-16 – Jacob Dreams of a Ladder to Heaven

Jacob, fleeing from his brother Esau and on his way to his uncle Laban, stopped for the night after sunset. He laid his head on a stone for a pillow and dreamed of a ladder from earth to heaven with angels ascending and descending on it. God appeared above the ladder, reminding him of God's promise to his grand-father Abraham and to his father Isaac; the promise of land and descendants. Furthermore he was given the assurance that God would not forsake him.

On waking, Jacob was awed by the wonderful dream – and not surprisingly so. As a homeless wanderer fleeing for his life, alone in an inhospitable environment, unsure of his future, God had appeared, giving him comfort through the promise of blessings beyond belief.

The ladder between heaven and earth was a symbol of the connection between the two, even in that place of desolation. It affirmed to him that God knows our circumstances at all times and is more than ready to reverse the situation.

This was a Prophetic Dream which was indeed fulfilled in God's perfect timing. Jacob needed to do nothing to make it happen but simply trust God that it would. This, no doubt, gave him strength to go on, knowing that God is faithful to his promises.

3. Genesis 31:10-13 – Jacob dreams of striped and spotted sheep mating

Jacob had a hard life working for his uncle Laban. Laban took advantage of him, cheating him by changing his wages several times in order to prevent his leaving to return to his homeland. Laban realised that he had profited from God's continued blessing of Jacob. The last straw came when Laban agreed that Jacob could keep for himself speckled and spotted sheep and goats of the flock while the plain black ones were Laban's, but Laban withdrew all the existing speckled and spotted from the flock and gave them to his sons.

In the dream God instructed Jacob to return to his homeland assuring Jacob that God would be with him as promised.

Jacob told Rachel and Leah that he had seen in the dream how to breed the flock to produce more speckled and spotted animals in order to regain his just rewards for the years of labour for Laban for minimal wages.

This is a Common Dream. Jacob had been wrestling with the problem of how to gain compensation in order to be able to leave Laban and return with his family to his home country.

He had slept and when he awoke he knew what to do. He then claimed that God had shown him in a dream how to do it, which is quite true when we acknowledge that God gives us wisdom and guidance in our sleep.

There are also elements of Confirming Dream in it – as for a long time Jacob had wanted to leave Laban but been duty bound to serve him. The dream confirmed that he should make plans to leave, so Jacob bred with the flock as he had been inspired to do and prospered enough for him to be able to return to his homeland with assets honestly acquired.

4. Genesis 31:24-29 – God appears to Laban in a dream

God warned Laban in a dream not to speak to Jacob, either good or bad; in other words, 'Leave Jacob alone.' But Laban ignored the dream and pursued Jacob, accusing him of theft and abduction, presenting himself as a loving parent and grand-father and a generous and gracious man who would have thrown a farewell party for them if they had only told him.

This was a Warning Dream. Laban ignored the warning, being a bitter and vengeful man, but God was faithful to his promise to Jacob, protecting and prospering him further.

5. Genesis 37:5-7 – Joseph dreams of the sheaves of corn

Joseph had a dream that his brother's sheaves gathered around his sheaf and bowed down to it while Joseph's sheaf stood upright in the centre.

There is much symbolism in this dream. The brother's occupation was to gather grain and tie it into sheaves to sell or for their personal maintenance; so grain symbolised their labour, wealth and nourishment. Joseph's sheaf stood upright. This symbolised strength, pride and honour. The brother's sheaves bowed down indicating that they were weak, burdened or humble. Wheat is also a symbol of resurrection and new life and corn a symbol of fertility. All this conveyed clearly to his brothers and to us that Joseph was proud, arrogant and thought himself superior to his brothers.

Many would classify this as a Prophetic Dream but it was, in fact a Transcendent Dream revealing Joseph's inner potential for fulfilling God's purpose for his life and for the future of Israel.

God had told Abram that his descendants would be enslaved in a foreign land for four-hundred years[11], but God would bring them back to the Promised Land with great possessions. Joseph was instrumental in bringing his family, the descendents of Abraham, Isaac and Jacob, to Egypt[12]. After Joseph's death, probably thirty years later, the Israelites were enslaved by the new Pharaoh[13] and four hundred years later, delivered by Moses[14]. If it were a Prophetic Dream, Joseph would have dreamed, either of the famine, the re-homing of his family, Israelite enslavement or deliverance.

6. Genesis 37:9 – Joseph's Dream of the Sun, Moon and Stars

Joseph dreamed that the sun, moon and eleven stars bowed down to him. This time his father and mother were included in honouring him. This reinforced the previous Transcendent Dream. Transcendent Dreams do tend to reiterate the message of God's purpose in bringing us to fulfilment.

7. Genesis 40:8-15 – The Dream of Pharaoh's Head -butler

After Joseph was wrongly accused and imprisoned, the royal butler – who was in prison with Joseph – had a dream which had troubled him. Being in prison, they could not consult an

---
11 Genesis 15:12-16
12 Genesis 47:1-6
13 Exodus 1:5-14
14 Exodus 12:40,41

interpreter of dreams but Joseph assured him that God would give him the interpretation, so the butler told Joseph his dream.

He dreamed of a vine with three branches which budded, blossomed and yielded three clusters of grapes – which the butler pressed into pharaoh's cup and presented the wine to him.

Joseph, inspired by God, recognised this as a Prophetic Dream and gave the butler the interpretation, which was that in three days he would be reinstated to serve pharaoh as he had done before.

The process of the vine producing wine through the natural process from the branches budding... to the grape clusters ripening... to the juice being extracted... and fermentation taking place as it was poured into the cup to produce wine was greatly accelerated. Possibly, for this reason, Joseph figured the number three to be days rather than months or years.

The Prophetic Dream was fulfilled as Jacob had said it would be and as God had given him to understand.

8. Genesis 40:16-19 – The Dream of Pharaoh's Baker

The same night, the royal baker in prison along with Joseph and the head butler also had a dream. Encouraged by the favourable interpretation of the head butler's dream, the baker told Joseph his dream.

His dream was that on his head he was carrying three cake baskets. The uppermost basket was filled with all sorts of baked foods for Pharaoh, but the birds were eating it out of the baskets on his head.

This too, by God's inspiration, Joseph interpreted as a Prophetic Dream. He told the baker that in three days Pharaoh would call for him and he would be hanged on a tree and the birds would eat his flesh.

When we analyse the baker's dream we see that it is loaded

with symbols. The baker's job was to produce bread and cakes for Pharaoh's consumption. But the birds were gorging on the bread and cakes – that which was for Pharaoh's table alone.

Bread is the basic food for all people. Grain products are the first solid foods given to babies and are a part of every meal throughout life from the poorest to the most affluent. Bread is 'The staff of life'.

Cakes represent indulgence, luxury and excess. Carried in baskets on the baker's head the bread and cakes were elevated out of reach and out of sight of those around, symbolising inaccessibility.

Birds of the air are symbols of the creatures from the heavens. Consuming what were rightfully Pharaoh's staple foods and delicacies was a treacherous offence. If the baker had chased the birds, it would have been different, but elevating Pharaoh's fare for the birds to consume was unforgivable. Thus Joseph interpreted it as an appalling dream, prophesying death.

As with the butler's dream, the interpretation of the bakers dream was accurate and three days later the baker was put to death.

9. Genesis 41:1-4 – Pharaoh's First Dream

Pharaoh dreamed that seven fat cows came out of the River Nile and fed among the reeds. They were followed by seven lean cows that ate the seven fat cows.

10. Genesis 41:5-8 – Pharaoh's Second Dream

Pharaoh had a second dream that same night. He dreamed that seven full ears of grain were growing on one stalk followed by seven thin ears, blighted by the east wind. The withered ears swallowed up the plump ears. He woke troubled by the two dreams.

11. Genesis 41:15-27 – Joseph Interprets Pharaoh's Dreams

None of the magicians or wise men of Egypt could interpret Pharaoh's dreams. Then the butler remembered that two years before, Joseph had correctly interpreted his and the baker's dreams; so Pharaoh sent for Joseph and told Joseph the dreams. Joseph told Pharaoh that God alone gave him the interpretations and that the two dreams were the same. He proceeded to interpret them.

The seven fat cows and the seven full ears of grain foretold seven years of plenty and the seven lean cows and seven blighted ears of grain foretold seven years of drought that would follow the years of plenty. The fat cattle fed on the lush grass growing along the banks of the Nile. This is clearly a sign of prosperity and abundance. The lean cattle eat the flesh of the fat cattle. This is a sign of something being grossly abnormal. Cattle are not carnivores and certainly for any animal to resort to cannibalism is a horrific sign. No wonder Pharaoh was disturbed by his dreams.

In understanding Egypt's culture of that time, they knew that out of the Nile came the fertility and the very life of Egypt, as it did in that desert land. The Nile god was represented by an ox and in many of their carvings of ancient Egypt, the ox was often accompanied by seven cows.

Jacob interpreted the seven to represent years, for seven days or seven months prosperity followed by famine would not make sense. It therefore had to represent years.

This we now know to be a Prophetic Dream as it was fulfilled as Joseph had predicted. Joseph quite rightly gave God the glory throughout his life. He knew that God was with him[15] and was working out God's purposes in and through him.

---

15 Genesis 39:2

12. Genesis 46:2-4 – God Appears to Jacob in a Vision of the Night.

God spoke to Jacob in a vision of the night, or probably a dream, reminding him of God's covenant relationship to Abraham and his father, Isaac, and telling him not to be afraid to go down to Egypt, for God would make Israel a great nation there. God gave Jacob the assurance that God would go with him and bring him back again.

This was a Confirming Dream for Jacob, who had been anxious about the long journey and without a doubt, fearful. Having experienced so much adversity in his life he probably wondered if this trip would follow the pattern of disappointment and distress.

Much comforted by the dream, Jacob travelled along with all his possessions to Egypt and was reunited with his son, Joseph.

13. Numbers 12:6 – God Speaks Through Dreams & Visions

Miriam and Aaron, the older sister and brother of Moses, criticised him for marrying a Cushite woman. This was a smoke-screen for the real issue of jealousy. Miriam accused Moses of spiritual arrogance. Moses was in fact, an extremely meek and humble man. It is very often a fact that people accuse others of the very sin of which they themselves are guilty. God confronted Miriam and Aaron head to head, telling them that God speaks to others through dreams and visions, but to Moses God speaks clearly and face to face.

14. Deuteronomy 13:1-3 A Severe Warning

God warned that we are not to heed dream interpretations that deny God's supremacy, direct us to reject God or that promote idolatry. God is central to the whole of creation, and unless God is central in our lives we are misaligned. We are commanded to love God with all our heart and soul[16] from and at the centre of our being.

15. Judges 7:12-15 – Gideon and the Midianite's Dream

Gideon was called by God to lead a small Israelite army against the vast Midianite and Amalakite armies camped in the Valley of Jezreel. Facing overwhelming odds, Gideon was naturally afraid. One night Gideon slipped into the enemy camp and there he overheard one of the Midianite soldiers telling a fellow soldier his dream. He dreamed that a loaf of barley bread tumbled into the Midianite camp, struck the tent of the Midianites causing it to collapse and turn upside down.

The fellow soldier interpreted the dream saying that the barley loaf represented Gideon's army and it meant that by God's hand, the armies of Midian would be defeated by Gideon's men. Gideon was greatly encouraged by overhearing the interpretation of the dream, and worshipped God.

The three-hundred-strong army of Israel, led by Gideon, rushed into the Midianite camp that night, armed with nothing more than a torch in a jar in their left hands and a trumpet in their right hand. At the signal they broke their jars, shouted, 'A sword for the Lord and for Gideon!' They blew their trumpets and watched as the enemy took fright, lashed out at one another with their swords, killing many and the remainder fled.

The dream was a Prophetic Dream given by God to give Gideon confidence and assurance of victory by God's power alone.

16. Kings 3:5-15 – God Questions Solomon in a Dream

Solomon loved God and offered a thousand burnt sacrifices to God over the years in thanksgiving for God's grace and mercy shown towards his father, David. God then appeared

---
16 Deuteronomy 6:5

to Solomon in a dream and asked him, 'What shall I give you?'

Solomon was acutely aware of his immaturity and inexperience in the challenging and awesome responsibility which lay before him as king of Israel. He asked God for an understanding mind and the ability to discern between good and evil in his task of governing God's people.

God was pleased at Solomon's recognition that the tribes of Israel were God's people and not his and that he had not asked for prosperity, prestige or power. God then granted him wisdom beyond anyone before or since. God also gave Solomon wealth and honour as no other king had in his day.

This dream had the elements of a Common Dream, a Vision in a dream and a Prophetic Dream. The Common Dream element was the result of Solomon being at that time anxious about his role as king and this played on his mind even as he slept. The Vision element was God appearing to him in the dream with a question and a clear and direct message of consolation and promise of the gift of wisdom. The Prophetic element was the unasked for gifts of wealth and military success.

17. Job 4:12-21 – Eliphaz' Vision of the Night

Eliphaz told Job of the spirit of knowledge that came to him in a dream vision. The supernatural presence of the messenger caused fear and dread because he did not know at first whether the spirit was good or evil, divine or demonic. When the spirit spoke, he realised from the message that it was from God; for it spoke of the majesty, power and divine authority of God. Demonic spirits do not revere God. What he was saying was: that according to human standards, Job may be considered blameless, but from the standard of divine righteousness no mortal is guiltless. Holiness transcends ethical standards.

This was a Dream Vision for Elephaz' enlightenment more than for Job, as Elephaz and the other two friends of Job were standing in judgement of Job. God gives dreams to the dreamer not to a third party. We do need a third party's help on occasions to interpret our dreams, but not to do our dreaming for us.

18. Job 7:13-15 – Nightmares from God

Job recognised that nightmares are also from God. God does not only comfort the afflicted but on occasions, afflicts the comfortable, as God did with Job. We need to be challenged to realise our full potential and stretched in order to grow emotionally, mentally and spiritually; it is for our own good and spiritual growth. A loving parent disciplines the errant child: punishment teaches us obedience and suffering is the consequence of breaking the law. How much more do we not suffer when the holy, righteous spiritual laws of God have been broken? God's laws stand firm – in fact, we cannot break them but are ourselves wounded through kicking against them.

Nightmares warn us of what is wrong in our lives so that we can be aware of it and get back on track and experience the peace of God.

Note that at the end of Job's suffering, when he had learned the spiritual truths of God's majesty, power and authority, God blessed him abundantly and restored to him double of what he had lost in the time of his suffering. (Job 42:10,12)

19. Job 33:14-17 – Elihu Reminds Job that God Speaks Through Dreams

Elihu had remained silent while Eliphaz, Bildad and Zophar, Job's three friends, accused Job of having deserved his suffering. Elihu spoke up at last with wisdom and spiritual insight, saying that God communicates with humans in many ways which we often do not perceive or understand. One of the ways in which God communicates is through dreams in order to warn us of things in our life that hamper spiritual growth.

Elihu was referring to Warning Dreams and Nightmares, but all dreams which we listen to, interpret and acted upon will assist us in realising our full potential.

20. Jeremiah 23:25-32 – False Prophesies through Dreams.

Jeremiah is not condemning the belief that dreams are a means of revealing God's word to us as individuals; he is warning that there are false prophets and false analyses of dreams.

Dream interpretation can be open to abuse. We need to qualify the interpretation of our dreams alongside other ways in which God communicates God's will and purpose for us. Dreams are not always clearly understood, but God's Word to us is plain and clear in the Bible. We must not value the interpretation of dreams more highly than God's revelation through the Scriptures.

To dream of having an affair with the spouse of one's best friend would in no way be a Confirming Dream; it would probably be a Wish Fulfilment Dream. It would also be a Warning Dream, even though you may awake with a feeling of contentment rather than shame, because in no way would God condone that relationship as we will know if we measure it against Scripture.

21. Daniel 1:17-20 – The Spiritual Gift of Dream Interpretation

A group of Israelite youths were brought to the Babylonian king's palace to be trained in the ways of the Babylonians. God gave Daniel, Hananiah, Michael and Azariah gifts of knowledge and understanding – and to Daniel the additional gift of comprehension and interpretation of visions and dreams. The spiritual gift of dream interpretation is more than simply learning to analyse our dreams: it is a supernatural ability to know what the dreamer has dreamed without being told what the dream was and understand what it means.

Even though we may not have the spiritual gift of dream interpretation, we can and must still seek to understand what God is telling us through our dreams. We may not hear God speak to us in our waking state because of distractions in our world. Dreams break through the screen of worldly preoccupation and logic to reveal the inner workings of our psyche: our unconscious, preconscious, subliminal and supra-conscious mind.

22. Daniel 2:1-13 – Nebuchadnezzar's First Dream

King Nebuchadnezzar of Babylon dreamed a dream that disturbed him greatly. When he awoke he could not remember the content of his dream. He called for magicians, astrologers and sorcerers, who were the wise men of the kingdom, to recall the dream for him and tell him what it meant.

In the ancient world, dreams were considered to be extremely important, especially the dreams of kings, priests and prophets. When the wise men could not interpret his dream, for they did not know what he had dreamed, Nebuchadnezzar was enraged. For the wise men it was not unreasonable to demand to know the dream before giving the interpretation; for humanly speaking this was simple; all they needed to do was consult their dream manuals for the interpretation. But knowing the content of a dream without being told required the supernatural gift of knowledge, which they did not have. Nebuchadnezzar possibly inferred from their refusal to interpret his dream as disloyalty and tantamount to treason. He was so angry that he ordered all the wise men in the kingdom to be slain.

23. Daniel 2:14-23 – Daniel Prays for Wisdom

Daniel had divine wisdom and knew that God could give him the spiritual gifts of knowledge and understanding to know and interpret the king's dream correctly. He asked his friends to pray with him concerning the mystery of Nebuchadnezzar's dream. That night God gave Daniel a vision of the king's dream. He is overjoyed by this and bursts forth with a prayer of praise and thanksgiving.

It is right to acknowledge God for every blessing we receive. God inhabits the praises of his people[17] for praise and thanksgiving enthrones God in our hearts, placing God at the centre of our being whence our words and actions issue. 'Central' is God's rightful place.

24. Daniel 2:24-35 – Nebuchadnezzar's Dream

Daniel, in humility, acknowledges that God has graciously revealed to him the essence of the king's dream. Nothing is hidden from God, and when we want enlightenment we need to go to God for insight, for God is ever present and all knowing[18].

Not only did God reveal the contents of the dream, but God revealed to Daniel the state of the king's mind, his thoughts and emotions that night.

In the dream Nebuchadnezzar saw an enormous statue with head of gold, its chest and arms were silver, its abdomen and thighs were bronze, its legs were iron and its feet were made of clay and iron.

A rock was cut and struck the statue's feet, smashing them. The statue toppled reducing to dust the whole statue from head to toe. A wind blew the dust away and the rock which had struck the statue grew into a mountain that filled the earth.

25. Daniel 2:36-45 – Daniel Interprets Nebuchadnezzar's First Dream

Daniel said that the statue's head of gold was king Nebuchadnezzar. The next kingdom to rise, symbolised by the statue's chest and arms of silver, would be inferior to Babylon. The third kingdom symbolised by the statue's bronze abdomen, would rule over all the earth. The fourth kingdom, symbolised by the iron legs would shatter the other kingdoms. There followed a divided kingdom symbolised by the feet of clay and iron.

---
17 Psalm 22:3
18 Psalm 139:1-12

The rock cut from the mountain but not with human hands, would be the kingdom of God which would destroy all worldly kingdoms and stand forever.

This was a Prophetic Dream for the statue represents four successive world powers which history confirms. The head of gold represented the Babylonian empire under Nebuchadnezzar, who was an absolute autocrat. He was succeeded by the limited Medo-Persian Empire. The bronze abdomen represented Greece, which was weaker than the preceding empires. The legs of iron represent Rome, strong as iron and breaking all others, yet weaker for it was divided. The feet of clay mingled with iron foretold the democracy in later times. The rock cut from the mountain was a messianic prediction.

God's kingdom comes with power to destroy all kingdoms of the world and grows to fill the earth.

26. Daniel 4:4-18 – Nebuchadnezzar's Second Dream

Though contented and flourishing at the time, Nebuchadnezzar has a second frightening dream. He dreams of an enormous tree, touching the sky and visible to the ends of the earth. It stood in the centre of the land. The tree was magnificent, with beautiful leaves and abundantly fruitful providing food for creatures. Animals and birds found shelter beneath it and in its branches.

An angel descended and ordered that the tree be stripped of fruit and foliage, its branches cut off and the tree felled. Its stump was to be bound with iron and bronze and left in the ground for seven years, to live like a wild animal, be drenched with dew and have the mind of an animal throughout that time.

The purpose of this was that all may know that God is all powerful, reigning supreme over all creation.

27. Daniel 4:19-26 – Daniel Interprets Nebuchadnezzar's Second Dream

Daniel was distressed at having to inform the king that he was that tree, great and powerful now, but to be driven out for seven years, to experience life as a beast with the mind of an animal, eating grass and drenched with dew, until he acknowledged that God was the Most High God.

Nebuchadnezzar's dream was a Prophetic Dream as was foretelling the period of his insanity. He had set himself up as a god and sought to destroy other religions in order to increase the number of his own worshippers. Daniel warned the king to acknowledge Almighty God as the one true God and that obedience might avert the fulfilment of the prophetic message.

28. Daniel 5:10-12 – The Gift of Interpretation of Dreams

King Belshazzar, Nebuchadnezzar's son was troubled by a vision. His mother told him of Daniel who was filled with the spirit of God and had the spiritual gifts of wisdom, knowledge, understanding, interpretation of dream, explaining riddles and problem solving. Daniel was called and was able to decipher and interpret the meaning of the writing on the wall.

It was a warning that the king had been observed by God, judged and found wanting.

29. Daniel 7:1-14 – Daniel Dreams of Four Beasts

Daniel dreamed that four winds churned up the sea and four beasts came out of the sea: one like a lion, the second like a bear, the third like a leopard and the fourth a terrifying creature with ten horns. As he watched, a small eleventh horn grew out among the ten and uprooted the first three horns.

Thrones were set up and the Ancient of Days, robed in white

with hair white like wool sat upon a flaming throne. Millions attended him as the court was seated and the books opened.

Creatures were thrown into the blazing fire while others were stripped of their authority and allowed to live for a while.

A human form came down in clouds of glory and into the presence of the Ancient of Days. He was given authority, glory and power to reign all nations. He was worshipped by all and his kingdom is eternal and indestructible.

30. Daniel 7:15-28 The Interpretation of Daniel's Dream

Still in the dream, Daniel asks one of the celestial beings in the judgement hall the meaning of the dream. He is told that the four beasts from the sea are four kingdoms that will rise on earth. The saints of God, or the holy people would possess the kingdom of God and have authority over the nations on earth.

The fourth most terrifying beast with the ten horns, iron teeth and bronze claws would be a forth kingdom that would appear on earth and devour the earth. The ten horns are ten kings that will come from that kingdom. The eleventh little horn would be another king who will subdue three kings and speak against the Most High God, oppress the saints and try to change the set times and the law. His power will be taken from him and he will be destroyed. Power will be given to the saints and God's kingdom will be everlasting. All rulers will then worship and obey God.

This too was a Prophetic Dream foretelling what would be in the end times with the establishment of God's kingdom on earth. This is the kingdom that we pray for each time we recite the Lord's Prayer: 'Thy kingdom come on earth as it is in heaven' – where God reigns supreme, served by angels and saints and worshipped in obedience by all the earth, having cast all opposing powers into the fires of hell.

31. Joel 2:28 – Spiritual Gifts Include Dreams and Visions

Joel prophesies that a time will come when God's Spirit will be poured out on all people. All will have the gift of prophesy, seeing visions and having dreams. This has to mean prophetic dreams as everyone has always dreamed all types of dream from common dreams, nightmares, warning dreams, wish fulfilment dreams… to déjà vu experiences, but prophetic dreams and visions are not common to most people.

This prophesy of the outpouring of the Holy Spirit happened on the day of Pentecost[19] and continues to occur as people turn to God and receive a baptism in the Holy Spirit[20].

32. Matthew 1:18-21 – Joseph Told in a Dream of Mary's Innocence

Joseph was a kind, loving and just man. He was sensitive to Mary's feelings but also compliant with Jewish law. When he discovered that his fiancée, Mary, was pregnant before they married or had come together at all. He assumed that she had had sex with another man and decided to end the relationship in accordance with Jewish law, but quietly without destroying her.

A messenger of God came to him in a dream telling him not to be afraid to marry Mary as the child was divinely conceived in her by God's Holy Spirit, and instructing him to give the child the name Jesus, meaning Saviour. As a deeply devout man he was receptive to the divine visitation and obedient to God.

Into Joseph's Common Dream came a Dream Vision and Psychic Dream. The knowledge of Mary's pregnancy must have troubled him. Being a just man, he wanted to do what was decreed according to Jewish law, which ruled that he should divorce the unfaithful wife or break off the agreement with his

---
19 Acts 2:1-17
20 1 Corinthians 12:1-13

fiancée. All this was no doubt playing on Joseph's mind as he went to bed that night. As he wrestled with this in a Common Dream, God broke through giving him the Vision of the angel of the Lord and the Psychic Dream message that the child Mary was carrying had been conceived supernaturally by the power of the Holy Spirit. This reminded him of the messianic prophesy of Isaiah[21], so he married Mary and supported her and the child as though Jesus were his own son.

33. Matthew 2:12 – The Magi Warned in a Dream

Wise men from the east followed a star to pay homage to the newborn king – the infant Jesus. When Herod heard of this he called for the wise men and asked when they had seen the star. He then told them to report back to him when they had found the child.

Having found Jesus they were warned in a dream not to return to Herod, so they returned to their country by another route.

Was this an instance of Psychic Dreams? Had the whole group of wise men dreamed the same dream; or was it that they all had different Warning Dreams which they shared with one another then interpreted the dreams as a caution for them all not to return to Herod? Whatever type of dream it was, they did well to follow its leading.

34. Matthew 2:13-15 – Joseph Warned to Flee to Egypt

After the wise men departed, Joseph was again visited in a dream by the angel of the Lord and told to flee to Egypt with Mary and the infant Jesus. He did not delay in doing what he had been instructed in the dream, thus fulfilling prophesy[22] and saving the life of the child Jesus.

---

21 Isaiah 7:14
22 Hosea 11:1

This again was a Dream Vision and Psychic Dream, for he could not have known that Herod was planning to slaughter every male child under the age of two. He simply trusted the dream message without understanding it and obeyed without question. Learning by experience – his first reassurance had been affirmed, so it was easier to respond promptly.

35. Matthew 2:19-21 – Joseph Told to Return to Israel

After the death of Herod, Joseph was again visited in a dream by the angel of the Lord, as the angel had promised to do[23]. He was told to return with Mary and the child Jesus to Israel, as it was now safe to do so. Joseph, obedient as always, prepared to do as he was told.

This was the third recorded Psychic Dream that Joseph had concerning the safekeeping of the child Jesus. Though not his genetic offspring, Joseph was still given the authority and responsibility of a father to care for and protect the child, Jesus.

36. Matthew 2:22 – Joseph Warned in a Dream

Being lead as he was, Joseph did not relinquish his intelligence or intellect to become a puppet of God. When he discovered that Herod's brutal son, Archelaus was reigning in Judea, he was afraid to go to Israel as he had been instructed to do. But God appeared again in a dream, warning him not to go to Bethlehem in Judea, but to take Mary and Jesus to Galilee.

This was a Dream Vision: God again appearing to him, and a Warning Dream which Joseph heeded as he had done with all the previous dreams concerning Mary and Jesus. He took Mary and Jesus to Galilee where Jesus grew up in safety.

---

23 Matthew 2:13

37. Matthew 27:19 – Pilate's Wife's Dream Concerning Jesus

Pontius Pilate's wife sent a message to Pilate telling him to have nothing to do with the trial of Jesus as she had suffered a night of bad dreams concerning these events.

Legend has it that Pilate's wife, Claudia Procla, had shown interest in the Jewish faith. She may well have heard Jesus preach in the streets of Jerusalem and seen the wonders he had performed there. She surely had heard of him and his words and deeds.

As the wife of the Roman governor of Judea she would have known of the events of that night concerning Jesus arrest and trail. Had she gone to bed that night troubled by the proceedings taking place in Jerusalem and had disturbing dreams?

The dream which had caused Pilate's wife much suffering through that day was indeed a Nightmare.

38. Acts 2:17 – Dreams and Visions are Gifts by God's Spirit

Peter, in his speech on the day of Pentecost, reminded the crowd who witnessed the manifestations of the Holy Spirit's outpouring upon those followers of Jesus who had gathered in the upper room for prayer, that this was a fulfilment of the prophesy of Joel.[24] Among the gifts of the Holy Spirit were the seeing of visions and dreaming of dreams.

This, I am sure, referred to Prophetic Dreams, for everyone dreams all types of dream, but prophetic dreams come from the Spirit of God for human enlightenment to spiritual truth, as do visions.

---

24 Joel 2:28

39. Acts 9:10-17 – Ananias Directed in a Vision

God called to Ananias in a vision and told him to go to Saul of Tarsus, who was living at that time on Straight Street, with a man named Judas. He was reluctant to go, because he had heard that Saul was persecuting the Christians, but God assured him that Saul was chosen by God to bring the gospel to the Gentiles.

Ananias went and found Saul where God had indicated. He laid hands on Saul and prayed for him. Saul's sight was restored; he was baptised and received the infilling of God's Holy Spirit.

40. Acts 9:12 – Saul told in a Vision of Ananias' Coming

God told Ananias that Saul had, in advance, been given a vision of Ananias' visit to lay healing hands on him for his sight to be restored.

When God calls us to do something that we may be nervous about, for fear of failure, rejection or ridicule, God not only goes with us to enable us to fulfil the mission, but also goes before us to prepare the hearts and minds of those to whom we are sent.

41. Acts 10:3-8 – Cornelius' Vision

Cornelius was startled by a vision of an angel of God calling his name and telling him to fetch a man called Simon Peter from Simon the tanner's house, and to bring him there. He obeyed at once and sent two of his servants to fetch Simon Peter from the tanner's house.

Here again is an example of obedience without question and we have the outcome recorded for our edification, and for the expansion of the Christian church.

42. Acts 10:10-16 – Peter's Vision

The following day Peter went up on the rooftop to pray. He fell into a trance and had a vision of a sheet, filled with birds, animals and reptiles, being lowered from heaven. He was commanded three times to kill and eat what was in the sheet – all unclean animals to an orthodox Jew. He refused saying that he had never, and would never, eat what was forbidden by Jewish law. But the angel told him not to call anything unclean that God had purified.

Here again, God had gone before to prepare Peter for the summons by a gentile, Cornelius, whom Peter would not have entertained had it not been for the vision.

This appears not to have been a dream but a vision while in a trance or reflective state. The only thing that I would liken it to would be a Waking Dream.

43. Acts 16:9 – Paul Directed to go to Macedonia

Paul has a vision of a man from Macedonia calling him to come over to Macedonia to help the Macedonians. He immediately prepared to go to Macedonia.

Visions and dream messages must be acted upon or God will cease to speak again in that way.

44. Acts 23:11 – Jesus Came to Paul in a Vision by Night

The previous day Paul had experienced a gruelling inquiry at his trial before the Sanhedrin. The following night the Lord stood before Paul and told him that he would be going to Rome to testify about Jesus as he had done in Jerusalem.

Paul was, no doubt emotionally and physically exhausted and anxious for his life, for the Jews were so angry at his having dared to accuse them of hypocrisy that they were ready to attack him physically there and then. He was removed from their presence so they then plotted to kill him. He may have had some doubts as to whether or not he was in the wrong.

The vision in the night, or dream, was given to Paul to encourage him and give him the assurance of God's presence and protection for his mission to continue.

This was a Common Dream, addressing his anxieties over the events of the day, with a Prophetic Dream element: telling him what lay in the future; and a Confirming Dream telling him that he was still on track.

45. Acts 27:23,24 – An Encouraging Vision in the Night

Paul was sailing to Rome when a violent storm struck. The ship was in danger of being driven onto sandbanks. After several days of being battered by a raging storm, the men gave up all hope of being saved. That night Paul had a vision or dream that an angel stood beside him and told him that he, Paul, would arrive safely in Rome to stand trial before Caesar. Furthermore, all who were on the ship would survive the storm, though the ship would be lost.

This was both a Common Dream/Vision of the Night and a Prophetic Dream. The Common Dream element was a result of the events of the past few days playing on Paul's mind. He must have been as fearful as all other men on board, with the storm raging around them and battering their ship. They had needed to pass ropes under the ship to hold it together, thus the ship's cargo had been thrown overboard to lighten the vessel; and finally the ship's tackle was thrown overboard. It was natural that the situation would affect their dreams if they managed to get any sleep at all.

The Prophetic element gave Paul assurance and he was able to encourage the others with the message he had received from the angel. He must have awakened with a sense of peace knowing that God was giving him the assurance of protection and safe deliverance to Rome, to stand before Caesar.

Though these last seven scripture reference do not refer to the encounters as dreams, but either as visions in the night or simply describing the incidents as messages from God, I have included them in the list of dream references. I have done so because the prophesy of Joel[25] and Peter's reference to that prophesy on the day of Pentecost[26] indicate that with the outpouring of God's Spirit upon all who serve God – young and old, slave and free, men and women – all would see visions and dream dreams, implying that this would be the way in which God would direct or communicate with the people of God in the post-Pentecost Church Era.

As Christians, we are now living in the post-Pentecost Church era and can therefore expect God to communicate with us, not only through our dreams but with visions. As we practice recording and analysing our dreams to hear God speak to us and guide us, we will also find that our spiritual senses become more receptive to God's leading and it should become easier for us to see, hear and perceive God's truth on the invisible, spiritual plane.

Visions today are a lot more common than most people realise. People don't seem to want to share with others the fact that they have been given a vision from God, probably for fear of ridicule, scepticism or being thought weird or to have hallucinated. The vision is usually one of angels, or an angel, for angels are God's messengers. Many folk on their death-bed see an angel, or are given a vision of a deceased loved one waiting to usher them into the hereafter. This is a gift from God for their comfort and peace.

There is nothing to fear from seeing a vision, for God would not permit harm to come to any of his faithful children who seek a more intimate relationship with God, and desire to know and do God's will, but it is as well to be warned that the enemy can counterfeit God's message. The simple test is that if it glorifies God or conveys God's love, it is a gift from God: if it undermines or is contrary to the word of God it is not from God.

---

25 Joel 2:28
26 Acts 2:17

'Follow the way of love' says Paul, 'and eagerly desire spiritual gifts, especially the gift of prophesy.[27]'

---

[27] 1 Corinthians 14:1

*'The Helper, the Holy Spirit,
whom the Father will send in my name,'
(said Jesus) 'will teach you
and bring to your remembrance
all that I have said...'*

John 14:26

6. Dream Recall

What word would you say is of prime significance to the whole Bible? Is it love, as the majority of the congregation called out in answer to that question? I don't think so. Is it faith, as some volunteered? Faith is important in knowing and experiencing God in our lives, but not the key to knowing God's purpose for creation or for our spiritual growth. Is it hope, as others there tentatively suggested? Faith, hope and love, remain[28] we know, but the word 'remember' I believe is the core message of the Bible and the key to a strong and growing relationship between us and God.

If Eve had remembered God's word of warning[29] the world would be a very different place. God placed the rainbow in the sky after the flood, as a sign of God's covenant with the world and as a sign that God would remember the promise.[30] God also made a covenant with Abraham, repeating the covenant with Isaac and with Jacob so that they may never forget the promise God had made them.[31] When the Israelites groaned under the burden of slavery in Egypt, God remembered that pledge made with the patriarchs: Abraham, Isaac and Jacob, almost half a century earlier.[32]

Moses instructed the Israelites to remember the day of their deliverance from slavery in Egypt[33] and it is still celebrated annually in the Passover feast in every Jewish family, as a reminder of who they are and to Whom they belong.

Jesus, at the Passover meal, on the eve of his crucifixion, distributed the bread and wine among his disciples, commanding them to do likewise, in remembrance of him.[34] We as Christian's continue the celebration of that last supper in Holy Communion as an act of remembring Jesus.[35] It is the sacrament which unites Christians of all denominations

---
28 1 Corinthians 13:13
29 Genesis 2:17, 3:3
30 Genesis 9:12-17
31 Genesis 22:17-18, 26:2-4, 28:13-15
32 Exodus 2:24, 6:5
33 Exodus 13:3
34 Luke 22:19
35 1 Corinthians 11:25

throughout the world – even in our diversity of styles of worship.

Fortunately for us, God remembers his promises and is faithful in keeping them. God has also promised not to remember our sins if we receive God's Holy Spirit and remember to keep God's commands.[36] Jesus committed scripture to memory and was able to quote it to the devil when he was tempted.[37] He chastised the Sadducees for not knowing the scriptures.[38] We too will find it a blessing and a help if we remember God's word to us. So remembering is vital to a growing and a deepening relationship with God.

Remembering Your Dreams

Do not forget that God speaks to us through our dreams. Even if it is not a Prophetic but a Common Dream, our dreams communicate to us that which is hidden in our heart and mind. We need to take our dreams seriously to discover the inner depths of our psyche. The first step in learning to analyse our dreams is to remember them.

Some people simply do not remember their dreams on waking. In fact, unless we consciously make a point of recalling the dream, it is often lost within about ten seconds of waking, and unless we not only call to mind, but write down or tell the dream, it becomes fuzzy within a few hours and is lost within a day.

Dreams are most likely to be forgotten by those who do not take dreams seriously. Also, a person may sleep so deeply, due to medication or an alcoholic nightcap, that the dream is lost in the time it takes to emerge from that deep sleep.

Some deep sleepers do not remember anything at all during the night; not even a trip to the bathroom or responding to a remark made by a wakeful partner. I had a friend who complained that his wife often got him to agree to all kinds of requests or suggestions in that semi-wakeful period first

---

36 Jeremiah 31:33-34, Hebrews 8:10-12
37 Matthew 4:1-11
38 Matthew 22:29

thing in the morning or after they had settled at night – things that he would never have agreed to if he were fully awake and in his right mind. He was a heavy sleeper and would drop off the minute his head touched the pillow. As much as she insisted that he had agreed to her suggestion, he insisted that they had not discussed it and certainly did not remember agreeing to her request.

Recently there was a case of a man who strangled his wife as he slept, dreaming that he was fighting with an intruder. There was also the account, some years ago, of a sleep-walker who beat his wife to death out in the garden while he was cleaning out the filter of their swimming pool in his sleep. Having walked in his sleep, he knew nothing of what he had done until the next morning when he awoke to find his pyjamas saturated with blood and his wife lying dead in the garden.

These are two extraordinary cases. Sleepwalking is not common. But not remembering night-time restlessness or wakefulness is quite common. Talking in one's sleep is rather more common than sleep-walking, but the speech of the talker is usually indistinct or garbled. Not remembering dreams is most common.

The first step for a person who insists that they do not dream or for someone who seldom remembers their dreams is to want to remember them. On retiring for the night ask God to speak to you in your dreams and to bring to your remembrance those dreams when you awake in the morning or through the night. Any distraction will cause the dream to fade, so make a point of holding onto the dream until you get a chance to record it. An alarm clock is a jolt into the new day and can cause the dream to flash away as the mind demands: 'What time is it? What day is it?' Try rather to waken gently with a clock-radio tuned in to peaceful music. I find that classical music and instrumentals work the best as music with lyrics, the voice of an announcer or a news report jars me out of dream picture mode.

If we want our dreams to guide us into a deeper knowledge of self and realisation of our capabilities, it is essential that we be open and transparent before God. As you go to sleep ask God to speak into your dreams, bring healing to any brokenness within you, to work his perfect will in you and to enable you to remember that which is important. Trust that God will not permit any destructive influence to harm you.

It is possible to control our dreams to some extent. We can influence our dreams by giving ourselves pre-sleep instructions (as Megan had done, described in the example of Transgression Dreams or as I described in my example under Nightmares, referred to in Chapter 4 – Types of Dreams).

Many people who are involved in dream studies encourage lucid dreaming in order to influence the progress and outcome of one's dreams. I would not support the manipulation of lucid dreaming if you want to learn what God is revealing through the subconscious activities of your mind. It would be like throwing away an unopened letter from a loving parent and writing one to yourself to replace it. Of course, the natural human tendency is to control our own lives, and that includes the dramas enacted in the theatre of our soul. If we want to discover our God-given talents, gifts, abilities and potential, as well as God's purpose in and for our lives, let God direct and bring to the surface that mystery of who and what we are and where we are going. Let us learn to enjoy and seek to understand our dreams, as ridiculous as some may seem to be.

You will find that the more you practice remembering your dreams, the easier it becomes and the more dreams will be remembered. You will even find that you begin to remember dreams in spite of time delays in recording them. But in the mean time, keep practicing, and even if the dream is lost, retrieve and record the little bit that you do remember.

Recording Your Dreams

For recording your dreams, I would encourage the use of a Dreams Journal. In that way you will be able to look back and see how dreams have indeed foretold your future, guided you into a deeper knowledge of yourself and given you insights into God's purpose for your life. A Dreams Journal is any notebook that you are comfortable using. Some people like to use a notebook that has alternate blank and lined pages so that they can draw the dream and write about it alongside. Keep the journal in a safe place where no prying eyes can find it: you will then feel more comfortable about being totally honest in recording dreams and feelings about them.

It is important to record the date and events of the previous day to put your dream into context. I suggest that you record your dream first; leaving a space for the date and events of the day before to be filled in later, or you may lose part of the dream as you bring to mind the events that preceeded the dream.

Alternatively, record significant events at the end of each day, then the next morning describe your dreams. At the back of this book you will find some dream worksheets that I use in my Dreams Workshops. Try each of the different types of worksheet to see which style you prefer. You may well find that different types of dreams will require different methods of recording them. You may copy or print off copies for your own use, but keep them in a binder so that you can refer to them later.

On waking from a dream, go through the dream in your mind. Write down first the dominant thought or impression, tone or atmosphere of the dream; then emotions during the dream and your feelings on waking. Draw the dominant dream symbol, or list the symbols as they come to mind – characters; objects; colours; words; actions – as many as you can remember. If you cannot remember the whole dream, simply jot down the bits you do remember.

One member of my dreams study group, who was an artist, always kept a supply of watercolour paper in a tray with water and a paint-box in the bathroom. If she awoke during the night, or when she rose in the morning she would go through to the bathroom, take out a sheet of watercolour paper, blot it off and paint the dream. The result would be a misty picture on the damp paper. Asked why she painted wet-into-wet, she would reply, 'Dreams are misty so I find that works well for me.'

We are not all artists, but that does not matter. Some non artistic members in the group tried it and found that it was very helpful for remembering their dreams. Others saw things later in the artistic rendering of the dream; things they had not realised were there, which they found most significant.

If you do not fancy using watercolours or getting up to go to the bathroom in the night, try keeping a drawing pad and wax crayons or oil pastels beside you bed for drawing your dream. Ignore the inner voice that tells you that you cannot draw. It lies – everyone can draw and paint. You are not trying to create a masterpiece, simply doodling your dream.

Later in the morning – in your quiet time – write out the dream, using the key words and phrases you wrote down on waking to jog your memory, asking God to help you to remember what is important.

In dream work we are in fact listening to God who sees deep into the hidden recesses of our innermost being. In analysing our dreams we discern what God has exposed – both the hidden possibilities or potential and blockages to spiritual growth. If we are to benefit from our dreams we need to be prepared for the truth, be totally brutal and honest in your interpretation of symbols rather than succumb to the temptation to put the 'best' or highest spiritual meaning to them. We grow most through honest assessment, accepting a challenge to change and being stretched beyond our perceived limitations. So doing, you will be astounded and enriched, blessed and a blessing as you glorify God through reaching out to uncover your full potential and God's purpose for your life.

Reflecting on the Dream

I cannot stress sufficiently the importance of reflecting on your dreams and the significance of the elements and symbols in the dream and on what they mean to you. It is your dream and the dream is speaking to you about the issues in your life, your hopes, fears, gifts and potential. Rushing to the nearest Dream Dictionary may be the easy way out, but the interpretation of dream symbols by the author of a Dreams Dictionary is a general explanation – not what is of personal significance to you, as the one who has had the dream.

By all means, refer to a Dream Dictionary as an aid to help you expand your thoughts on the symbols in your dream, but not as the final answer to the meaning of your dreams. What you will probably find more helpful is a thesaurus or ordinary dictionary to look up related words or different meanings to the same word. (See the Worksheets at the end of this chapter that I use as examples of different ways of recording dreams. I expand my thoughts as I did under Dream Objects and Symbols in Worksheet # 2 – Jacob's Dream, as I imagined how Jacob could have recorded and reflected on his dream.) When studying your dream objects ask yourself, 'What does this mean or symbolise for me?' or 'what springs to mind from that word?'

It is also helpful to have a dreams companion or spiritual director with whom you can share your dreams. This needs to be someone not telling you what your dream means, but asking questions enabling you to unpick your dream, exploring various avenues of thought and helping you to see connections between your life and the dream symbols. The purpose of this book is not to give specific predictions or forecasts but to help you in understanding yourself and your dreams; it is not a directory from someone who does not know how you think or what it should mean for you.

The Atmosphere of the Dream

When you go to the theatre, the first things you notice as the curtain rises, is the atmosphere of the opening scene. The ambience of a restaurant; the cover of a book; the feel of a room all tell you much about what to expect. So too, the atmosphere of your dream sets the mood for understanding the content of your dream and giving you clues as to the type of dream.

You may therefore find it helpful to record first, when reflecting on your dream, the atmosphere of the dream, your and other character's emotions in the dream and your feelings relating to the dream on waking. Note that these are three separate issues. You may have had a frightening dream but woken to feel elated that the threatening element was under your control. So the mood of the dream would be tense; your emotions in the dream would be anxiety; and the feeling on waking may be jubilation.

Emotions in the Dream

How would you describe your emotions in the dream, and the emotions of the other characters? This is perhaps more important than identifying the atmosphere of the dream, but the two go together. Imagine dreaming of a violent storm and the emotions of all characters being fear, terror, panic, anger... but you are calm. Is that not significant? It could indicate that there is some potentially destructive element in your life, which would cause most people extreme anxiety, but you are calm, suggesting that there is nothing to fear, for all will be well. Think of Paul's experience (Acts 27:23,24)

Fear and anxiety are the most common emotions in dreams and anger ranks next. Fear, anger, and sorrow occur twice as often as pleasant emotions. It is important to note that the emotions we experience in our dream are usually reflections of our true feelings. Such feelings may not have been able to be expressed during the day and as a result they come out in our dreams. This is why it is also important to record the activities of the previous day to see if the emotions of our dreams are linked to events.

Once you have identified your emotions in the dream and the emotions of your dream characters, ask yourself the questions: How does this relate to what happened yesterday? What was it in the dream that made me feel that way?

If you do this, you will understand the root of that dream emotion and probably know how to resolve the disturbing element of the day before.

Common Feelings in Dreams

Sensations that are commonly experienced in dreams usually relate to our physical condition. Sexual frustration or abstinence can lead to dreaming of a sexual encounter and arousal; hunger can be felt when a meal is missed, the last meal was inadequate or on the first night of fasting. Paralysis or a sensation of numbness can be experienced in a dream if you have been lying in such a way as to restrict the flow of blood to a limb. Pain can pierce our dream to alert us to the presence of physical hurt; one can dream of being suffocated if breathing is being restricted. A full bladder will affect our dream and cause us to seek release. Fortunately, most of these sensations cause us to wake up in order to relieve the discomfort or accept it if it cannot be alleviated.

Immobility or the inability to move or run is another very common sensation or dream experience, however this is not due to physical restriction but to be interpreted as a sense of no escape from whatever it is that you think is threatening you. On waking or recording your dream, identify the perceived threat and look at ways in which you can deal with it, or view it as a challenge – something to be tamed. See the way in which my sister Clair dealt with the lion that I described under Nightmares in Chapter 4 – Types of Dreams. Identify also the symbolic significance of your pursuer in chapter 10 – Dream Characters; Animals in Chapter 12 or in individual listing in Chapter 14 – Common Dream Images.

Feelings on Waking

What were your emotions on waking? Were you disappointed at being roused from your dream? Did you want the dream to continue? You may want to try to drift off again to continue with that dream if there is no urgency in getting up.

Described below are some of the more common emotions experienced on waking from a dream.

Anger towards one of your dream characters is a common emotion. My mother regularly appeared at breakfast in a sombre mood. When asked what was troubling her she would reply that one of us had offended her in some way – it was usually me. When asked what was troubling her she would relate what we had done to offend her. Knowing that it was not true, we would then realise that it happened in her dreams.

Anger towards a person close to us, as in the case of my mother's mood over breakfast, could be a carryover of the dream or relate to a perceived offence during the preceding day.

Get over it. What is in your head is not necessarily in their heart, but it is important, so record it in order to analyse the source of the anger and address it.

Disappointment is another common feeling on waking if the dream was one you really enjoyed. You would be saddened that it was only a dream.

Relief is also a common waking feeling. It is usually associated with dreams that are not welcome. You will feel relieved that it was only a dream and you are not standing naked in the middle of town, but snug in bed.

Fear is often experienced in that waking moment from a nightmare. Fear that it was not a dream but that there is a real threat lurking in the shadows. Is there really a burglar in the house or did I dream it? Is there a demon skulking in the darkness that somehow crept into my dream? The only way to deal with that is to switch on the light, get up and make a warm drink, satisfy yourself that there is no intruder, living or otherwise; read something light; sing a hymn of praise; pray…

whatever helps to distract your mind and calm your spirit.

Sorrow can be felt if the dream was a reminder of what has been lost. Dreaming of a deceased loved one, or finding a lost treasured possession stirs up the memory of the loss.

Joy is yet another common feeling we can experience on waking from a pleasant dream, as is peace after a refreshing night's sleep filled with pleasant dreams.

Examples of Completed Dream Worksheets

Below I have used four of the dreams recorded in the Bible to illustrate how you can use four of the different types of Dream Worksheet that you will find at the back of this book. Of course, I have used my imagination where facts are not recorded, like the day and month of the dream, (the year is about right.) The dreamer's waking feelings and what the objects may have meant to him or her are pure speculation. I could not get into his or her head so I got into my own instead and filled out the worksheet as though they had been my dreams. I have also used contemporary jargon and cliché's like 'property ladder' and 'ladder of success' which would not have been used by the dreamer of three thousand years ago.

In the case of the dream of Pontius Pilate's wife, I took the liberty of giving her a psychic dream and recording it as she may have if she had been a secret follower of Jesus (as some believe she was) and dreamed the trial of Jesus before it happened. All that we know is that she said that she had had a dream about him that had caused her great suffering. The dream may have come to her before the night of the secret trial. If she had dreamed the events of that night before they happened and a week later heard on the news that the proceedings had been as she had dreamed them, she could have made a note, as I did, that it was in fact a Psychic Dream.

Do this with your dreams. Go back to them and make added notes as you remember additional facts, have further enlightenment or recognise the fulfilment of the dream.

Dream Worksheet #1 – The Dream
(Jacob's Dream – Gen. 28:12-16)

Sketch of the Dream:[39]

---

[39] Print of the watercolour: Jacob's Dream by Heather Truter-Buchanan 2001

Dream Content: (Relate the Story) I dreamed that a type of ramp, staircase or ladder stretched between earth and heaven. Angels were going up and down the steps. As I watched, God appeared and said, 'I am Jehovah, the God of your grandfather Abraham and your father Isaac. The ground you're lying on I will give to you and to your descendents; and your offspring will be like the dust of the earth, and you will spread to the North, South, East and West. In you all families on earth will be blessed. Know this: I am with you always and will keep you wherever you go and I will bring you back to this land for I will not leave you until I have done what I have promised.'

Dream Setting & Atmosphere: Earth below and heaven above; the mood was awesome with a glorious aura of holy light and intense purpose!

Dream People:
Angels
Jehovah God
Me

Who/what they symbolise
Angels - Servants of God & messengers to people on earth
God - Light – guidance; Love; Generosity; Provision;
Me - (Jacob son of Isaac & Rebecca) My name means 'deceiver'

Dream Objects:
Stairs …steps…ladder or ramp
Rock pillow
Heaven & Earth
Plants

What they symbolise or possible interpretation:
Stairs - Going up/down in the world?
Ladder - Ladder of success? Property ladder? The lad!
Ramp - Rave? Rampage/rampant /wild/uncontrolled?
Rampart – defence, protection?

Incline - My 'inclinations'? to Swindle?
Rock pillow - an obstacle; rock solid – stable; 'rock bottom'; 'hard headed'...
Heaven - God's dwelling; 'heaven sent'; ethereal; cloud nine; bliss; paradise...
Earth - 'Down to earth'; basic; earthy; simple; soil; dirt; Adam; 1st man...
Plants - Two of them, one at my feet and the other to the left of where I lay.
Leaves - growth; health; strength; prosperity;
Flowers - the plant at my feet had two pretty blooms = beauty
Tendrils - the plant at my feet also had tendrils reaching out towards me
Berries - fruit; fruitfulness

Any other Details: (e.g. Numbers; Colours)
Yes, I think there were 8 or 9 angels – 6 or 7 fully grown and 2 little ones. Is that significant?
The dominant colours were a bluish-mauve haze surrounding me with beams of golden light radiating down from God above the staircase/ladder.

Emotions in the Dream: Joy & harmony

Feeling on Waking: Overawed & blessed

Context: (Events, or Dominant Thoughts of the Previous Day/s)
I had deceived my father, lying about my identity; tricked my brother for the second time, stealing Esau's blessing and birthright as elder son, and now I was fleeing in fear for my life. I am a coward and not worthy of our father's blessing. On the way to uncle Laban to seek employment there I had nowhere to lay my head for the night, so I slept on the ground with a rock for my pillow. How low can you go?

What type of dream is this? This must be a Prophetic Dream

What is it telling me about myself/what I need to do?
I am not worthy of my father's love or forgiveness, yet my Heavenly Father loves me – so much that God comes to me when I'm at my lowest, affirming His purpose for my life, promising me undeserved blessings multiplied – not only to me, but through me to my descendents!
This tells me of the grace and mercy of God, but also that God is LOVE! Wow! I need to trust God and hold onto that promise He gave me. With God's help, I will not fail Him.

Dream Title: Affirmation on Life's Journey

Date: 7th Tishri 1929 BC

On later reflection: 1870BC – Confirmed! But could the two plants have symbolised my 2 wives - my beautiful and beloved Rachel's & plain but fruitful Leah? Could the 7 grown angels point to my children by Leah:- Reuben; Simeon; Levi; Judah; Issachar; Zebulun & Dinah & the cherubs indicate my 2 cherished sons by Rachel: Joseph & Benjamin?

Dream Worksheet #2 – Action Dream
(Jacob's Dream – Gen 31:10-13)

What was the first thing that came to mind on waking?
Wow Thank you Lord.

Atmosphere: Springtime – bright

Emotions: Happy & Frolicking

Characters: 1) Me; 2) Herd of Goats; 3) God

Actions: I was observing the scene before me
The Goats were all mating enthusiastically
God was directing the proceedings

Speech: God called my name and I answered, 'Here I am, Lord.' Then God said, 'Notice that all the Billy-goats that are mating with the nanny-goats are striped, speckled and mottled; for I have seen all that your uncle Laban is doing to you. I am the God of Bethel where you anointed a pillar and made a vow to me. Now leave here at once and return to the land of your birth.'

Objects: Nothing but the flock of goats - all mating vigorously.

Colours: Green grass; blue sky; white, brown, black spotted, speckled and mottled goats

Numbers: A vast number – the whole flock

How does all this relate to the previous day, past week or significant events in my life?
Laban has been cheating me since I came to him 21 years ago. His son's were complaining that I had prospered at their father's expense. I confronted Laban and negotiated with him. I suggested that from now on all speckled, spotted and mottled goats and sheep would be my wages and the white sheep and

goats in my flock he could regard as stolen. He agreed but when I wasn't looking he removed all the speckled, spotted and mottled animals and sent them off with his sons.

What is the dream telling me? That God is with me and telling me it's time to leave.

What type of dream was it? This was a Common Dream

Dream Title: The Mating Game

Date: 12th Adar 1908 BC

Dream Worksheet #3 - Remembered Fragments
(Pharaoh's Dreams - Gen. 41:1-8)

What was the first thing that came to mind on waking?
I was perplexed and greatly troubled

What fragments of my dream do I remember? I remember a river. I remember also dreaming of fat cows and thin cows. I awoke and had another dream of full ears of corn or grain and some blighted ears of grain. There was also a biting wind blowing.

Draw the dream fragments or symbols:

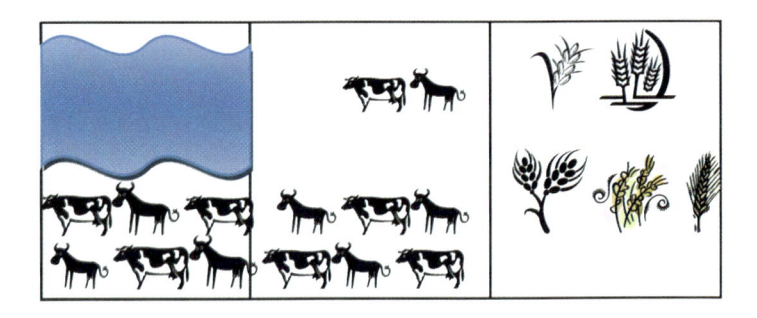

Expand on or link the fragments to get the whole story:
It must have been the river Nile that I dreamed of. There were 7 cows and they came up out of the Nile. They were fat and healthy. Now I remember – 7 skinny cows followed – coming out of the Nile. They ate the fat cows but remained skinny. I awoke then fell asleep again and had a second dream. There were 7 full ears of grain on one stalk, and 7 ears of grain blighted by the east wind.

What in the dream is related to the previous day, week or event on my life?
Nothing at all that I can think of. There is nothing troubling me and that is what is so strange. I need someone to come and

interpret the dreams for me. I will call for all the magicians of Egypt to come and interpret those weird dreams.

Type of Dream: The magicians didn't know, but Joseph told me the meaning of the dream and that it was a Prophetic Dream. We will see... I'll appoint him Minister of Agriculture.

Dream Title: Bad Times Ahead

Date: 8th Heshvan 1885 BC

On Later Reflection: (3rd Tishre, 1878 BC) - It has been exactly as Joseph predicted those may years ago. We have enjoyed the most wonderful weather, livestock had increased as I never beieved possible and crops flourished beyond my expectations. Joseph is an excellent administrator and the barns are overflowig with grain and produce. I can't believe that it won't continue.

(15 Heshvan 1872 BC) – Six years of famine! ... And one more to go, if Joseph's predictions are true, and I have no reason to believe otherwise. I am truly thankful that I took his advice, and more so that I trusted him, giving him oversight of the gathering, storing and fair distribution of grain. Because of what he has done for us, I rewarded him by giving his father, brothers and their children the best and most fertile part of the land of Eygpt, in the Nile delta.

Dream Worksheet # 4 – Interview with My Dream
(Claudia Procla's Dream – Matthew 27:19)

1. **What did I feel when I awoke from the dream?** I awoke in a cold sweat, distressed and deeply troubled.
2. **What is the mood of this dream?** Frightening!
3. **What was my prevailing emotion in the dream?** Dread
4. **Who are the characters in the dream?** Pilate, Herod, Caiphas, The crowd and Jesus
5. **What are the emotions of the various characters in the dream?** Pilate, my husband – Bewildered, puzzled,mystified. King Herod – Elated, crafty, ambivalent, indecisive. Caiphas, the High Priest – secretive, scheming, devious. The crowd – fickle, lusting for blood, hyped up, excitable, volatile. Jesus – Submissive, meek, serene, tranquil, calm
6. **What are these characters doing?** Pontius Pilate – Sending Jesus from pillar to post. King Herod – preparing the palace great hall for entertainment. Caiphas – calling together people who might testify against Jesus. The crowd – gathering in the square to watch the proceedings. Jesus – being dragged along, spat upon, whipped, stripped, humiliated then crucified
7. **What personality facets does each of the dream characters display?** Pilate – 'Passing the buck'; being a 'people pleaser' . Herod – Detached. Caiphas – He personifies devious entrapment, is critical and hostile. The crowd – fickle!. Jesus – Like a lamb: submissive, resigned, yet displaying inner strength
8. **What are the characters personalities, attitudes & actions telling me about myself?** Pilate – Yes, I suppose there is an element of 'people pleaser' in me. The Herod in me is an inclination towards arrogance and pride. Caiphas – I must watch out for being judgemental

and condemnatory. The crowd reflects my tendency to allow others to influence my actions. The Jesus in me is bringing out a devotion to God and a longing to serve.

9. **What symbols are important in this dream?** Caiphas's Breastplate of Judgement; Herod's crown of authority; Pilate's judgement seat of power; the crowd's anonymity.
10. **Where are the warnings in this dream?** Being judgemental without knowing all the facts is unjust; absolute power corrupts; discarding principles for popularity is perilous; being swept along by the crowd is brainless.
11. **Is there a helping or a hindering force in the dream?** No! They are all swept along as if by an evil force.
12. **How am I being encouraged through this dream?** I am encouraged to speak out for what I believe. No more will I be a secret follower of Jesus.
13. **How am I being challenged through this dream?** I am being challenged to do something, anything, to stop this heinous crime!
14. **Who or what is the adversary in this dream?** The Devil is using them all!
15. **If so, where is it coming from?** Greed, pride, fear?... I don't know.
16. **What or who is being harmed?** Jesus is being set up.
17. **Who or what is being helped or healed?** No one – they all have their own blinkered agendas and are blind to the truth.
18. **What am I avoiding or what would I like to evade?** In my own life, I have avoided confrontation or voicing my own opinions. I have seen myself as a mere woman – a chattel – and no more than Pontius' obedient wife, here to meet his demands. Since istening to Jesus, I realise that I am of worth to God.
19. **What actions are being carried out and by whom?** None are taking any action but all are passing the buck, hoping that someone else will do the evil deed.

20. **What relation does this dream have to recent events or concerns I have had lately?** I have noticed that the Pharisees have lately been growing more hostile to Jesus teachings. I've been concerned for his safety.
21. **Does this dream clarify events in my waking life?** Yes – I'm deeply troubled about what's happening in Jerusalem right now. There have been rumours about a plot to have Jesus convicted of treason.
22. **Is this dream telling me that there is something I need to deal with in my life?** Is God telling me to confess to Pontius that I am a follower of Jesus?
23. **Is this dream giving me some guidance in how to deal with those concerns?** Not really
24. **What choices should I make as a result of working with this dream?** For a start, I will warn Pontius not to have anything to do with the trial of Jesus.
25. **What type of Dream was it?**
    This was a horrifying nightmare! *

Dream Title: Black Friday

Date: Friday 3rd April 33AD

*__Thursday 9th April 33AD__ – I now realise that this was a Psychic Dream as all the events of my dream happened exactly as I dreamed it the night before the trail and crucifiction of Jesus.

The Vision

*Sit on the bank of a river,
in reality or in fantasy,
and watch the water flow...
If you know how to look without reflections
the river will speak,
not to your brain but to your heart,
creating a silence in your spirit,
and a wisdom
that your conscious mind will never grasp.*

*Only look.
And creation will speak to you
of life and death...
and love...
and self...*

and God...

Anthony de Mello: Wellsprings – a book of spiritual exercises

7. Philosophy of Dream Interpretation

Interpreting our dreams is a little more complex than understanding the messages of the world around us. We have grown up in our world and learned from infancy what a smile means; what a frown means. As we develop and grow, we explore our surroundings and our perception of it broadens. We take in an infinite number of sights, sounds, textures, smells and flavours increasingly assimilating information and learning to read the signs and symbols around us without thinking much about the process.

As you read this book, you do not need to decipher each letter, for you have learned through practice to recognise immediately each word as a whole, and phrases come together to form pictures in your mind. We do not need to stop and think about the word 'smile' or 'frown' – we see the facial expression in our mind as we read the word, whereas the letters or words in a strange language mean nothing to us: αγαπε will mean nothing if you do not read Greek, but maybe, written in Latin lettering you may know that it is agape, meaning 'love'. Likewise, שלום is simply a bunch of strange symbols if you do not know the meaning of the Hebrew characters. It is shalom, which in Hebrew is 'peace'. Now you have a picture in your mind of love and peace and what 'love' and 'peace' mean to you. So pictures are used for universal symbols which are immediately recognised in every language and culture.

Thus: ♥ ☝☠ ☝☝ ✖ ➡🍱 🚹 🚹 ♿ ⓘ ☎ ✉ £ $ € ✓ ✗ + − = ∞ 🐑 ✝ ✡ ☪ need no explanation.

When we go to the theatre, actors use familiar gestures to help us to interpret the story that is enacted before us. Even if we do not understand the language of the opera we get the gist of it from the gestures and props. And of course, ballet is all costumes and actions.

In our dreams, it is a little different. Often a lot of it does not make sense because dreams use different symbols. Dreams use the pictures stored in our psyche: the collective unconscious, preconscious, subconscious, subliminal and supra-conscious pictograms drawn from personal past experiences stored in our individual minds.

What does 'mother' mean to you? What picture emerges for you with the word 'father' or 'teacher'? I had a colleague who could not say the Lord's Prayer as we know it. He would say, 'Our Mother which art in heaven…' for Jake grew up in a home where his father beat and sexually abused him. He could not imagine a father who could understand and love him in a generous, gracious, merciful and undemanding way. He simply could not picture God as a loving Father, and could therefore not call God 'Father'. His mother on the other hand, gave him a clearer picture of what God is like.

If I say the word ring, what do you see? Maybe you do not see but hear a bicycle bell, or a church bell or a door bell or an old fashioned telephone. All are very different objects, each having special significance for different people. A little boy may immediately hear a bicycle coming down the road; a priest the church steeple and call to worship; an old man his telephone; the young woman a large diamond engagement ring; a wild-life conservationist may picture the ringing of the legs of birds of endangered species. For circus folk it may conjure up the smell of grease-paint or lions and elephants for it would mean to them the arena in which the clowns entertain us and the animals perform. It may not even be circular in shape but square as for a boxer or wrestler. It could also be a symbol used to represent something having no physical shape like eternity, continuity, having neither beginning nor end. So you see – one simple word can have a variety of immensely diverse meanings to different people.

So too, the interpretation of dreams is intensely personal to each individual. We can therefore, not refer to a Dreams Dictionary in order to uncover our individuality, the hidden depths of our soul and God's purpose for us, in order to understand our dreams; because, unlike a normal word dictionary, we don't seek to know the meaning of the word but the interpretation of the symbol for us as unique individuals. A normal dictionary or thesaurus can be helpful, and indeed a dream dictionary will be a help, but we each need to unpick every symbol to discover the meaning peculiar to ourselves.

In Chapter 14 – Common Dream Images, I list many objects commonly appearing in our dreams and suggest what they could symbolise, but the list is far from exhastive. This is where a dictionary will help, but common sense and practice are also needed.

Dream symbols can be seen as all that the dream encompasses. Just as in a theatre the stage, properties, sound effects, lighting, characters and costumes are all part of the story, so in the theatre of the soul, we need to take note of all the elements in the dream. We watch the drama as it unfolds; note the actions, the dialogue, the message and finally the outcome or ending. The play has ended but we still need to analyse the drama that has been enacted before us in the theatre of the soul.

The Mood

Mood begins with self. Mood is part of our temperament. Each of us has a basic disposition to being optimistic or pessimistic, joyful or gloomy, expectant, excitable, melancholic, sentimental, romantic... the list seems endless.

Secondly, our mood on any one day is governed by the circumstances which surround us. Our disposition can change in an instant through some small comment, gesture or news – bad or good. Thirdly, we are influenced by the mood of the environment which we enter.

Keeping the theatre image before us, we enter the playhouse in a certain frame of mind, carrying with us the pressures or pleasures of that day. The atmosphere in the theatre either lifts our spirits or sends a message of gloom. As the play unfolds, the mood of the story draws us in to become a part of the tale.

So too with dreams – The mood of the day is taken to bed with us and the dream either reinforces the mood or draws us out of it to reveal to us the truth of the situation and how to deal with it.

Therefore, in dream work, record your mood before you went to sleep, or better still, what preoccupied your mind that day and what you did before retiring for the night. Did you watch a horror movie on TV, have an argument with your spouse, do your devotional reading and pray or listen to relaxing music? Each of these activities affects your dream stories.

What was the mood of the dream and is it related in some way to your frame of mind before dropping off to sleep? What was your emotion on waking? Were you relieved that it was only a dream? Were you sad to wake up and realize that it was not real? Did these feelings confirm or differ from your pre-dream mood? What is this saying to you?

The Setting

As in the theatre, the setting is important, as is the first general impression you receive as the curtain rises. What is the setting in your dream? Is it indoors or out? day or night? dark or light? morning, noon or evening? lavish or scanty? What does each of these settings convey to you? What does the setting in the theatre of your soul tell you about your dream?

The Scenery

What is the next thing you notice? Is it the building, the furniture and stage props? What about the other elements or objects in the play? All are significant; all are part of the telling of the story. Colours may also be significant, as are numbers. Like the setting, so too the objects in your dream are important for understanding the message that is being conveyed.

Thirdly, you become aware of people. Who are they, and what are they saying and doing?

As you follow the dialogue and actions the story unfolds and becomes clear. You leave with much food for thought and you are never quite the same thereafter. At worst you are bored or annoyed at having wasted your time in coming to this performance or it may have gone right over your head. At best you experience something delightful, expand your knowledge, are challenged, motivated and enriched.

So too as you watch your dreams unfold night after night. You can simply sleep though them and ignore them or you can watch and listen to them, analyse them, be enriched and grow spiritually.

Write down whatever impressions come to you from the dream. What impact does the dream have on your senses, particularly sight and sound? You will seldom be aware of touch, smells and even less, taste, but if you are, those senses are especially significant. Write out your dream, describing the mood; the setting; the furnishing and objects; the people; the dialogue and actions.

Objects

Buildings and interiors: whether the play is enacted in the town square, the drawing room of a stately home or in a hairdressing salon; a forest or courtyard garden, if it is an outdoor scene; and, rarely on stage, but frequently in our dreams, planes, trains, ships and motor cars may feature. These are all important for giving us clues as to the meaning of our dreams, as do items of furniture and other objects – perhaps more so in our dreams than as stage props.

All objects that are noteworthy need to be listed and then each studied in turn for what it means to you and what it symbolises in the context of the dream. Think also of clichés and connecting thoughts associated with the object – e.g. dreaming of clouds = 'clouded vision'; 'head in the clouds'; 'under a cloud'; 'on cloud nine'…or could it be 'pillar of cloud' = God's guiding presence by day; or 'storm clouds' – then you may think through 'What does 'storm' suggest to me… and what does the cloud look like?' Are they feathery clouds? – analysing your associations with 'feathery' and 'feathers' could lead you on to 'birds of a feather'; 'feather her nest'; 'feather in his cap'; 'show the white feather'; 'flying feathers.'

Dreams and the Five Senses

Sights

Dreaming is almost exclusively a visual experience. All that we see in the theatre of our dreams needs to be noted in order to discover the significance and meaning of each dream.

Sounds

Usually what we hear in dreams comes into our dream from the outside world, like an alarm clock, the baby crying or the ringing of the telephone. It usually wakes us, but not always. Sometimes it can simply be incorporated into our dream. Some people will respond to conversation without waking and seldom remember hearing the speaker or giving an answer. However, what you remember of conversations or sounds in your dream need to be noted as you record and reflect on what you heard and what was significant about it, what was said and by whom. Dialogue with your dream characters, as you reflect on the dream after waking. Ask them why they said it and 'listen' for the answer. It will come.

Touch

Feelings are also usually influenced by outer stimuli, like being cold, hot and uncomfortable or tangled in the bedclothes. If the dreamer feels the bite of the tiger it will most likely be something in the bed pricking him. If you feel something that is not an influence from the outer world, question it closely.

Smells

It is interesting to note that dreamers seldom report on smell in their dreams. I certainly have a vivid memory of a dream about roses and a shallow dish of pink rose essence or oil. I remember the strong scent of roses from the rose essence, but this is the only memory of the sense of smell in my dreams that I remember. Perhaps in waking life we do not have as much interest or see the significance of smell as we do of sight (shapes, size, colours, numbers), unless it is overpowering, offensive, stimulates our other senses or has emotional connections.

Aromatherapy is widely used to aid meditation and certain aromas are soothing and help us to relax in preparation for sleep or to counter insomnia; so fragrances may also enhance our dreams. Our sense of smell is profoundly associated with memory, stirring the preconscious mind, certainly affecting the subliminal area of our psyche and possibly even registered in the collective unconscious. It has been noted in psychological tests that people react strongly to certain smells, though perhaps without knowing why. In some cases it was subsequently found that the scent was associated with a good or bad experience in childhood.

Taste

The sense of taste is unlikely to come into our dreams, as it is generally only activated as we eat. If you do dream of taste and flavours, simply treat it as an added stimulus enhancing the message of the dream.

Actions in Dreams

Activities and actions in the dream need to be observed and noted. Ask: Who is doing what to whom? and what do these actions convey? If the action is between two or more people, observe how the subject is responding. If it is an independent action, what is it telling you about the character (you as that character)? Note what its significance is in the dream story and in your waking life.

Dream actions and activities are significant in that they signify intensity and urgency, as in 'a walk in the park' or 'running towards the finishing line'. They also denote security (or insecurity): 'I stood my ground'... 'He left me standing'; comfort, or discomfort: 'Best sleep on it' ... 'I won't take it lying down'; authority, position or control: 'I leapt to my feet when the boss entered'... 'He sat at my feet.'... 'When he says

'Jump!' I ask, 'How high?"

In analysing dream actions three basic considerations need to be taken into account:
1. Is your own body the driving force as in walking, sitting, swimming or flying like a bird?
2. Is the driving force a vehicle apart from you but in your control – as in driving a car, riding a horse, flying a plane, rowing a boat?
3. Are you being transported – as on a bus, in a taxi, on a sea cruise, flying in a commercial aircraft or driven along by the wind as in a yacht?

Sexual Acts in Your Dreams

Human beings are sexual creatures. We indulge in sex not only for procreation but for pleasure, and not only in the peak of the fertile cycle nor only in our productive years, but are responsive at any time and well beyond fertility. We are sexual beings because we are spiritual beings. Sexuality and spirituality are closely related. Created in the image of God – 'male and female God created them and said be fruitful and multiply'.[40] That's sex, isn't it?

But the newly created human had no mate, so God took some flesh and bone from that human and made woman. The divided human became two separate beings, man and woman, male and female, needing to come together to find completion, companionship, fulfilment[41], and in order for them in turn to create new life.

In animal reproduction the male assumes a dominant position. Only in human sexual union are both parties equally affirmative and receptive – facing one another and jointly fulfilled in attaining mutual satisfaction. A spiritual experience is not unlike a sexual experience. In a spiritual experience God unites with our human body in mutual reciprocity between God's Spirit and our human soul. And in the merging we experience a climax of utter joy, exhilaration and fulfilment. It

---
40 Genesis 1:27
41 Genesis 2:20b-24

is a life-changing and fruitful experience.

One of my friends experienced a baptism in the Holy Spirit and came to me in great excitement to declare that the encounter of being infilled by God's Spirit was the best orgasm that he had ever experienced – not confined to the genitals but pulsing through his whole being.

Human sexual intercourse was invented by God and sanctified to be a unifying, elevating and fulfilling experience within the bond of commitment. Unfortunately, it is open to corruption and when indulged in for self-gratification it can be unfulfilling, robbing us of the enriching experience it is meant to be.

What has all this to do with dreams? you may be wondering. Simply, that in the theatre of the soul, sex plays a vital role, because we are spiritual and sexual beings, created by God to reach our full potential. Coitus symbolises the blending of masculine and feminine qualities: the merging and unifying of intellect with intuition; thinking with feeling; will with emotions; wisdom with compassion; doing with being.

It could also indicate, for a woman, a desire to assimilate her masculine qualities (forcefulness, aggression, judgment, logic, ambition…) and for a man, the need to recognise his feminine qualities (gentleness, nurture, sensitivity, empathy, care…) in order to achieve balance of the male/female qualities to become more whole.

If the dream partner is known to you, it could signify a desire or need to incorporate the virtues or character of that person. It may also be the role or occupation of the partner that is significant. For example, dreaming of sex with someone in the caring profession could symbolise a desire to espouse a more caring nature.

Dreaming that you are masturbating could indicate that you are too self-sufficient or independent and need interaction with others to find fulfilment and creativity.

A homosexual act, in your dream, could symbolise an imbalance of the masculine/feminine qualities and a desire to engage more of the traditionally accepted same gender qualities.

Indulging in sex with a child does not necessarily indicate paedophilic tendencies but that the dreamer needs to adopt a more child-like faith, unless the dreamer is hostile and aggressive in the act. Then it would indicate a warning against a destructive approach to responsibilities or a tendency to dominate.

Rape is an aggressively violent act of the domineering male forcing himself onto the passive or resistant female. It could be a warning that the dreamer is forcing his or her will in an antagonistic, insensitive and destructive way. It could also indicate that an undesirable activity is being forced onto you.

Note too, that any dream about sex could simply be a Common Dream, reviewing a desire entertained or suppressed in waking life.

Questioning Dreams

It is far more important to ask the right question than to have the right answer. Questions lead to examination, exploration, discovery, invention, creativity and, ultimately, to knowledge. Through asking the right questions of dreams, we come to a deeper knowledge of self and what God reveals of Godself. (See Dreams Worksheets # 4 where questions are asked of the dream.)

As you work with your dream symbols, you will be learning to look at the world around you with different eyes. Your spiritual eyes will be opened to see a broader view of all things. Jesus taught mainly through parables. What is a parable but a picture painted in symbolic language using common elements to open the spiritual eyes and ears of the listener to a different facet – the mysteries of the truth of the invisible spiritual realm. 'See,' said Jesus, 'the farmer is sowing seeds – some fall on the pathway and are eaten by birds; some fall on rocky ground and are unable to take root; some fall in uncultivated earth and will be choked by weeds – but some fall on good, rich soil and will yielding an abundant crop.'[42]

What is a seed? For the purpose of his parable, Jesus said that the seeds are the word of God, the words Jesus spoke and the gospel his followers would spread[43]. But we can expand it further and even take it in a new direction. A seed is the essence of the parent plants. It encapsulates life and is a symbol of ongoing life, regeneration, creativity, evolution. It is vulnerable and totally dependent on a receptive host and environmental influences. It is a starting point, dormant yet with infinite potential.

So too, are the creative words of God, 'Let there be…and there was…[44]'; the Word of God – the Scriptures[45]; Jesus, the Word of God becoming a human being[46]; and the word coming to us by the Holy Spirit in the gifts of prophesy[47], wisdom, understanding… not forgetting that nature is not silent in declaring God's message to the world, and perhaps to the universe[48]. Our dreams are seeds encapsulating the essence of our being. Our dreams are speaking to us. Are you listening?

Spirituality is dependent on the use of symbols for there is nothing in the visible realm that adequately communicates spiritual truths, yet to gain an understanding of the spiritual realm we only have material objects as illustrations. All religions make use of objects or pictures to help the worshipper to see into the spiritual realm. The Christian church makes use of many symbols in worship: Water, wine, bread, a bowl, a jug, a towel, palm branches, ashes, a crucifix, a cross, the fish, candles, incense, icons, banners, liturgical colours, numbers…

Working with dream symbols helps us to break out of the constricting mould of pre-conception. There are people who cringe at the sight of a pentagram, and some who frown on the symbols used by other religions. I knew a group of Christian teenagers who thought that an elderly member of their church

---
42 Matthew 13:3-23
43 John 15:26, 27
44 Genesis 1:3,6,9,11,14,20,22,24,26
45 Psalm 19:7-13; 119:103-105…
46 John 1:1-5,14
47 1 Chronicles 17:3
48 Psalm 19:1-6

was a witch as she collected porcelain owls. They declared that owls invoked evil on that house. Lay aside prejudice and bias in seeking to understand your dreams. Think, for example of your opinion of snakes and scripture references to snakes – they are not all bad![49]

---

[49] Numbers 21:8-9 Proverbs 30:18-19 Matthew 10:16 John 3:14

One of life's most fulfilling moments occurs in that split-second when the familiar is transformed into the dazzling aura of the profoundly new.

Edward B. Lindaman: 'Thinking in the Future Tense'

8. Colours, Gems and Metals

On Mount Sinai, Moses received a vision of the Heavenly Sanctuary. God gave him the blueprint for building the Tabernacle, modelled on the Temple in Heaven, to be the place of worship and communion with God for Moses and the Israelites as they journeyed through the desert.[50] God was not only particular about the design, materials and furnishings, but also most specific about the colours of the cloth and embroidery threads to be used for the hangings and priests' garments as well as the jewels to be set into the breastplate of the High Priest. If these details were so important in the construction of the Tabernacle then they must have spiritual significance.

Below is a plan of the Tabernacle, or worship tent, that the Israelites set up in the wilderness. It is not drawn to scale, but simply serves to give you an idea of the layout of the furnishings.

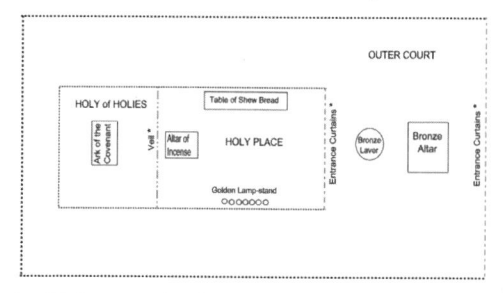

Plan of the Tabernacle (worship-tent) in the Wilderness

The outer perimiter of the Tabernacle was of fine twined linen without ornimentation.[51] The inner sanctuary comprising the Holy Place and Holy of Holies was constructed of hangings of fine white linen decorated with cheribum woven into the fabric and embroidered in purple, scarlet and blue thread. The Veil, and Entrance screens were of linen curtains embroidered with purple, scarlet and blue thread.[52] Furnishings in the inner sanctuary were gold.

Note colours, gems or metals that come into your dreams and explore the meaning of them for your life.

50 Exodus 25:8,40 Exodus 26:30 Acts 7:44 Hebrews 8:5
51 Exodus 27:9-15
52 Exodus 26:1-6 & 27:16

The Significance of Colours in our Dreams

Many people insist that they dream in black and white. Perhaps it is because we take more notice of the people, places and actions and don't notice the minor details like colours. There are, however, occasions when we become aware of a striking colour. With practice we can learn to notice and remember colours, or bring them into our dreams.

Not only do colours enhance the image but colours have a psychological effect on us. Some colours are soothing while others are stimulating; some are depressing, whilst others have healing or regenerative properties. It has been noted that meditating on colours influence us emotionally and physically.

It has also been found that the seven endocrine glands that secrete hormones into the bloodstream communicate between the body and soul. We can associate the seven colours of our visible spectrum with those seven endocrine glands. I will therefore list the colours with their general western cultural associations, their association with each of the endocrine glands and the physical and emotional influence that each colour has on us as well as their liturgical use in the Christian Church and the spiritual implications of each colour. At the end of the descriptions of colours there is a diagram of the endocrine system.

We all react differently to different colours, so you will need to register your own reaction to the colours that you see in your dream and then interpret the significance of that colour in relation to the rest of your dream.

Red

Red is the lowest or least refracted colour of the visible spectrum and the first of the three primary colour. Related to the endocrine system, the first of the spiritual centres in the body are the gonads or sex glands. These are the male testes and female ovaries. The gonads are a mass of tissues arising from the primordial germ cells within which the ova and spermatozoa are formed. When we link the seven colours of the visible spectrum to the seven endocrine glands in the body, red is the logical colour associated with the gonads and reproductive organs.

Crimson is the colour that enfolds and influences our early development in the womb as it is the colour that the foetus sees as mother walks in the bright sunlight. Crimson is therefore associated with sexuality, generative power, life-blood, birth, passion and intense human emotion.

A spiritual association with the colour scarlet is blood. It is related in particular to life-blood,[53] the blood of sacrifices[54] and wine. It is also associated with flames of fire, signifying God's presence and power.[55] Scarlet was one of the four colours used for the hangings in the entrance to the Tabernacle[56] the curtain between the Holy Place and the Holy of Holies. It is a symbol of Jesus' sacrificial blood.[57]

Red is the liturgical colour for the season of Pentecost which marks the birth of the church. It symbolises the flames of fire seen on the day of Pentecost when the Holy Spirit descended in power on the disciples gathered in Jerusalem. Red is also the liturgical colour for services commemorating the Martyrs, indicating the blood of sacrifice.

Scarlet is also the most primitive of colours associated with hunting, blood, violence, aggression, danger, emergency and fire. Red is the colour that gets our attention and stimulates us to action. Other associations – 'Red letter day'; 'Mars - the red planet'; 'Paint the town red'; 'Hearts and Roses'; 'Valentine's Day'; 'Poppy Day'; 'Red alert'; 'Communism'; 'Seeing red!' What does red signify to you?

Pink

Pink is a subtle tint of red. It is a soft, sweet, cute, endearing, feminine colour. The lighter the tint of pink, the more delicate

---
53 Genesis 4:10, 9:4
54 Leviticus 17:11 Exodus 24:6-8 Hebrews 9:12-22
55 Genesis 15:17 Exodus 3:2; 2 Chronicles 7:1 Acts 2:3
56 Exodus 25:4 26:1,31, 36 27:16 28:5,6,8,15 35:6,23,25 38:18,23
57 Hebrews 9:11,12

its implication. It says, 'Handle with care!'

Orange

Orange is a secondary colour and next on the colour spectrum. It is a combination of red and yellow so its hue can vary from red-orange to yellow-orange. The colour represents balance, duality, diversity, merging of opposites, hope, affability and friendliness.

Orange is a logical colour to associate with the pancreas, the second spiritual centre in the endocrines system. This gland produces and secretes digestive enzymes which keep the body supplied with fuel to produce and maintain stores of energy.

Red-orange is a warm colour, but not as hot as red. It is the colour of burning coals, warmth, energy... Flames signify God's presence and power.[58]

Yellow-Orange is the colour of brightness and the sun. It awakens in us enthusiasm. It is also an earthy colour – the colour of resin, amber, copper and bronze.

There is no spiritual significance attached to the colour orange and likewise no liturgical importance or use. Orange however will no doubt have significant associations for you and you will need to explore these as you interpret what it symbolises in dreams or visions.

Yellow

Yellow is the second primary colour. It is brighter than orange but not as warm. It is a happy colour glowing with light and joy.

Yellow is the colour associated to the third spiritual centre of the endocrine system, the suprarenal glands, which are situated above the kidneys. They release adrenalin which stimulates the body's fight or flight mechanisms.

It is thought that yellow stimulates the mind, enhancing intellect, mental activity, creativity and energy, and is therefore a good colour to dominate a place of study. It displays self-

[58] Genesis 15:17 Exodus 3:1-6, 2 Chronicles 7:1 Acts 2:3

confidence and emotions of joy and happiness. This colour has both positive and negative connotations. On the positive side it is a warm, bright, happy colour. It is the colour of sunshine, spring, daffodils, ripening fruit. On the negative side it may symbolise fear and the inability to make a decision or take action.

Yellow has no spiritual significance and is not a colour used liturgically. As yellow stimulates intellect, could this be why it is not spiritually noteworthy – The tree of knowledge forbidden to Adam and Eve as it would kill an intimate and dependent relationship with God?

Green

Green is a mixture of the second and third primary colours: yellow and blue. In nature it is the colour of leafy trees, grasses and healthy growing plants. The significance of the hue is hope, growth, fertility, vigour, positive change, and health. Emerald green is the colour of healing and seen in healing auras, by those who perceive them. Olive green symbolizes wisdom.

In the endocrine system, green is the colour related to the forth spiritual centre. It is said to stimulate the thymus gland and is restful and soothing to the nervous system bringing a feeling of peace and harmony. The thymus is a temporary organ present in babies and continues to grow to reach its largest size at the time of puberty, it then ceases to grow and gradually dwindles to almost disappear in adults.

Used liturgically green symbolises spiritual growth and is used in many churches in the season from the week after Pentecost to the week before Advent – focusing from the birth of the church to the end of the church age – the period of church growth.

On the negative side, green can suggest envy, jealousy, materialism, deceit, cheating, greed, stinginess, avarice or striving to gain recognition.

Red, orange, yellow and green are earth or temporal colours.

Moving up the colour spectrum we see the heavenly or spiritual colours of blue, indigo and violet.

Blue

Blue is the third primary colour. It is a cool colour – associated with the sky, heavens, water and seas. The earth is seen from outer space as a blue planet because of its atmosphere and bodies of water. Blue is associated with the human will and is therefore associated with devotion to God, peace, tranquillity, contentment, loyalty, wisdom, heaven, eternity, truth, loyalty and openness. The deeper the colour blue, the stronger the spiritual connotation.

In the endocrine system, the thyroid gland is the fifth spiritual centre. It is situated at the base of the throat and shaped like a butterfly or bow tie. It produces a hormone that controls the body's metabolic rate and body temperature: the rate at which cells burn fuel from food to produce energy. Blue is the colour associated with those functions.

Blue is not generally used liturgically in churches; it is however stipulated in the Bible as the colour for the robe of the High Priest.[59] It is also one of the four colours used in the entrance to the Tabernacle, and the curtain into the Holy Place.

Indigo

Indigo is a deep rich blue with a tinge of violet. It is the colour of midnight, mystery, secrecy, obscurity, depths and the heavenly realm.

In endocrinology, it is the colour related to the sixth spiritual centre or pituitary gland, The pituitary is located at the base of the brain just beneath the hypothalamus; though no bigger than a pea it is considered the most important in the endocrine system. It is known as the master gland because it produces the hormones that control all the other endocrine glands.

Indigo is the colour of contentment, fulfilment, wholeness,

---
59 Exodus 28:31

'shalom' peace. It is associated with divine protection and the aura of a spiritual person functioning primarily with a spiritually awakened sixth sense.

Violet

Violet is the highest or most refracted colour on the visible spectrum. A purple aura has the maximum vibration. Purple is the colour associated with royalty, spirituality and law. It is a colour rarely found in nature except in a few flowers and one species of mollusc.

It is associated with the the seventh and highest spiritual centre: the pineal gland located in the centre of the brain. It develops as an outgrowth in the brain to reach its peak as the size of a pea in the seventh year. It then begins to shrink in size to around age fourteen. In adults it is about the size of a grain of rice and calcified. It is thought of as the mystery gland as not everything is known about it as yet. It is believed to have a strong influence on our spirituality. René Descartes, a 17th centuary phiosopher, was convinced that it was the seat of the soul. It is also called 'the third eye' as it is light and seasonally sensitive, secreting a hormone that regulates sleeping and waking.

Purple is the liturgical colour used in many churches during advent and lent – celebrating the coming of Jesus as King and recalling his suffering and death on the cross.

In the Tabernacle, purple was used as one of the four colours of the curtains forming the entrance to the Tabernacle and the hanging at the entrance to the Holy Place.

The veil between the Holy Place and the Holy of Holies was woven from blue, purple, scarlet and fine white linen, embroidered with cherubim.[60] The four colours, purple, red, white and blue represented the four facets of the nature of Jesus and the four-dimensional focus of the Gospels of Christ. Purple for Christ the Messiah and King of kings as emphasised in Matthew's Gospel; Red for the facet of the Suffering Servant

---

60 Exodus 26:31

and Saviour as represented in Mark's Gospel; White for the humanity of Jesus, the Son of man as portrayed in Luke's Gospel; and blue represents His deity as Son of God which is the emphasis of John's Gospel. Purple in dreams may then symbolise God's authority.

Brown to Beige

Brown is an earthy hue. Humans created out of the dust of the earth[61] resemble the colours of soil ranging from chalky through the pale beige of beach sand to dark rich tones of humus rich soil and almost black earth.

Brown is a combination of the three primary colours: red, yellow and blue, so we find that browns will have a red-brown, yellow-brown or blue-brown hue, depending on the dominant primary colour. If you study skin tones, even in darker skins, you will see that they too fall into three basic complexions of sallow, ruddy or cool.

Brown is also the colour of roots, tree trunks and branches, most seeds, nuts and berries. Brown therefore symbolises humanity and life from the earth or worldliness. Beige stands for neutrality, basic essentials or an unbiased position. Whatever the shade of brown or beige of your flesh, it represents nudity or bareness.

---

61 Genesis 2:7

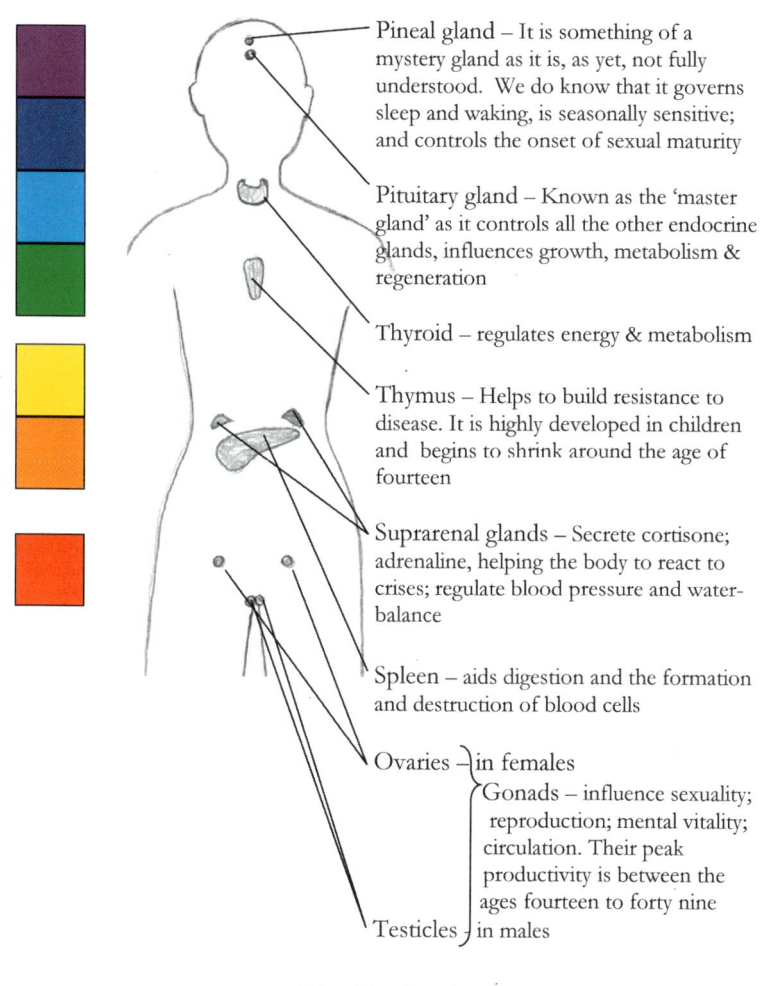

Pineal gland – It is something of a mystery gland as it is, as yet, not fully understood. We do know that it governs sleep and waking, is seasonally sensitive; and controls the onset of sexual maturity

Pituitary gland – Known as the 'master gland' as it controls all the other endocrine glands, influences growth, metabolism & regeneration

Thyroid – regulates energy & metabolism

Thymus – Helps to build resistance to disease. It is highly developed in children and begins to shrink around the age of fourteen

Suprarenal glands – Secrete cortisone; adrenaline, helping the body to react to crises; regulate blood pressure and water-balance

Spleen – aids digestion and the formation and destruction of blood cells

Ovaries – in females
Testicles – in males
Gonads – influence sexuality; reproduction; mental vitality; circulation. Their peak productivity is between the ages fourteen to forty nine

The Endocrine System

White

White is not an absence of colour, but all colours reflected from the object. White light is pure and bright. A white garment has no stain or blemish. White therefore represents purity; cleanliness; virginity; innocence; perfection; simplicity; clarity; truth; honesty; dignity; integrity; enlightenment; awareness; transformation.

White has a cooling effect on the body and enlarging effect to the eye. White objects therefore look larger than black, a room painted white looks more spacious that one with dark or patterned walls and furnishing, and white clothing makes the wearer look larger than they are.

White is the liturgical colour for the days between Christmas Eve through to Epiphany; Easter morning through to Whitsun Eve, which is the day before Pentecost; Transfiguration and Saints' Feast Days.

White invites creativity, like a blank sheet of paper. It calls forth inspiration, and stimulates the imagination – new beginnings, reawakening and a fresh outlook on life. Think of: 'pure as the driven snow'; 'little white lies' implying acceptable fibs; 'white magic' = sorcery in which the devil is not invoked; 'white witch' = one who practices white magic; 'whited sepulchre' = wickedness concealed under a cloak of virtue.

Grey

Grey is neither black nor white, or both black and white in varying shades and tones. Grey is non-committal, insipid, indecisive or neutral. Does the grey in your dream lean more to the black or to the white? It could symbolise lack of clarity, confusion, ambivalence, ill health or limited vision.

Black

Black is the result of absorption of all light and reflection of none. Black is our colour of mourning. It denotes death, grief, evil, falsehood, error, corruption and despair. Black, being the absence of light, implies total lack of vision.

Black is the liturgical colour used for Good Friday. Associations: 'black hole'; 'black mood'; 'black as the ace of spades'; 'black arts'; 'black magic'; 'black market'; 'black-out'; 'black sheep'; 'black widow.' All these associations convey either: ignorance, corruption, deception, evil, renunciation or death, as construed by Western culture.

Black, on the positive side, also conveys a sense of mystery, unknowing, as yet un-revealed profundity; beyond understanding; the unknown and unknowable; obscurity; anonymity and secrecy.

When analysing the meaning of colours in your dream, be as honest as you dare and try to avoid choosing the 'best' interpretation. Ask yourself the question: 'What does this colour mean to me?' 'Do I like it or don't I?'... 'Why do I like/dislike it?'... 'What is it telling me in the context of the dream or about the object so coloured?'

You could also ask yourself, 'What colour do I project to the world and what colour would I like to project.'

Gems and Metals
Gemstones

Gems from the earth symbolise hidden treasures in our fallen nature. These relatively unimpressive rough rocks need to be cut and polished before their beauty can be seen. They symbolise something within you which is rare, precious and of great value, but it needs to be brought to the surface, shaped and then polished. Some of the most traumatic times in our lives have shaped us for excellence.

From a humanistic point of view, many believe that gemstones influence our lives, having supernatural characteristics and virtues associated with each. Amulets and charms have been used to ward off evil spirits or disease, promote healing, bring good fortune or impart power. These are the gems that are said to influence each of the twelve months of the year:

>January: Garnet – constancy
>February: Amethyst – sincerity
>March: Bloodstone – courage
>April: Diamond – innocence
>May: Emerald – success
>June: Agate – healing
>July: Cornelian – contentment

August: Sardonyx – happiness
September: Chrysolite – sanity
October: Opal – hope
November: Topaz – loyalty
December: Turquoise – prosperity

Because of their value, gems have been used as a medium of trade, as gifts to monarchs and loved ones on important occasions. Gemstones are valued for their durability, beauty, lustre, brilliance and colour.

God instructed the names of the twelve tribes of Israel to be engraved each on a specific gemstone and set in the breastplate of judgement to be worn by the High Priest.[62] God was specific about the order, the gem and the tribal name.

Carbuncle Levi	Topaz Simeon	Sardius Reuben
Diamond Naphtali	Sapphire Dan	Emerald Judah
Amethyst Issachar	Agate Ashur	Jacinth Gad
Jasper Benjamin	Onyx Joseph	Beryl Zebulin

Breastplate of the High Priest

The New Jerusalem, the heavenly city of gold with walls of jasper and gates of pearl has foundation stones of precious gems.[63] The names of the twelve apostles are inscribed on those foundation stones.[64] Ten of these foundation stones are the same as the gemstones on the breastplate of the High Priest as described above. The interesting thing is that the twelve signs of the zodiac, according to Eastern belief, with their corresponding precious stones are identical to the twelve foundation stones of the City of God, the Heavenly Jerusalem.

---
62 Exodus 28:15-21
63 Revelation 21:9-21
64 Revelation 21:14 Matthew 10:2-4 Romans 1:1

Aries the Ram	Amethyst Paul* (replacing Judas)
Taurus the Bull	Jacinth Simon the Zealot
Gemini the Twins	Chrysophase Thaddaeus
Cancer the Crab	Topaz James son of Alpheus
Leo the Lion	Beryl Matthew the tax collector
Virgo the Virgin	Chrysolite Thomas
Libra the Balance	Carnelian or Sardius Bartholomew
Scorpio the Scorpion	Onyx or Sardonyx Philip
Sagittarius the Archer	Emerald John, son of Zebedee
Capricorn the Goat	Agate or Chalcedony James, son of Zebedee
Aquarius the Water-carrier	Sapphire Andrew
Pisces the Fishes	Jasper Simon Peter

* Paul was the only follower, after Pentecost, who was called an apostle. Though Matthias was elected to replace Judas, by the remaining disciples casting lots, nothing more is heard of him in the Bible. Saul, later renamed Paul was chosen by Jesus, as were the other apostles. See Romans 1:1-5, Acts 1:20-26, 9:1-6,15, Mark 3:14-19

Metals

Metal is mined from the earth. It is a symbol of strength, permanence, durability and achievement. Some metals are used in the making of jewellery, others to give strength in construction and many other uses, too many to mention here. If metals come into your dream, think about with what you associate that metal. I will mention here only gold, silver, copper and bronze.

As with the jewels in the ephod of the High Priest and the

colours of the curtains of the Tabernacle, so there is significance in the furniture and metals used. The metals used were gold, silver and bronze, consecrated for use in the Tabernacle by waving them before the Lord.[65]

Gold

Gold is the most precious and beautiful of metals. It is incorruptible and highly malleable. It symbolises wealth, prosperity, high rank, status, spirituality and the holiness of God. Gold was used in the making of the Lamp-stand, the table of shew-bread and the Altar of Incense in the Holy Place and in the Holy of Holies in the Tabernacle. Gold completely covered the wood frames for the furniture in the Holy Place, while in the Holy of Holies, the mercy seat and cherubim were of solid gold.[66] The Holy Place in the Tabernacle, and later in the Temple is the place of worship and the Holy of Holies symbolizes the heavenly Throne Room – God's holy habitation.[67] Gold denotes deity and wood represents humanity. Therefore the details for the construction of the tabernacle given by God to Moses on Mount Sinai[68] were important. Every detail was significant and the Tabernacle, as the place of worship, symbolised God's people coming into the presence of God, and wood overlaid with gold – humanity covered by God's deity.

Silver

Silver stands for purity. Silver was used in the construction of the Tabernacle for the rods, posts and hooks that held the curtains which surrounded the Tabernacle. The silver used was the silver collected in the census of all Israelites as a ransom for their lives.[69] It thus represents humanity and the price of redemption. Though precious, silver tarnishes and blackens

---
65 Exodus 38:24-31
66 Exodus 37
67 Isaiah 6:1 Revelation 4
68 Exodus 24:12 – 25:9
69 Exodus 30:11-16

if neglected. Mirrors are backed with silver and the spiritual symbolism of silver is humanity reflecting the image of God – clearly or dimly according to darkening by corruption.

Copper

Copper is a natural element, sometimes occurring in lumps, but now more often smelted from rock. Though naturally soft, it is hardened by hammering. Firing restores its ductility. Copper is an excellent conductor of electricity and heat, this is why it is used as a base for the best cooking pots.

Bronze

Bronze is a metal alloy made from copper and tin. It is much harder than brass and has been used for making tools. In the Tabernacle, all tools and implements and the bases for the poles supporting the curtains surrounding the Tabernacle were of bronze. The Altar of Burnt Offerings symbolising initial commitment and offering of self to God was wood overlaid with bronze, and the Laver for washing, which is symbolic of baptism or entry into the church, was made from bronze mirrors.[70] Bronze therefore symbolises judgement.

---

70 Exodus 38:8

Where can I go from your Spirit?
Or where can I flee from your presence?
If I ascend to heaven you are there;
If I make my bed in Shoel, you are there.
If I take the wings of the morning
And settle at the farthest limits of the sea,
Even there your hand shall lead me,
And your right hand shall hold me fast.
If I say, 'surely the darkness shall cover me,
And the light around me become night,'
Even the darkness is not dark to you;
The night is as bright as the day,
For darkness is as light to you.

Psalm 139:7-12 (NRSV)

9. Numbers in Dreams

Though you may seldom be aware of numbers in your dreams, it is well to take note of them when they do occur, as numbers are usually symbolic and highly significant. From the beginning of time numbers have fascinated statisticians, mathematicians, scientists, philosophers, theologians, artists, musicians, architects, and anyone who would seek to comprehend the mysteries of the universe. All agree that the universe is founded on a numeric system.

If the hairs on our head are numbered, and if one sparrow doesn't fall to the ground without God knowing it, numbers must be important. We see numbers featuring prominently in the Bible, more extensively than you may realise. Many books have been written on Biblical numerology. In fact, every Hebrew letter has a numeric value, and those who have converted the Hebrew Scriptures to their numeric values have described the Bible as a mathematical masterpiece.

Numbers may not appear directly in your dreams, but it is as well to note the number of objects or people. If something is repeated a number of times that too is significant and the frequency needs to be noted.

I will touch briefly on the significance of certain numbers. This is enough to give you something to go on as you work with your dreams and start to interpret them. If this intrigues you and you want to know more you can undertake a more intensive study of numerology later.

In the dreams recorded in the scriptures, numbers represent time, as in pharaoh's seven fat and lean cows and seven full and withered heads of corn, seven stood for seven years. In the dreams of pharaoh's baker and cup-bearer the three baskets and three branches represented three days. But elsewhere in the Bible, numbers mean more than counting years or days. Here follow some examples in nature and references to numbers recorded in the scriptures to indicate the significance of each numeric value.

Zero – O is the number of eternity, infinity, perpetuity, time without end. 'In the beginning God…' God and nothing! God, therefore is symbolised by the O of eternity. The name God in Hebrew 'Elohim' is plural = all of creation is encapsulated in the mind of God. Out of nothing God created the universe and all that time encompasses in creation. From the atom to the as yet undiscovered knowledge – all were present in that vacuum out of which creation emerged.

For the mathematician, zero is the absence of quantity or magnitude. It is the number at the centre out of which all positive and negative numbers flow in ever increasing intensity.

O is a perfect circle, and like a ring having no beginning or end. The earth is not only circular but spheroid which is a multitude of circles joined. The further East one travels the closer one gets to the West. Were the wheels of Ezekiel's vision[71] spherical, for they went in all directions without turning? O is the shape of every star and planet, all eggs and the pregnant womb.

One – 1 stands alone, single, solitary, individual, singular, unique. It represents a unit, complete, perfect, harmony in unity, agreement, having no copy. It is the number of authority; supremacy; power; primacy; first, last, and only word, incomparability; dominance; domination. God is one, standing alone among the gods - unique and complete. God created *'adam'* (human) in God's image: male & female.[72] The original human (before 'woman' was taken out of 'adam') was one person all inclusive and complete. Jesus is the second Adam[73] needing no opposite other to complement him. Therefore God, Jesus and the original Adam all stand apart, unique and unparalleled.

Two – 2 II ☯ is a symbol of plurality; duplicity; division; balance; stability; equilibrium; complementing; dialectical; opposition; polarity; duality. Examples of this are: Heaven and

---
71 Ezekiel 1:16,17
72 Genesis 1:27
73 1 Corinthians 15:45, 49

earth; God and human; spirit and flesh; Adam and Eve; male and female; good and evil; black and white; life and death; visible and invisible; spiritual and carnal; sacred and secular; physical and metaphysical.

On the positive side the two are in harmony and balanced – complementing one another. On the negative side they could be in opposition, creating tension and discord.

In the Bible, two is a number used to emphasize importance, to reinforce the message, as in Jesus words, 'Verily, verily, I say unto you.' or 'Truly, truly I say...[74]' There have to be two witnesses in agreement before judgement is passed. Two therefore signifies witness and truth. The poetry of the Bible uses parallelism (laying two identical thoughts side by side) to create metre and to reinforce the meaning. Look at Psalm104 for example. Joseph's two dreams of bowing corn sheaves and heavenly bodies[75] and Pharaoh's two similar dreams of fat and lean cattle and corn, told them that the messages were important. Thus, recurring dreams need to be taken seriously.

Two similar objects in your dream could be: a) stressing importance; b) stating truth c) indicating a need for harmony and balance, or d) a warning of opposition, tension or discord. In interpreting your dreams you need to look at all the facets of meaning and record them. You may know at once what it means, but it is more likely that it will become clear later.

Three – 3 III △ ▲ is a number of great strength and creative force. III is the God number reflecting the three-fold Godhead – Father, Son and Spirit; and the three-dimensional nature of God – Holy, Just, Love[76] symbolised by the triangle ▽ pointing downward. The upper line represents God's holiness as the platform from which God's justice and love in equal strength flow downwards and draw upwards. Created in the image of God, human beings also reflect the three-fold personhood – soul, mind and body. The three components

---

74 John 1:51; 3:3,11; 5:19,24,25; 6:26,32,47,53; 8:34,51,58; 10:1,7; 12:24; 13:16,20,38; 21:18 (plural in original Greek, 'verily, verily' or 'truly, truly' in AV & RSV)
75 Genesis 41:32
76 Jeremiah 9:24; Exodus 33:19,20; 34:5-7; Deuteronomy 10:14,15,18

of the human mind are will, intellect and emotions. Human nature is in essence three dimensional - sinful, judgemental, covetous. As opposed to the nature of God, humans function in their fallen nature of sin, judgement and lust.

In the natural world, three is the comprehensive number e.g. solid, liquid, gas; water ice, steam; nucleus, cytoplasm, membrane; yolk, albumin, shell; head, thorax, abdomen; larva, pupa, adult; father, mother, child; animal, vegetable, mineral.

Concepts have three components – past, present, future; beginning, middle, end; good, better, best. In artistic composition three is the perfect number: three objects; three primary colours – red, yellow, blue; three tones – black, white, grey. In presentation, whether in speech or writing, there are three components: introduction, body, conclusion…

Scriptural triads are: Abraham, Isaac, Jacob; Three angelic visitors brought a promise of a creative miracle to Abraham and Sarah.[77] The Holy family – Mary, Joseph, Jesus; Three gifts of the magi - gold, frankincense, myrrh; Jesus' three-fold mission – prophet, priest and king. Jesus' first miracle, turning water into wine, occurred on the 3rd day of the wedding feast.[78] Jonah was three days and three nights in the belly of the fish – prefiguring Jesus' death, burial and resurrection.[79] The nine spectacular spiritual gifts[80] are in three sets of three – 3 revelation gifts = wisdom, knowledge, discernment; 3 utterance gifts = prophesy, tongues, interpretation of tongues; 3 power gifts = faith, miracles, healing. In short – thought, word, deed; mirroring God's creative power – God is… God said… it happened.[81] Peter's vision was repeated three times.[82]

In dreams and visions, three symbolises the Seal of God, presence; creative power; completion = perfection and/or fulfilment of God's purpose.

Four – 4 ☐ ✞ this is the perfect earth number. There are

---

77 Genesis 18:1-14
78 John 2:1-11
79 Jonah 1:17; Matthew 12:40
80 1 Corinthians 12:8-10
81 Genesis 1:1-3 etc.
82 Acts 10:16

four seasons; four winds; four points of the compass; four elements – water, air, earth, fire; four stages in the life cycle of insects – egg, larva, pupa, adult. Four is a number for stability – animals walk on 4 legs; furniture generally stands on four legs; buildings have 4 outer walls; a quadrangle has four sides and four corners; sports fields are four sided.

In Scripture the four gospels: Matthew, Mark; Luke and John each highlight the four-fold nature of Jesus: Messiah; Saviour; Man and God. the four faces of the cherubim likewise reflect the four-fold nature of Jesus: Lion (King of the Beats); Ox (scarificial animal); Man (Adam as created in the image of God); Eagle (Deity - exalted).

Christ's relationship to the world is by the sign of the cross – from heaven to earth and arms stretched wide encompassing all in sacrificial love.

In a dream four symbolises the world, order, stability, permanence, reliability or the seal of Christ on the world.

Five – 5✭Five is seen by some to be a demonic number: the five pointed star extended into the pentogram, viewed as a pictogram of the goat's head, symbolising the devil and power.

Biblically it is not a sinister number: Five loaves for the feeding of the five thousand. Five gold tumours and five gold mice was the guilt offering required by the Philistines.[83] Five shekels apiece was the price of redemption of the firstborn of the Levites.[84] Five rams, goats and lambs were required for a peace/fellowship offering.[85] David picked up five smooth stones to come against Goliath.[86] The woman at the well had had five husbands until Jesus came along and dispensed the living water to quench her thirst.[87] Five times Paul had been beaten and survived.[88] At worst, five falls short of perfection; at best it denotes a means of grace.

In nature, we have five senses – one short of what God

---

[83] 1 Samuel 6:4
[84] Numbers 3:47, 18:16
[85] Numbers 7:17, 23, 29, 35, 41, 47, 53
[86] 1 Samuel 17:40
[87] John 4:18
[88] 2 Corinthians 11:24

provides by his gift of grace. We have five digits at the end of each limb and the human shape has five extensions ✱ ★.

Five is seen to symbolise imperfection, incompleteness, grace, redemption. It is the number for potential transformation. In dreams it can symbolise anticipated change.

Six – 6 ✡ ✳ is the number of human spirituality. It elevates the (imperfect) human to be a fully complete human. Restoring what was lost in the fall of humanity – the kernel of spiritual life. The presence of the sixth (and missing) sense of inspiration, intuition, instinct, insight, extra-sensory perception, inner harmony – adding the nucleus of spirit to the human soul.

Biblically it is the ideal human number. Humanity created on the sixth day, six days given for work, six years of service[89]; six stone water-jars transformed into jars of wine at the wedding at Cana.[90]

Six is the number of harmony, stability, beauty; the shape of the hexagon ⬢, a cube, a snowflake❋.

The six pointed Star of David ✡ is made up of two intersecting triangles: the Jewish symbol – God and Israel united in covenant. What most Jews do not realise is that it is also a symbol of the triune God coming down to humanity and triune human merging into God. Six symbolises human perfection, but falls short of heavenly perfection. The number of the unholy trinity is 666 – the beast, the false prophet, the anti-Christ, striving to dominate the world without God, whereas God's purpose is to establish the Kingdom of Heaven on earth.

Seven – 7 is a mystical number; the sacred number, the heavenly number. The Biblical mysteries emanate from the number seven; the greatest mystery being Jesus deity and humanity, 3+4 = 7 Emanuel, God with us. Seven is the Kingdom of Heaven number: 3 (the God number) + 4 (the earth number) = 7 'Heaven & earth combine, angels and men agree... our God contracted to a span, incomprehensibly made man.'[91] The

---

89 Genesis 1:31, Exodus 20:9, 21:2, 23:10, Leviticus 25:3, Deuteronomy 15:12, 18, Jeremiah 34:14
90 John 2:6
91 Charles Wesley – Hymn 109:1 Hymns & Psalms (1983)

book of the Revelation of Jesus Christ, which is John's vision of heaven, revolves around the number seven. God's day is the Sabbath, the seventh day, and God invited humanity to enter into God's Sabbath rest[92] to rest in the finished work of Christ.

The Jewish seven branched candlestick is a symbol of the seven-fold Spirit of God[93]: the Spirit of Power – Wisdom and Understanding; Counsel and Might; Knowledge and Submission. The candlestick was filled with olive oil for fuel[94]. Olive oil is a symbol of the Holy Spirit.

Relating to the world, we have seven days of creation: God [3] + World [4] = 7; seven church dispensations before the rapture.[95] Many Bible scholars believe that we are in the seventh dispensation, the age of materialism. These seven ages relate to the seven churches of Revelation Chapters 2 and 3.[96]

There are seven colours in the rainbow; seven musical notes to the scale; the stages of human development are in seven-year phases. Seven in a dream indicates a heavenly revelation related to earth.

Eight – 8✷ Eight is the number for evolution, resurrection, a new beginning. 8 on its side is the symbol for infinity ∞ (evolution - the ever onward thrust in time unfolding)

In music, the eighth note of the octave is in fact a new beginning in the musical scale.

According to the scriptures eight people went into the ark; and from those eight the earth was re-peopled after the flood.[97] The day after the Sabbath is technically the eighth day and both the day of Jesus' resurrection and the day of Pentecost – the birth of the church. Eight, not seven, is the Jesus number (God + man = Jesus... 3+5=8) Substituting the numeric values for the letters in the Greek alphabet, the name Jesus adds up to 888. (θεσουσ 10+8+200+70+400+200=888) Other names Jesus

---

92 Genesis 2:1 Hebrews 4:1-11
93 Revelation 1:4, 4:5 Zechariah 4:2-6,10 Exodus 37:17-22 Isaiah 11:2
94 Exodus 27:20
95 Apostolic; Martyrdom; Holy Roman Empire; Crusaders; Reformation; Missionary Age; Materialistic Age
96 Ephesus = opened; Smyrna = suffering; Pergamum = linked; Thyatira = sacrifice; Sardis = escaping; Philadelphia = brotherhood; Laodicea = opinionated.
97 Genesis 6:18; 9:18

called himself are also all multiples of eight; and finally, the last book of the Bible called 'The Revelation of Jesus Christ' contains exactly 888 words in the original Greek text.

Eight in a dream probably signifies a new beginning.

Nine – 9 Finality! Nine is the last and greatest of the single digit numbers. No matter by what number it is multiplied, the sum of its numbers is reduced to 9.

13579 x 9 = 122211 and the sum of these numbers 1+2+2+2+1+1 = 9. 2468 x 9 = 22212 and the sum of these numbers 2+2+2+1+2 = 9

As in converting the Greek letters to their numeric values described above, Hebrew letters of the first four words of the Hebrew scriptures – 'In the beginning God…' add up to 999; and '…created the heavens…' add up again to 999. The Bible is the final word! Pertaining to the wrath of God poured out at the end of the age on the rebellious people[98], there is certain finality about the wrath of God, for the numeric value of the words 'My wrath' are 999. The numeric value of the word 'amen' is 9, and for Jesus strongest emphasis 'verily, verily' is 99

At Jesus crucifixion, there was darkness over the land to the ninth hour, and at the ninth hour, Jesus gave up his spirit.[99] With a cry, 'It is finished!'[100]

Nine months from conception to birth for the maturation of a human infant.

Nine in dreams signifies finality, completion, the end of the matter!

Ten – 10 Returns to unity ten-fold. See also the ten plagues of Egypt[101]; Ten Commandments[102]. Multiples of Ten: 20 = 2 x 10; 30 = 3 x 10 etc. 40 is particularly significant as it is the earth number ten fold and represents the fullness of time. The flood continued forty days.[103] Forty days was the time required

---

98 Psalm 94:7-11, Hebrews 3:7-11
99 Matthew 27:45-54, Mark 15:33-38, Luke 23:44-46
100 John 19:30
101 Exodus 7 – 11
102 Exodus 20:1-17
103 Genesis 7:4

for embalming[104]; Moses spent his first forty years in Egypt, he then fled to Midian where he spent forty years, and his last forty years leading the Israelites through the wilderness to the Promised Land.[105] Moses was on Mt. Sinai forty days and nights receiving from God the Ten Commandments and the blueprint for the Tabernacle[106]; the Israelites wandered in the wilderness for forty years, until the generation that left Egypt (except for Joshua and Caleb) had died off.[107] Jesus was tempted by the devil in the wilderness and fasted 40 days and nights.[108] More accurately than nine months, forty weeks is the human gestation period.

Eleven – 11 is one short of perfect administration. Eleven disciples remaining after Judas hanged himself.[109] 'The eleventh hour' symbolises completion 'in the nick of time'[110].

Twelve – 12 is the perfect number for administration. There were twelve tribes of Israel[111] and twelve disciples of Jesus to establish the Church and continue the work of Jesus on earth.[112] Twelve is also six doubled, four trebled, or three quadrupled.

In time there are twelve months in the year, twelve hours of day and twelve hours of night. There are twelve signs of the zodiac.

Twelve is the age at which Jewish boys celebrate their 'bar mitzvah' - their launch into adulthood.

Thirteen – 13 is regarded by many as the number that carries a stigma – the number of ill-omen for the superstitious or the number for sin or rebellion. What does it mean to you?

---

104 Genesis 50:3
105 Acts 7:23, 30 Deuteronomy 34:7
106 Ex 24:18, 34:28, Deut 9:9, 10:10 Acts 7:44
107 Numbers 14:33, 32:13
108 Mark 1:13 Luke 4:2
109 Matthew 28:16 Mark 16:14 Luke 24:9,33
110 Matthew 20:6, 9
111 Genesis 35:22; 49:28
112 Matthew 10:2 Luke 6:13

*All the world's a stage,
And all the men and women merely players:
They have their exits and their entrances;
And one man in his time plays many parts,
His acts being seven ages...*

Shakespeare: As You Like It

10. Dream Characters

The characters in our dreams are perhaps the most important elements, for they are generally extensions of self, playing different roles and expressing different facets of our personality on the stage of our subconscious in the theatre of our dreams. The dreamer is usually the main character on stage, but sometimes the dreamer is in the audience, watching the drama unfold. Other characters play a part and these are usually, though not always, known to the dreamer.

Known characters could be that person, and the dreamer is replaying a recent encounter but improving the outcome or bringing it to a satisfactory conclusion. Rarely do they actually represent the person you are dreaming about but what that person signifies to you. Most characters are usually archetypes of self.

What the dream character is doing is as important, if not more significant than which of your characteristics he or she reveals. Reflect on what emotions are being displayed by that character and what you feel about what he or she is doing.

Our Multiple Identities in the Theatre of the Soul

We have several identities; are different things to different people, and fulfil different roles in diverse situations. Though we are adults, we will always be 'my child' to our parents. As time goes by, we grow into other roles and adopt other identities in the eyes of our parents and other significant people in our lives – helper, companion, carer and many more. To our spouse we are mate; lover/beloved; opposite other; companion; partner; friend and, depending on the relationship, several other associated roles, like cook, housekeeper, gardener, chauffeur, childminder.... We are always parent, teacher, enabler... to our children.

For the dreamer each character symbolizes a different personality type. These usually represent the facets of the dreamer's own nature. To understand the dream we need to consider what that person suggests to us. For each of us the character could symbolize something different. Sometimes we may dream that a) the person known to you is a stranger in the dream or b) a stranger becomes a known person in the dream. For example – a) our husband/wife comes into our dream as a stranger, friend, sibling, parent... or b) our dream husband/wife is actually unknown to us in waking life. The way to interpret this type of dream is that a) there is something about our husband/wife that is strange or unknown to us or some facet of our masculine/feminine side is hidden from us; b) the personality trait of the stranger in our dream is being realised in us.

Besides our humanity there is also an 'animal' side to our nature. Think for a minute: if you were an animal, what animal would you be? Besides our perceived animal type or temperament, there are also different types of behaviour or moods which humans display associated with animal behaviour: cheeky monkey; mother hen; pig; sloth; tiger; stud; mouse; rat; cat; squirrel etc.

Identifying ourselves with the dream characters can give us a greater understanding of our nature, calling or role in life, and God-given potential which we are perhaps not realising. As an example let us look at the parable of the good Samaritan as though it were enacted in the theatre of our soul as a dream. Then identify with each of the characters below and list your similar qualities, weaknesses or potential in each. We can do this with many of the biblical accounts and parables – to our enrichment.

Our Many Selves in the Good Samaritan Parable[113]

Jesus is the teacher and counsellor, lovingly listening and hearing the unspoken need behind the question. He challenges in order for the enquirer to learn more about himself and grow

---
113 Luke 10:25-36

to discover his calling in life.

Descendants of Adam reflect the image of rebellious, godless, sinful humanity[114]. Jesus is our model – for the work of the Holy Spirit is to transform us into the image of Christ[115].

The Lawyer is a scholar, enquirer, seeker after truth and challenger. Perhaps he did not realise his spiritual hunger, but Jesus did.

In coming to Jesus, even with a wrong motive, we are challenged and learn about our human responsibility in society and discover many more facets of human nature.

The Traveller was on a journey through life, as are we all. Think of your present journey in life.

The Robbers – There is within each of us that which robs us of our wholeness: wearing masks, selfish, self-seeking, lack of concern for strangers, hostile, envious, prejudiced, fearful…

The Wounded Man – We all bear wounds, for at some time in our life we have been emotionally battered, bruised, helpless and dependent on others for care, help and support. What wounds do you still carry?

The Priest was unconcerned about that which did not directly affect him. We have all at one time or another said, 'That's not my job, my concern, my business. I haven't the talent or spiritual gift for that.' We may not have the gift but we do have the responsibility to react to needs around us.

The Levite was curious about the wounded man's plight, but not prepared to do anything about it himself. This reflects the human nature to be drawn to the scene of the accident or read about it with interest or morbid curiosity but not to get involved.

The Samaritan was concerned, caring, reaching out where he saw the need, doing what he could do – then letting go. It is important to let go once we have done all that we can do then passing the subject on to receive the next phase in the healing or growing process. There is in some of us a tendency to want to hold onto the person whom we have helped,

---
114 Genesis 3 & 6 - 9
115 2 Corinthians 3:18

subconsciously keeping them in need of us. The more helpful thing to do is give others the opportunity to serve (and to be blessed in so doing) and to hold them accountable.

The Innkeeper did more than his job. He accepted an added responsibility in caring for the wounded man. He was also held accountable. We too need to accept responsibility when a need comes to our attention and remember that God is the one who holds us accountable if not man.

The Healed Person – Through the ministry of others we are healed of our wounds and grow to become more whole individuals.

Doing the same with our dream characters we learn a lot more about who we are and our responsibilities in the world.

Common Dream Characters
Personality

Persona is that which represents the person externally. We recognise the person by their role, personality traits, mannerisms, speech, features, attitude, facade and appearance. The person's clothing: uniform; hairstyle; makeup; even nakedness or inappropriate dress reveal how we categorise a person. These are the costumes and masks of the various 'actors' in the theatre of your dreams.

Self and the Shadow-self

Your higher being is the image in which you were created. God created each of us in God's own image and according to God's plan for a specific purpose. The world, our environment and life's experience moulds us into the pattern of the world and our inborn sinful nature distorts or shatters the image God prepared for us. Dreams show us the distortions and reveal the higher ideal for our spiritual identity. See the characters in the chapter on Dream Symbols and ask, 'What is this character telling me about whom I have become and what I should be?'

There are very few dreams where we do not take centre

stage. We are the hero, the protagonist and the dream revolves around us. This is as it should be because each of us is at the centre of our own world, observing, acting, reacting, responding to the stimuli that we encounter. In the theatre of the soul while we sleep, we play out our hopes and fears; we make sense of the uncertainties and tackle the challenges that confront us.

The shadow-self is the hidden or denied secret facet of our personality which we conceal from the world or fervently deny, but it is part of us and sticks to us like a shadow. When we recognise and face it, it ceases to have power over us. In our dream it is: the tramp; gypsy; murderer; prostitute; drug-addict; alcoholic; paedophile; rapist; cripple... The shadow self is almost always of the same gender as the dreamer. To a woman she can appear as her sister; mother; daughter; the witch; old woman; fairy-godmother; princess; queen. To a man he may appear as his father; brother; son; a wise old man; little boy; king; priest; professor. He or she may be someone known or unknown to us, pursuing or confronting us.

Family Members

Family members feature most prominently as characters in our dreams. It is important to look at the dream characters in the context of the dream as a whole. If the family members are not performing to character, reflecting the personality of the person in life, but acting out a different role or displaying other characteristics, they are probably portraying a facet of the dreamer's own character.

Archetypes

Psychiatrists recognise a general storehouse of information shared by all human beings. Carl Jung refers to it as the collective unconscious. Sigmund Freud called it 'the archaic remnants of inherited beliefs.' These stored memories have not been learned nor are they associations with a person's upbringing, environment, cultural influence or religious teachings. For example, demons or monsters are the universal means of portraying fear.

These archetypical characters appear in legends, myths, in fairy tales and on the stage of our dreams. They represent the various facets of our nature or those things that we perceive as threatening our well-being.

At the theatre, we identify with the characters and either like or loathe them. We appreciate the way they react to the situation in which they find themselves or wish they would respond differently. If you stop to think about it, those traits we dislike in others are often the very shortcomings of which we ourselves are guilty. And the qualities we admire in another are the virtues that we believe we possess. As you try to discover the significance of your dream characters, look first for the archetypical association, then the facet of your nature in that character.

Some archetypical characters are: father; mother; step-mother; step-father; child; step-children; ugly sister or step-sister; prince charming; princess; angel; devil; good fairy; wicked fairy or gnome, goblin; dwarf; giants; witch... to name but a few. They are part of every nation's legends and folklore. Certain animals also feature in myths and fairy-tales like: a lion; bull; lamb; goat; pig; wolf; bear; dragon; monster; snake; vampire ... etc. what do each of these mean to you?

Besides people and archetypical creatures, there are also several archetypical objects like: a cave; mountain; river; road; rainbow; lamp; goblet; rose; apple; mirror; star; sun; moon; fire... etc. What do each of these symbolise for you?

In trying to understand your dream, think first what the person, animal or object symbolises generally then think of what it means to you personally. In Chapter 14 – Common Dream Images you will find suggestions that will help you to interpret your dream characters and objects.

Undesirable Characters

All too often unwanted undesirables sneak into our dreams. We would prefer to distance ourselves from them and pin the identity onto someone known to us who fits the description. Unfortunately, these nasty characters may also represent facets of our lower nature. It is to our advantage to own them, unmask them and cast them out forever – either into the desert, into the deepest sea or into outer darkness. But it is also a relief to discover that not all are bad.

These objectionable characters that make an entrance on the stage of our dreams are there because we have created them and given them their roles to play. We do not like them, but we put them there whether or not we acknowledge their existence. They represent the facets of our nature that we would rather not own, or maybe we tell ourselves that they do not exist or they have been expelled. I remember going on a church camp and playing the ball-game called 'Four Square' one evening. I was doing really well until I took a swipe and missed the ball. A naughty swear jumped out of my mouth and it shocked me perhaps more than it did the other campers. A stunned silence fell. I tried to cover it with a 'shot' um…'shoot' um… 'sherbet'… but it hung in the air like a foul odour or worse, like a lump of cow dung lodged in their ears. I couldn't un-say it no matter how hard I tried.

I remember a word of wisdom I once heard: 'If you tip over a cookie jar, cookies fall out… If you overturn a garbage bin, garbage falls out and if you put buttons in a toffee tin you can't expect toffees to fall out when you turn it over. What you put into the container will spill out when it's upset.' Oh, dear, that '$#!+' swear had been buried deep down in the bottom of the memory box from a previous life and I hadn't realised that it was still lurking there ready to spring out and pull its ugly face at me.

What undesirable characters lurk in the dark corners of your psyche? I have heard it said that we are all capable of murder. Our dream villains may surprise us, but knowing who they are we can, with God's help, unmask and eject them.

No matter how frightening the dream or obnoxious the undesirable character is, what is far more important is the self-awareness that results from interpreting the significance of that character. Get in tune with your inner spirituality and uproot the blockages to experience wholeness.

Clothing and the Persona

Clothing represents not only the external identity but the activity of the person. Garments are our protective covering. A uniform identifies the person with a role and allegiance. Attire relates to attitude and personality. '…give them a garment of praise instead of a spirit of heaviness'[116] 'put off the old nature and put on the new'[117] Note the outfits of players on stage and of the characters in the theatre of the soul. (See the various items of clothing in Chapter 14 – Common Dream Images)

Occupations

More than who the people are, what our dream characters do is usually most significant. It is necessary to view the occupation in the context of the dream. The dreamer is the only one who can accurately interpret the meaning of the occupation. For a lecturer to dream of a teacher may be work-related and mean something quite different from what it may suggest to a student. For someone who is not connected to education it may indicate that he needs to learn something. To dream of a doctor will not have the same meaning for someone in the medical profession, but for a healthy person it may suggest that she needs to attend to her health. For a person who is ill it could simply be a dream of re-living a recent medical check-up or anticipating a visit to the surgery.

Many occupations can be viewed as authority figures, as they represent people who are experts in their field and in command of the situation in the parameters of that profession.

---
116 Isaiah 61:3
117 Colossians 3:9-14

You need also to observe what the character is doing; who is playing the role – you, a stranger or someone you know. Is he performing a role that he is not equipped to do in real life? The occupation of the dream character could be telling you to bring that facet into your own life. To dream that you are a preacher could be telling you to speak of your faith to others, or if a friend or relative who is a banker in life is lecturing could be saying, 'Put your money where your mouth is.' (Be true to your word or uphold what you say). Dream occupations need to be teased out.

In reflecting on your dreams, dialogue with your dream characters: ask them who they are, what they are doing and what they want from you. What is the message they wish to convey?

*Then the angel showed me the river
of the water of life,
clear as crystal,
flowing from the throne of God
and of the Lamb
down the middle of the great street of the city.*

*On each side of the river,
stood the tree of life
bearing twelve crops of fruit,
yeilding its fruit every month.*

*And the leaves of the tree are for the healing of
the nations.*

Revelation 22:1-2 (NIV)

11. My World

Our material world is comprised mainly of the buildings in which we live and work; the gardens, parks and countryside we have for relaxation, recreation and restoring our inner being; and the vehicles we drive or make use of to transport us on our journey through life. These all feature prominently as the setting in the dream theatre of our soul.

Buildings

Buildings represent the activity or occupation carried our in that particular structure. An office is a place of administration; a factory a place for the manufacture of commodities. A house represents the dwelling place of the individual or family.

A house can therefore represent your body – the habitation of your soul or your mind where your personality, intellect, emotions and will reside, as also your memories, hopes and aspirations.

The most common building in our dreams is a house. It is usually your permanent or temporary home – the place of abode that you occupy in your dream even though it may not resemble your residence in waking life. It may, on occasions be the home in which you grew up. If this is the case, you will probably be a child again in that setting, and this will possibly relate to a childhood experience linked to that time.

Dream-structures could also represent our personal state of consciousness. They can be the mould that others have pressed us into or state-of-being that we have built for ourselves. Frameworks or an incomplete edifice represents what we are in the process of building, or the tasks that we are involved with at that time.

The type of structure also gives a clue to the inner activity of the person. A hospital represents illness and healing; a school relates to lessons being learned; a police station, to offence and accountability; a courtroom to justice issues, guilt, being judged, convictions; and a prison is associated to limitations, restrictions, control, oppression. But it is as well to note that any building will have different associations for different people. An architect, a town planner, a teacher, a parent and a student will each have different interpretations for the schoolhouse in their dreams.

When interpreting the significance of the dream building, you need to take into account whether you are inside or outside, involved, detached or observing. You need also to examine various aspects of the structure. Is it large or small, old or new, a period or a modern building? Is it light and airy or dark and gloomy? Is it in good condition or is it in need of repair or renovations? Is it well furnished, cluttered or bare? Is it tidy or untidy, functional or lavish? The answers to these questions give us an insight into the state of our consciousness. Size, quantity and quality are important in dreams. A large spacious building indicates a broad mind; a single room structure – single-mindedness; many inter-leading rooms – exploring many avenues of thought.

The structural material of your building may also be significant. Most buildings are made of earth, stone, brick or concrete. These materials are of the earth and related to our earthly or worldly pursuits. Earth is connected with our human body – created from the dust of the earth and returning to dust in the end.[118] It may also symbolise the conscious mind or our worldliness, 'down to earth.'

A house built of wood, bamboo or grasses indicates a living, growing awareness as its construction is of organic material. A glass house indicates openness, transparency or exposure.

It may also be interesting to note the contours of the building and look up the significance of that shape as well as the other structures and details in Chapter 14 – Common Dream Images.

Other factors to be considered are: Is the building in a crowded, built-up area or isolated? Is it standing alone or adjacent to other structures? If so, what are they and what do they symbolize. Is it out in the country? Is it surrounded by trees, plants, flowers, water or is it in a desert place? Are its

---
118 Genesis 2:7, 3:19

foundations deep or shallow? Is it built on sand or rock?[119] Note also any characters that may be present, or is there an absence of the people who should be there? What does this indicate to you? All of these details are significant in interpreting your own present physical, psychological or emotional state and how to use the knowledge to your self-development.

The Great Outdoors

Whether it is a garden, a park, the open countryside, farmland or woodland – the great outdoors is, for most of us, a place of peace and tranquillity, recreation and relaxation, retreat and renewal of our inner being. It is a place of beauty where growth and fruitfulness occurs.

Vegetation can range from a single flower or leaf to a jungle or forest. Plant life symbolises growth and increase. Healthy plants means vigorous spiritual growth or mental development. Dying or dry vegetation means mental or spiritual deficiency or degeneration.

Roots – indicate cultural or family background; stems and branches – your extensions, interests or expansion; leaves – your general physical, mental or spiritual health and well-being. Buds on the plant – symbolise potential; promise; prospect. Blooms – generally signify fulfilment and beauty but the types need to be noted and the personal significance for you, of that particular flower. Fruit symbolises fertility; fruitfulness; productivity; abundance; satisfaction; accomplishment.

The garden of the house in your dream is the place of personal growth where your individuality is cultivated, habits are acquired, decisions are made and personality is formed. Adam and Eve were placed in the Garden of Eden[120] where they were given freedom of choice and boundaries; opportunity to grow in their spiritual relationship with God; time to get to know and trust one another; to relate to the animals in their care; to be strengthened in character by resisting temptation and to find fulfilment in their world.

119 Matthew 7:24-27
120 Genesis 2:7-25

It was a place for new discoveries; identifying species and naming them.[121] In naming something you give it a separate identity and relate to it personally. Through the sin of Adam and Eve, humanity was barred from paradise[122] but in Christ we are re-admitted and nurtured in this world[123] looking forward to the perfection of paradise in the world to come.[124]

Gardens in your dream symbolises all of the above elements – new life; exploration; discovery; personal encounters; fellowship; harmony; passion; love; growth; fruitfulness; regeneration; nurture; beauty; potential; fulfilment as well as temptations and transgression.

Note also the potentially destructive factors – neglect; weeds which choke and inhibit growth; disease; thorns which cause injury and pain; drought; rocks; insects that destroy (but there are also those that pollinate); sand with no nourishment;[125] poisonous plants (and healing herbs); the need for sunshine and shade, pruning, watering and fertilising.

As you reflect on the garden, ask: what is the season? Are the plants productive and in keeping with the season? Winter is necessary but a bare tree in summer signifies death; and fruit in winter symbolises premature and inappropriate behaviour. Note also birds and insects: Are insects pollinating or ravaging? Are birds singing or silent? Also examine your dream garden in the light of the scripture passages referred to in the footnote that you may interpret it in your own context.[126]

Vehicles in Dreams

Our body is the mobile home of our soul. We are on a journey through life, always on the move and in transition. The journey begins prior to conception and ends in eternity. The first phase of the journey begins when the ovum is expelled from the ovary to travel down the fallopian tube, and sperm ejected to

---

121 Genesis 2:19,20
122 Genesis 3:1-13, 22-24
123 John 15:1-16
124 Revelation 22:1-3
125 Mark 4:3-20
126 See also Psalm 1:3, Matthew 7:16-20, Mark 4:30-32

make its journey through the womb and up the fallopian tube where the two incomplete gametes unite to find fulfilment – first in union with one another, then in growing to maturity in preparation for the second stage of life's journey.

The second phase of the journey begins at birth when the foetus is painfully ejected from the womb, detached from its life-supporting placenta to continue growth to maturity and fulfilment in the world, in union with significant others along the way, and in developing its full potential on earth in preparation for the third phase of life.

The third stage of life's journey begins when we shed our earthly body, which is the life support system and earthly dwelling of the soul. We discard it because it is frail, degenerating or dysfunctional and a hindrance to life in the heavenly spiritual realm. We are then detached from the temporal world to enter the kingdom of heaven to begin a new journey of discovering life in eternity.

It is possible, though not common in our dreams to regress, relive or remember the first journey, and some folk have claimed to have had a dream or vision related to a previous life – this type of dream touches the pre-conscious. Most of our dreams relate to life in this world, but it is also possible in a dream to be projected into the hereafter.[127] God speaks through dreams and is ever equally present in the past, present and future. We are limited here on earth in time and space, and cannot experience the future except through a God-given dream or vision. This then would be a prophetic dream.

As the body is our vehicle on earth so our vehicle tends to take on our personality. We not only choose a vehicle to suit our temperament; we drive our vehicle by personality type. The timid person will drive tentatively, the aggressive person will drive in a hostile way and a hurried person will tend to speed. We identify with our vehicle saying, 'I scraped my bottom on the speed-hump' rather than, 'I scraped the bottom of my car while driving over a speed-hump' or 'That young man hit me as I was turning into Short Street.' rather than, 'The

[127] 2 Corinthians 12:1-4

Ford, driven by a young man, hit into my Peugeot as I was driving along Main Road and turning my vehicle into Short Street.' I am my car. When driving, we become one with our vehicle and your dream vehicle represents you, and how you are driving reveals much about your present journey in life.

The vehicles in our dream are usually our common or usual mode of transport. Thus, dreaming of travel generally symbolises progress, movement or purpose of the dreamer. Whether you are in control or being driven by something or someone will be significant. Consider the surface on which you are riding and the angle of elevation. Note also if the vehicle is appropriate to the surface; if not, what is it telling you? Answers to these questions will clarify your present life's journey.

Other things to consider when interpreting a dream journey, is the type of vehicle. Is it a train, airplane, motor vehicle, boat, or some other mode of transport? Each particular vehicle represents its function and is significant. A fire engine's purpose is to facilitate the extinguishing of flames; a bus is for the transport of many people.

Remember also that different vehicles have different meanings for different people. An ambulance means something different to an ambulance driver, a chronically ill person, a healthy individual and an ambulance maintenance mechanic. Interpret the dream vehicle with these personal implications in mind.

For additional explanations see the individual listings of buildings; features of a house under 'House'; plant life and vehicles in Chapter 14 – Common Dream Images.

Our birth is but a sleep and a forgetting:
The soul that rises with us, our life's star,
Hath had elsewhere it's setting,
And cometh from afar;
Not in entire forgetfulness,
And not in utter nakedness,
But trailing clouds of glory do we come...

William Wordsworth: Ode – Intimations of Immortality

12. Animal Life & The Four Basic Elements

All types of wild and domesticated animals as well as mythical creatures can often appear in our dreams. There are certain things we need to consider as we seek to understand their significance. First we need to recognise that our dream animals generally represent our lower nature: the beast, or 'animal' in us – that facet of our unredeemed nature with its basic animal instincts, temperament, urges, hostilities, fears…

To unmask our dream animals we need to remember that we are all unique and influenced by our environment, upbringing and personal experience. We all react differently to each animal entering our dream. Think through not only what that animal means for you, but what (hidden or clear) facet of your nature does the animal represent? It may help you to understand the symbolism of animals better if you asked yourself, 'If I were an animal, what would that animal be? If I were a bird, what bird would I be? What sea creature… what insect?'

Secondly, we can identify the area of our psyche that it relates to by categorising creatures according to their natural habitat within the four basic elements of earth, water, air and fire. Is it terrestrial, aquatic, a creature of the sky or an insect?

As related to terrestrial animals, the conscious area of the mind, which continuously interacts with the world around us during waking hours, is related to the earth, or our earthiness. If it is a burrowing animal, the subliminal area of the mind, which is below the threshold of consciousness, relates to that which is underground.

Aquatic creatures are associated with the collective unconscious region of the mind, where shared experiences of the whole human race are stored in our psyche, having come down to us from our ancestors. This is related to water – shallow and clear if it is recent and deepening and darkening as it recedes into the past.

Birds of the air are connected to the supra-conscious part of the mind, which is in tune with God and the spirit realm. The higher they fly the loftier the association.

Stinging creatures can be linked to the Preconscious area of the mind, which is the memory-bank where information is stored for possible recall when needed. This is related to fire. We say, 'Ouch!' when we are reminded of something we would rather forget. We may blush or get hot under the collar when remembering an embarrassing or a distressing event.

We will return to the four basic elements after looking at the four categories of animal life.

Terrestrial Animals

Dream animals are usually representative rather than the actual pet or creature. They represent the material, worldly and instinctive qualities divergent from our aspiring, spiritual being. Wild animals represent our untamed, primitive emotions which we are shown in the dream so that we may face them, control and tame them. They may also symbolise perceived dangers, potentially harmful emotions and negative influences around us.

Domestic animals represent the domesticated or socially acceptable behaviour in us. It could indicate that we are being controlled by public opinion, or the demands and expectations of others. A naturally feral animal that is tamed indicates that you have succeeded in restraining that which was uncontrolled in you.

Dreaming of a pet or trying to make a pet of a wild animal could indicate that we are indulging and nurturing that untamed aspect of our lower nature. It is important to remember that the interpretation of the animal in your dream depends on your relationship with it, or your feelings about it, in your waking life.

Fish and Aquatic Creatures

Being early creatures in the evolutionary progression, they represent the prehistoric conformity and dependence on God before the human fall into rebellion. Having water as their habitat, they symbolise early life when the earth was covered by water before dry land appeared, and also life in the womb. This relates to the embryo and foetus floating in the amniotic fluid. It indicates simplicity, innocence and early development.

Some people believe that if you dream about fish you will soon find out that you or someone close to you is pregnant.

In the first Century, when the Church was undergoing severe persecution, Christians drew the fish symbol:

It is called the Ixthos, which is 'fish' in Greek, as a secret symbol identifying them as Christians. Many Christians still have the emblem on car stickers, badges and brooches. At the highest level fish represent our spirituality or spiritual development, safe in the womb of God, as it were.

Ixthos in Greek, or 'JChThS' in roman lettering, represents the initial letters of Jesus; Christ; Theos (God); Saviour.

Water dwelling animals may also represent messages from our unconscious indicating to us how we navigate through the unknown depths of our mind, or through ancestral waters.

Need we be reminded once again that dreaming of fish will probably have a totally different meaning for a fisherman; a marine biologist; a chef; an artist or a pet shop owner?

Birds

Sky is associated with outer space or things above. Birds therefore represent the transcendent state of our being, soaring to the heavens.

The eagle is not only one of the four faces of the cherubim[128], but used to symbolise the spiritually rich gospel according to St John. Angels are depicted as having wings like those of an eagle, and the Holy Spirit is described as descending 'like a

---

128 Ezekiel 1:10 Revelation, 4:7

dove' on Jesus at his baptism.[129]

Birds are also symbols of our emotions, particularly love and romance. Lovebirds and doves are often pictured in love poems, on wedding cakes and valentine cards. Birds can also be a symbol of our sexuality – 'the birds and the bees.'

A caged bird symbolises constrained emotions or restricted spiritual expression. Parrots could be warning against gossip or a garrulous nature.

Flightless birds symbolise down-to-earth reasoning. Think about the many clichés pertaining to birds: 'bird-brain'; 'a bird in the hand'; 'birds of a feather'; 'bird's eye view'; 'for the birds.' If you dream of a fowl, think of a play on words – something is foul, 'falling foul of' or 'foul-play.'

Insects

Insects represent those little irritations in life. We say, 'He bugs me'; 'You're a pest'; 'I wormed my way in'; 'It's pricking my conscience'; 'stung by the scorpion sin'; 'These things are sent to try (test and strengthen) us.' Insects devour our crops; spoil our gardens; invade our houses; carry disease; contaminate our food; disturb our sleep; ruin our clothing and damage our property. But they are part of God's creation, one of the lower forms of animal life in the food chain and therefore provide nourishment for other creatures. Some insects are useful to us though – in pollinating flowers, aerating and fertilising the soil, producing honey and silk to name just a few benefits.

Crawling insects on the ground relate to our bodies of clay, the physical problems or material aspects of our life. Flying insects relate to the mind, to negative or destructive thoughts. Burrowing insects could relate to the subconscious.

When interpreting your dream symbol the main idea to consider is that you may currently be annoyed or 'bugged' by someone or a situation in your life.

In Chapter 14 - Common Dream Images, many terrestrial, aquatic, flying and creepy crawlies are listed and what they

---

129 Luke 3:22

may symbolize to us, but you need to work out for yourself what that creature means to you personally.

In conclusion, ask yourself, 'Does this creature represent something that I need to face, control, tame or avoid?' Ask also: Is it behaving according to its nature? A mouse chasing a tiger; a lamb eating a lion or fish flying are all significant to understanding the dream message, so something else we need to be aware of is the natural habitat of the animal.

The Four Basic Elements

The Bible describes the fifth day of creation as the emergence of aquatic and bird life on earth, and on the sixth day insects, animals and finally humans were formed. Thus animal life was the penultimate act of creation before the final act of creating human beings. Animals therefore symbolise the best-but-one of God's creative purpose: which was people created in the image of God to enjoy fellowship with their Creator. But primitive humans were and still are also evolving to reach their zenith in the image of Jesus Christ: God in human form. God is still at work in us to bring us to fulfilment of God's ultimate purpose.

Air

We think of air as everything above earth, from the air we breathe to the heavens and outer space. It the starting point of all that came into being. 'In the beginning God created the heavens (first) and the earth (after).'[130]

We cannot live without air. Air is the basic requirement for life and oxygen is our lifeline. Blood carries oxygen to every cell and organ in our body. When the flow of air is cut off that organ dies. We are told in the Bible that the life of the body is in the blood.[131]

In both Hebrew and Greek, breath, spirit and wind are the same word: ruach in Hebrew and pneuma in Greek, so in

---
130 Genesis 1:1
131 Leviticus 17:11

the text of the Bible these words are interchangeable.[132] Air therefore is the breath of God or the life of God's Spirit in the human spirit. Keep in mind that, related to this fact, when we are being driven by the wind, as on a yacht, and therefore travelling at the speed of the wind, one does not feel the wind's force. It is only when we are immobile or travelling against the wind that we feel the wind's resistance.

Air is also the element associated with the mind and mental activities, particularly related to the supra-conscious area of the psyche that is in tune with the infinite, all-powerful and all knowing God our Creator. Thoughts, dreams and aspirations are seen as unbounded and floating through the air. We call them: 'flights of fancy'; 'soaring hopes'; 'high ideals'; 'castles in the air.'

Water

Water symbolises the divide between the spiritual and secular world. The earth was enveloped in water and, after separating the light from the darkness, the next act of creation on the second 'day' was to separate the waters above the earth from the waters below[133] thus separating the secular from the spiritual realm.

Evolutionists tell us that life on earth began in water and as creatures evolved, the more advanced grew lungs and emerged from the water to become land creatures.

Note that in the Bible water represents transition. When the Israelites left Egypt (a symbol of 'the world') they crossed the Red Sea which parted for them, to begin their journey through the wilderness (symbolising our Christian journey on earth) then crossed the Jordan River into the Promised Land (symbolic of heaven).[134]

Jesus told Nicodemus that unless we are born of water and the Spirit, we cannot enter the kingdom of God.[135] This refers

---
132 Genesis 1:1; 2:7; 7:22 Ezekiel 37:9,10; John 20:22
133 Genesis 1:1,6
134 Exodus 6:6-8;14:21,22; Joshua 1:10,11; 3:7-17
135 John 3:5

to both natural birth, via the water of amniotic fluid first and then reborn of God's Spirit and through the waters of baptism, to be inspired (inbreathed) by the spiritual breath of God.[136]

In Baptism, water is used as a symbol of transition from worldliness to spiritual living.[137] Baptism also symbolises cleansing from original sin or rebellion against God. The new convert 'dies' to the world and is 'reborn' a spiritual being. Rising out of the water we rise to new life and spiritual living, a new birth and regeneration. The first nine months of human life are in water and at birth we leave the waters of the womb to begin to breathe the air of the new world into which we have been thrust.

Christians are born by water and blood – the water of renewal through baptism and sanctified by the blood of Christ on the cross.[138] And as the woman was created by God from the side of Adam,[139] so the Church, the bride of Christ, comes by water and blood from the pierced side of Jesus Christ,[140] the second Adam.[141]

Water is necessary to sustain life. Our bodies are 90% water. Plants deprived of water will soon wilt and die. Seeds need water to begin to germinate. We can live for many weeks without food, but only a few days without water before we become dehydrated and perish, so water is not only thirst-quenching but physically and spiritually life-giving. Jesus offers the water of life or life-giving water[142] to all who thirst, and those who trust in him will become fountains of life-giving water.[143]

The general appearance of the water is also helpful in interpreting the implications of your dream. Deep water signifies spiritual depths; clear water, clarity or transparency; turbulence will indicate turmoil in your spiritual life; dirty water may indicate corruption; muddy water – sins of the flesh; Note

136 John 20:22; Acts 2:2-4
137 Romans 6:4-11
138 Hebrews 13:12
139 Genesis 2:21,22
140 John 19:34; 1 John 5:6-8,11
141 1 Corinthians 15:45-49
142 Revelation 21:6
143 John 7:37-39

whether it is still or flowing, a large expanse or confined. And note too its colour.

Earth

On the third day of creation the dry land appeared, and all that would sustain life on earth.[144] Earth then symbolises the physical and material world. Humanity was created from the dust of the earth and in the end our bodies once again return to dust.[145] Following rebellion against the righteous laws of God, the ground became cursed and humankind was consequently blighted. Dreaming of earth, soil, dust, sand, rocks all relate to worldliness or earthiness.

Rocky paths and sandy roads indicate our present journey or walk in our secular or carnal nature. Mountains and hills relate to our aspirations or struggles to achieve our goals. Below ground, as with tunnels, pits, caverns or mines, represents the inner being or lower nature. Underground relates to the subliminal area of the mind which is below the threshold of our consciousness.

Gems from the earth symbolise hidden treasures in our earthy or worldly nature. These rocks need to be brought to the surface, cut and polished before their beauty can be seen. (See listings of Gems and Metals in Chapter 8)

Earth relates also to the conscious area of the mind which interacts with the world around us during waking hours. Think of related sayings and a play on words: 'down to earth'; 'soil' = get dirty; 'gorge' = gluttony; 'rock bottom'; 'on the rocks'; 'stony broke'; 'stoned'; 'rolling stone'; 'rock the boat'; 'rock solid'; 'Rock of Ages' = Jesus the unshakable foundation of the Church.

Fire

The sun and stars are balls of fire emitting light and heat. The core of the earth is also burning molten rock. Fire provides

---
144 Genesis 1:9-13
145 Genesis 3:17-19

heat and light, purifies and destroys. It is both comforting and destructive.

Fire is also seen to symbolise both the power and the wrath of God. Fire destroyed Sodom and Gomorrah, cleansing the cities of corruption. God spoke to Moses from a burning bush, yet the bush was not destroyed.

God's guiding presence led the Israelites by way of a pillar of cloud during the day and a pillar of fire through the night as they journeyed for forty years through the wilderness towards the Promised Land. Fire came down from heaven to consume the sacrifices offered by both Elijah and of King David.[146]

Fire may also symbolise uncontrolled temper, jealousy, hatred, lust. All these strong emotions are related to memory. Without a memory of pleasure, loss and desire, the fire of passion burning in the human heart would not be kindled.

---

146 Genesis 19:24 Exodus 3:1-3; 13:21,22; 1 Kings 18:36-38; 1 Chronicles 21:26

A Meditation

☯☪

Be still and know that I am God.
Be still and know that I am...
Be still and know...
Be still...
Be!

Psalm 46:10

13. Emotional Healing through Meditation and Lucid Dreams

When a tree is felled, we can tell its age by counting the rings in the cross-section of the trunk. Those growth rings record not only the age, but the life experiences of that tree. We note the years of high winds, and from which direction those winds came that bent the tree. We see evidence of a forest fire in its twelfth year and a lightning strike in its thirty-ninth year. We can count how many years of drought the tree suffered and the season of the flood – for all these traumas have left their mark as scars in the heart of the tree – invisible until the core is exposed.

Like those trees, we are influenced by our environment and each person's story is different, yet the same – our life, especially our childhood, is filled with both good and bad experiences that shape us and equip us as we grow to maturity. Traumatic occurrences leave their mark and often hamper us, preventing us from realising our full potential.

Dream analysis lays bare our soul and reveals those things that have fashioned us and the root causes of traumas we have experienced. These knocks in life can range from physical and psychological abuse through to the hurts inflicted by thoughtless remarks, criticism or false accusations. At the other end of the scale, over-protective smother-love can stifle our growth and prevent us from experiencing life in all its fullness.

Most of us have learned to suppress bad memories by pushing them into the shadows or denying the existence of the demons of the dark. We bury them deep in the preconscious or subliminal areas of our psyche – but the scars remain.

We may ask: how can God have allowed this to happen to me? The answer is simple: We are created perfect with all the necessary potential talents and abilities built into us to achieve God's purpose and reach our full potential. Unfortunately, we live in an imperfect world. Hostile forces impinge on us causing pain, bruising or sometimes even destroying our self-confidence or faith in others. Even the well-meaning restrictions or false expectations others place on us can disable us. Along with a hostile environment we may be locked into false assumptions of our inabilities and we begin to believe the message that the world sends us – that we are no good or incompetent.

As we reflect on our dreams, working with them to interpret their meaning and significance in our life, we will find that we come to a deeper self awareness and begin to grow to wholeness. However, in exploring the caverns of our soul, the gremlins in the shadows are exposed to the light; those things we have kept hidden reveal themselves and the secrets of the darkness come out trying to hold us back from reaching our full potential.

Is there any way out of the prison of painful memories and healing for a wounded psyche?

Denial buries incidents alive; and something buried alive causing it to fester in the darkness and generate resentment.

Unforgiveness locks both perpetrator and victim into the act, and blocks healing. 'Turning the other cheek' does not remove hurt. Blaming others for our problems is not helpful – we need to take responsibility for our own lives, actions and reactions. Seeking compensation cannot recover what was lost. So what do we do? Is there a cure for the wounds suffered in the past? – Indeed there is!

God dwells in eternity, which means that God is forever equally present at all times in the past, the present and the future. God's omnipresence means that we can, in our imagination, go back to that damaging event and ask for God's healing touch today. This is done through meditation or lucid dreams.

There is no difference between the healing of past hurts and the forgiveness we receive through the death of Jesus on the cross, his resurrection and ascension two thousand years ago. It is no different from the regeneration we experience as we receive the outpouring of his Spirit upon us and flooding our being at our spiritual rebirth.

Prayer opens the soul to God allowing the searchlight of the Holy Spirit to penetrate the dark corners of the psyche, to bring to the surface the painful experiences, to wash out the festering wounds of painful memories and allow God's healing love to flow through our being and renew what was damaged in our soul.

The Holy Spirit brings to our remembrance things forgotten and even those things that are unknown or hidden in the dark corners of our being. As the subliminal images begin to surface through our dream-work, and are processed and then assimilated by the conscious mind, we can bring them into the healing presence of God's Spirit to experience feelings of peace, renewal and wholeness.

We can never unsay what had been said nor can we wipe out the past, yet we can replace the negative images with positive ones or see it from a new perspective. A healed wound may leave a scar, but the pollutant and pain have gone. Excising the bad memories which have wounded our soul brings healing and makes us whole.

Physical healing begins when we acknowledge the presence of disease and seek medical help. Emotional healing begins when we recognise the need for healing and approach the Great Physician. The healings that Jesus performed were done by the request of the sick or friends of the infirm. To the paralysed man at the pool of Bethesda, Jesus asked, 'Do you want to be healed?'[147] We need to want to be healed and to seek it.

An important part of the healing process is to understand that forgiveness is at the heart of the fullness of life. So often when people came to Jesus for healing, before anything else he told them that their sins were forgiven and healing naturally followed. In fact, God's whole mission was to come into our world, experience our humanity, free us from the curse of sin and its consequences by suffering and dying in our place that we may live in fullness of life as God intended.

---
147 John 5:6

We need to let go of harbouring pain, bitterness, resentment, anger, hostility and self-pity, that through a new understanding we may take hold of truth, beauty, love, joy, peace, goodness … and experience wholeness.

Jesus said, 'Truly, I tell you, whatever you bind on earth will be bound in heaven, and whatever you loose on earth will be loosed in heaven.'[148]

---

[148] Matthew 18:18

Meditation Exercises:
Introduction to the exercises:

Choose a time when you know that you will have an hour undisturbed. Then to be doubly sure, switch off your phone, unplug the land-line, disconnect the front door-bell, and if necessary leave a note on the door saying: 'Be back later.'

Then sit comfortably in an upright chair and in a quiet place where there are no visual distractions, as there would be by a window looking onto a busy street. Better still choose a back-room overlooking a peaceful garden or close the curtains. Most people find it helpful to place a lighted candle in the centre of the room and to focus on the flame, an icon, or one of you favourite pictures of Jesus.

Picturing Jesus

Many people find that gazing upon an image of Jesus is helpful in their meditations. We all have our favourite pictures, be it an icon, a picture that we have become familiar with in our church or a modern photograph of an actor portraying Jesus. There are literally hundreds of representations of Jesus, but I have selected two for you to choose from, if you prefer, you may obtain your own illustration from a Christian bookshop or from the internet.

Exercise 1 – The Counsellor:

See Jesus come in through the door and sit in the chair opposite you.

Read through Psalm 139 you will find this on page 198 after the picture of Jesus, directing it to Jesus as though you are speaking to him openly. He listens, looking lovingly at you as you speak.

Ask him to go back with you to the beginning of your life; to that time when you were being formed in secret; back to your conception. He was there.

Hear him tell you that it doesn't matter whether or not your parents planned you; that God planned you, selecting the time, the day, the month, the ovum and the sperm to create you for God's divine and specific purpose, giving you the talents you have and challenges you would need to reach perfection.

Review your life going forward from infancy stopping at each milestone or hurtful incident to ask Jesus to show you what was happening there with the people who were present and why they spoke and acted as they did.

Ask him to forgive your own wrong doings and your bad attitude. Let go of your hostile feelings towards the perpetrator: your emotional hostility is hurting you, not the perpitrator. See Jesus reach out to heal your hurt, repair the damage and restore you to wholeness.

Continue until you feel a sense of peace and closure on that part of you life. Then receive Jesus' warm embrace and thank him for his love and the way that he is revealing to you the truth... strengthening you... bringing you to fullness of life... and continuing to shape you for his divine purpose. Ask him if you can come again tomorrow (or next week) to continue where you left off. Then keep the appointment.

Exercise 2 – The Picture Gallery:

Imagine Jesus is standing beside you in a long corridor with pictures of your life lining the walls. Some are pictures that you are fully aware of; others of which you are ashamed or find embarrassing. You wish they had not been taken, but they were. There are also many pictures that you did not know about and of which you have no memory.

'Come, let me show you what is behind each picture,' says Jesus as he leads you down the corridor.

As you look at each picture, you remember that occasion; what you were thinking at the time and how you felt. Jesus reminds you of what went before and led up to that event. Ask his forgiveness of those things that were not good.

He turns the picture around and shows you the truth from

another perspective, that of the other people in the scene: what they were thinking and feeling at the time; their confusion, motives, hopes, fears, frustrations and the scars of their own wounded lives. Ask Jesus to forgive them and help you to forgive them and bring healing into that situation.

You could also ask Jesus to remove that picture and replace it with one that reveals the situation as you and he would have liked it to be.

Exercise 3 – The Staircase:

Imagine that you are dreaming your own 'Jacob's staircase to heaven' dream with a few variations:

You are where you are now, sitting comfortably in your quiet place. You see before you a broad staircase reaching from the ground and leading up into the mists of the unknown future. Each step is a year in your life. Instead of angels descending and ascending there are some of the significant people of each period of your life on the stairs, going about their own business.

Read Jeremiah 1:1-8 and hear Jesus tell you that you were no accident. As God created Jeremiah for a specific purpose, so were you uniquely and beautifully created as part of God's perfect plan.

Jesus is standing at the foot of the stairs waiting to walk with you up through each stage of your life-journey.[149] Do not hurry but pause on each step to allow God to show you what is happening at each phase in your life. There are several landings on the staircase with a bench for you to sit and rest when you feel the need, until you are ready to go on, maybe even in a day or two. Jesus will be waiting until you are ready to continue.

The first step is the year of your pre-natal development to birth. God has selected your DNA and is moulding and shaping you – a beautiful, unrepeatable miracle of God's creating – in the warmth of your mother's womb. As God

---

149 Psalm 37:23-24 & 118:5-7

forms your delicate being he is healing the negative emotions and influences that bombard you from outside.

Jesus is present at your birth on the second step. He stills the pain as you are thrust from darkness into glaring light. He takes you in his loving arms to holds you close ready to lead you into the healing light of truth and forgiveness through each of life's new experience of the hurts you will encounter on life's journey.

Feel the warmth of his body close to your tiny frame. In his arms you continue to develop and discover your world. He is ready to minister healing at any and every stage as needed, to bring you to wholeness and fulfilment of God's purpose for your life.

On your first birthday he carries you onto the next step. Soon you are ready to walk, so he sets you down and takes your tiny hand in his. Close to Jesus' side you feel the warmth of his love as you interact with the people in your life in that second and third and every year that follows.

It is your first day at school. Jesus is beside you, your invisible companion, yet visible, tangible and audible to you alone as you share with him your thoughts and feelings. He is ready to heal your hurts and give you strength for each new challenge. He comforts you, wipes away your tears and brings healing to your soul.

At your own pace, move up sucessive steps to each year of your life's journey through into your teens. He knows your fears and hopes and dreams. He is there when you are tempted and when you fall; and he helps you to rise again, strengthened by his love.

Continue up your golden staircase, pausing when you need to break off for an hour, a day, a week or longer. Go on until you reach the present year, thank him there that he has healed the hurts of the past and will walk with you into the unknown future, holding your hand and guiding you in his way. Receive his promises: 'I will never leave you nor forsake you.'[150] 'Remember, I am with you always, to the end of the age.'[151]

---

150 Hebrews 13:5-6
151 Matthew 28:20

Exercise 4 – A Walk with God:

Read Psalm 118 and see God walking beside you through every stage as you review your life. You were not aware of his presence back then, and you did things your way and bad things bombarded you. But now, as you return to those scenes you see that God is beside you, not permitting the hurts to destroy you and helping you now to rise in triumph over your former adversity.

Memorise and carry in your mind one of the scripture verses that made a positive impact on you as you meditatively read through this Psalm, or hold onto one of the verses from another scripture passage in one of the other healing exercises.

Whenever a painful memory threatens to raise its ugly head, repeat the verse of victory.

*'The thief comes only in order to steal and kill and destroy,'
said Jesus. 'I am come that you might have life, and have it in
all its fullness and abundance.'*
(John 10:10 amplified)

Jesus said, 'I am the light of the world. Whoever follows me will never walk in darkness, but will have the light of life.'
(John 8:12)

Psalm 139(NIV)

1. O LORD, You have searched me and you know me.
2. You know when I sit and when I rise;
   you perceive my thoughts from afar.
3. You discern my going out and my lying down;
   and are familiar with all my ways.
4. Before a word is on my tongue you know it completely, O LORD.
5. You hem me in – behind and before;
   you have laid your hand upon me.
6. Such knowledge is too wonderful for me,
   too lofty for me to attain.
7. Where can I go from your Spirit?
   Where can I flee from your presence?
8. If I go up to the heavens, you are there;
   if I make my bed in the depths, you are there.
9. If I rise on the wings of the dawn,
   if I settle on the far side of the sea,
10. even there your hand will guide me,
    your right hand will hold me fast.
11. If I say, 'Surely the darkness will hide me
    and the light become night around me,'
12. even the darkness will not be dark to you;
    the night will shine like the day,
    for darkness is as light to you.
13. For you created my inmost being;
    you knit me together in my mother's womb.
14. I praise you because I am fearfully and wonderfully made;
    your works are wonderful, I know that full well.
15. My frame was not hidden from you
    when I was made in the secret place.
    When I was woven together in the depths of the earth,
16. your eyes saw my unformed body.
    All the days ordained for me were written in your book before one of them came to be.

17. How precious to me are your thoughts, O God!
    How vast is the sum of them!
18. Were I to count them,
    they would outnumber the grains of sand.
    When I awake I am still with you.
19. If only you would slay the wicked, O God!
    Away from me, you bloodthirsty men!
20. They speak of you with evil intent;
    your adversaries misuse your name.
21. Do I not hate those who hate you, O LORD,
    and abhor those who rise up against you?
22. I have nothing but hatred for them;
    I count them my enemies.
23. Search me, O God, and know my heart;
    test me and know my anxious thoughts.
24. See if there is any offensive way in me,
    and lead me in the way everlasting

ಸಿಆ

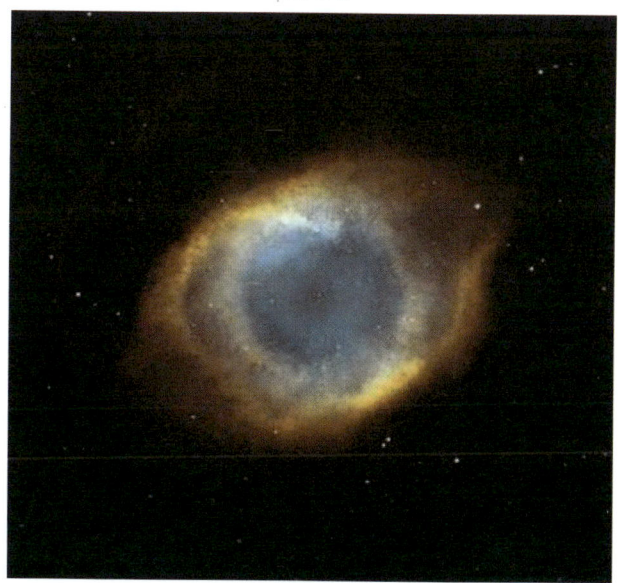

'The Eye of God'[152]

---

[152] This photograph of an event, which occurs only once every 3000 years, was taken by NASA with the Hubble telescope. It is called 'The Eye of God'.

A Bedtime Prayer

ೞಉ

*Now as I lie down to sleep,
I ask thee Lord my soul to keep.
Be with me through my dreams this night,
And wake me with the morning light.*

Author unknown

14. Common Dream Images

ৎ৹ A ৫ও

Abandonment: Dreaming that you have been abandoned may signify a subliminal state of anxiety or dependency which has emerged in your dream to bring it to a level of consciousness in order for you to deal with it by either letting go of it or working through the roots of feelings of insecurity. You may be in need of inner healing[153] if it relates to a past experience of being abandoned. If you dream that you have abandoned someone or something, it could either be a positive indication that you need to move on, or a negative sign warning you of neglect of an important issue or relationship: depending on your waking feelings – relief or distress.

Abdomen: A place of feelings and emotion. At times, on a subliminal level, we know that something is wrong even before symptoms appear. Think of the term: 'gut feeling.' What were your feelings associated with this dream? (See also Stomach)

Abduction: This is to do with fear and often occurs during times of transition or stress when the future is uncertain. Think of what is unsettling you or what you may be afraid of losing, either materially or emotionally. 'Do not be afraid, for I am with you…' says God.[154]

Abortion: It is common for someone who has had an abortion or miscarriage to have dreams about it. It may be an indication that inner healing is needed,[155] if not, it could indicate something with tremendous potential not being fully developed: giving up before the idea or project is completed. Alternatively, it could suggest that you are anticipating failure in some area; hesitant in pursuing a new direction in your life; hindering or obstructing your own spiritual growth.

Absurdity: Many of our dreams do not make sense. It may simply illustrate that life is a mystery and there is much,

---
153 See Chapter 13 - Emotional Healing through Meditation and Lucid Dreams
154 Genesis 26:24 also Joshua 1:9
155 See Chapter 13 - Emotional Healing through Meditation and Lucid Dreams

particularly in the spiritual realm, that we will never understand this side of heaven. You simply need to watch and wait for clarity. What you need to understand will be revealed in God's perfect timing.

Accident: This usually indicates a warning of something having gone awry.

Actor: To dream of a well-known actor could indicate you identify with them. Think of what you admire or despise in that person. Note the part that is being enacted – is it a comedy or a tragedy? Perhaps this dream could be revealing the role that you are playing in life; presenting yourself as other than who or what you are; that you are putting on an act or escaping reality. Ask yourself, 'What role am I playing? From what am I hiding or trying to escape? How do I want to be seen by others?'

Adultery: Dreaming that you are committing adultery could signify sexual urges that are longing to be expressed or it may indicate an unconscious betrayal. You might possibly be entangled in a situation that is not in your best interest or perhaps immoral or even illegal. If you dream your spouse or partner is having an affair it may indicate your insecurity or fear of being abandoned, or a suspicion playing on your mind. Alternatively, it could indicate a desire to connect to your opposite complementary nature. (See Man & Woman)

Advocate: (See Judge)

African: This can symbolise our roots or heritage. You will need to explore in your own mind what this person represents to you, personally.

Aging: Old age is a symbol of wisdom and experience, or outdated ideas. Consider analysing what it is that is aging in your dream.

Air: One of earth's four basic elements. It is associated with spirituality and creativity – related particularly to the supra-conscious area of the mind – *in tune with God, the Creator of the universe*. Turbulent air indicates confusion of spiritual thoughts. If the air is foggy or misty, it suggests that you thoughts are clouded. Is the air polluted? Have you allowed impure thoughts to poison your mind? (See 'Air' under The Four Basic Elements in Chapter 12. See also 'Breath' and 'Wind')

Aircraft: (See Airplane)

Airplane crash: This kind of dream is usually tapping into your fears or related to your waking reflections on real air crash disasters. The first question to ask yourself is: What have I recently been seeing, reading or hearing about an air-disaster? If it is unrelated to your personal fear of flying it may be associated to an unrelated fear of having lost control of a situation; lost hope; a loss of ambition; or loss of faith. Have high ideals come crashing down? It could be a warning of possible disaster.

Airplane: All vehicles symbolize your life's journey. Note first your feelings about the dream. A disturbing dream carries a warning, whereas if you are enjoying the experience it has a positive message. You need to note too whether you are in control of the airplane or if you are a passenger. With you in control it could indicate that you are 'reaching great heights'; 'flying high'; 'rising above the situation'; 'you have your head in the clouds' or are 'out of you element.' If you are a passenger it may suggest that you are being taken to new spiritual, intellectual or emotional heights. Are you landing in an aircraft? Come down to earth. Taking off? You could be about to rise to new heights. (See Travel; also Vehicles in Chapter 11 – My World)

Airport: Refers to religious pursuits; high standards; lofty principles. Being in an airport indicates a desire to be caught up in the spirit; to rise above your circumstances, your difficulties, worldly pressures or responsibilities. You may want to escape something which you feel is repressing you, holding you back; Meeting someone at the airport – someone you think needs to come down to earth. Are you missing your flight? – You may be missing an opportunity to raise your status or standards.

Alarm: What kind of alarm is it? Is it an alarm clock; fire alarm; siren? Reflect on what it may indicate – Wake up to some truth; a warning of some kind; being alarmed. What is causing you alarm? You may need to note the context of the dream.

Alcoholic beverage: 'Unholy' spirits; hindrance to spiritual growth; dulled senses. What effect does alcohol have on you?

Alien/s: Are you the alien in your dream? It could indicate that you are unfamiliar with your present situation or anxious about going into a strange situation. It may also be revealing that there is an undiscovered part of you needing to be realised. Are you perhaps escaping reality? Are your ideas outlandish? If you are encountering or being abducted by aliens, it may be that you are fearful of a new or strange situation, a change of job or a move. Is your space being invaded?

Alley: The mood and your feelings associated with this dream are important. Is it dark and menacing? Have you strayed into something unpleasant? Is there a dead end? Do you feel as though there is no way out? Think also of the positive: 'Just up my alley'

Alligator: (see crocodile)

Altar: A symbol of worship or sacrifice. What is on the altar? Does this indicate what you are worshipping or need to sacrifice? Consider the play on words – what do you need to alter?

Ambulance: This dream may be pointing to some urgent situation in your life or a warning of a crisis looming; prepare for an emergency; there is a need to act quickly; you are ready to be of assistance; help is on the way. Consider if there is something that requires your immediate attention.

Amputation: To dream of body parts being amputated signifies a threat of loss of what that member symbolizes for you. It indicates your feelings of powerlessness and helplessness. It may indicate a talent that you have been neglecting – 'use it or lose it.' It could also signify some activity that needs to be curtailed.

Amusement Park: To be in an amusement park could reveal that you may need to set some time for leisure and more enjoyment in your life. Let the inner child play. Consider how the things in the park may express some aspect of your life. Alternatively, you may have been too easily distracted lately and need to get serious.

Ancestors: This could be referring to inborn character traits; your genetic makeup or a preconscious state. Note also who the ancestor is and what they mean to you.

Anchor: An anchor is a symbol of stability and security. You may want a solid base. Alternatively, it could indicate that you are firm in your views and opinions, or it may be saying, 'This is the place to settle,' or 'Stay where you are for a while.'

Androgynous Being: This is a genderless individual, having both male and female qualities. It is an archetypical symbol. This is a person with a perfect balance of both male and female characteristics. (See both Man and Woman in listings below)

Angel: This is an archetypical symbol. They are spiritual beings; messengers of God; intermediaries between God and humans representing purity, goodness and protection. They are guides toward deeper spirituality and greater fulfilment in your life. Pay careful attention to the message that the angels are trying to convey to you. To dream that you are an angel could be a call to apply your higher self to serve others. Think of the appeal, 'be an angel and...'

Anger: Who is angry and for what reason? It could be a carry-over from a situation in your waking life. In the theatre of our soul on the stage of our dream we can vent our anger in safely. It may also stem from the subliminal level emerging to reveal the cause so that we may deal with it appropriately and creatively on waking.

Animals: (see Chapter 12 – Animals Life and the individual listings)

Antiques: Are they beautiful or valuable? This could signify potential; something original; genuine; classic; ageless; old traits, attitudes or behaviour; outdated ideas.

Ants: A symbol of frugality; provision; untiring; stockpiling;

strength. According to the Bible, ants are commended for their wisdom.[156] Though tiny, an ant can carry a load many times its own weight. They are always on the run laying up stocks - a symbol of diligence.

Ape: A symbol of lust; cunning; uncleanness; malice. Note the type, size and behaviour of the primate in your dream. What is your feeling about primates in general and this type in particular? Is the one in your dream behaving true to type or is it acting differently? How do you react to your dream primate? Generally primates are associated with the primitive state. We associate with them low intelligence; destructive behaviour; mimicry; agility.

Applause: This generally indicates approval and encouragement.

Apples: For most people this is a dominant religious symbol. It primarily represents knowledge and freedom of choice with positive or negative options. What do you associate apples with? Is the apple a symbol of movement to spiritual or emotional liberation, or does it symbolise for you passions run wild and its consequences? Are you being tempted in some way? Are you giving in to temptation and making harmful choices or are you being wise and enjoying the fullness of life? Note that there is no mention of an apple in Genesis 3:3. It was the fruit of the tree of knowledge of good and evil which was at the centre of the garden that was forbidden. Think also of some familiar sayings associated with apples: 'In apple pie order' = perfect order; 'the apple of my eye' = most loved person; 'an apple a day keeps the doctor away'; 'stealing apples' = a desire for the love of someone who is already committed to another; 'one rotten apple spoils the whole barrel.'

Apron: Wearing an apron suggests that you may be nurturing an idea or a project. It could imply submission, allowing others to tell you what to do. It may also symbolize a need for protection.

Aquarium: Water is associated with primordial life – at the beginning of creation the world was enveloped in water.

---
156 Proverbs 20:25

Aquariums represent fully contained ecosystems. We enjoy an aquarium because it soothes and relaxes us. Looking at fish in an aquarium could indicate that you are observing or envious of your Christian friends' spiritual devotion; wanting deeper theological teaching; aspiring to holiness; aestheticism; mysticism. It may therefore be a call for contemplation and relaxation or indicate a desire to retreat from the stress and complexity of daily life. (See also Chapter 12 Animal Life and the Four Basic Elements)

Archaeologist/Archaeology: This could relate to something buried from your past, or something in your subliminal or unconscious mind that needs to be brought to the surface; dig within yourself for the answer.

Argument: This may indicate inner turmoil or conflict. It could also be a warning of opposition or emotional tension.

Ark: Is it the Ark of the Covenant which was housed in the Holy of Holies in the Tabernacle and the Temple? This could be reminding you of your covenant with God, or God's promise to you. Is it Noah's Ark? If so, it could relate to the preservation of your animal instincts.

Armchair: Sitting in an armchair indicates security and comfort concerning a position in waking life and deserving respect. It could also signify a job completed and well done.

Armour: Armour represents protection and defence. Think about what protective measures you use and how you defend yourself when under attack. Are you feeling the need for protection? Are you anticipating an attack? 'Put on the whole armour of God.' (See Ephesians 6:10-18)

Arms: Related to service, they indicate your ability to reach out, embrace or care for someone or something. It may also represent a struggle or challenge in life. What is in those arms? How are they held? – cradled = care for it. Carrying a heavy burden? – What load are you carrying? Are the arms weak or strong? The right arm signifies an outgoing nature and is associated with masculine energy, while the left arm signifies a supportive or nurturing nature and is associated with feminine qualities. Losing or injuring either arm may suggest a failing or weakness in those characteristics. Consider also 'arm yourself' or 'armour' = implying a need to protect yourself; 'up in arms' = being angry or ready to argue.

Army: This can represent an overwhelming force working for or against you. You may feel outnumbered or under attack and unable to deal with or overcome this situation.

Arrow: Is the arrow being used for sport, as a weapon or a sign pointing direction? Depending on what kind of arrow it is, the interpretation differs. The arrow could symbolise precision; swiftness; a message coming to you; giving direction; Cupid's arrow through your heart = love coming your way; Satan's fiery arrows = accusations; or it may be a phallic symbol.

Art: What kind of art is it? Is it some form of art that you like or dislike? Pictures are representations of what you see or know. What does the picture represent to you?

Artist: If you are an artist it is indicative of the creative side expressing itself. The picture that you are painting may symbolize the way that you visualise your present situation.

Artwork: If you are purchasing a work of art, it suggests that you are seeking inspiration. If you are selling artwork, it shows your ability to express yourself and your beliefs.

Ashes: Could be showing that something is now finished and done with. It may also indicate that a relationship or venture is over and laid to rest. Put the past behind you.

Ashtray: Connected to your being a smoker it may be related to your efforts to give up the habit. To be using an ashtray suggests that you are trying to rid yourself of your old ways or need to extinguish a burning issue.

Ass: A symbol of stupidity or signifying a lack of understanding. (See Donkey)

Athlete: Are you being too competitive? Perhaps you are being a bad sport in a situation or you may need to cooperate more with colleagues or associates. What are you running from? What are you running towards? What is your goal? Are you simply racing against time? Are you under time pressure?

Think: 'It's not whether you win or lose, it's how you play the game.' 'Since we are surrounded by so great a crowd of witnesses, let us lay aside every weight and sin which clings… and run with perseverance the race set before us.'[157]

Attack: If you are attacking someone it shows pent-up emotions and anger. If you are being attacked it indicates a feeling of vulnerability and harassment with a need to defend yourself. You may also be faced with stress in your waking life. If it is an animal that is attacking you, it may be the animal within you that you are fighting. What does that particular animal symbolise for you? What qualities has that animal that you identify in yourself or someone you know?

Attic: This is connected to the higher self – a symbol of our spirituality. It also relates to the mind and stored memories. An attic full of lovely things may mean that you are achieving much and living up to your potential in life. To see a cluttered attic, is a sign of confusion and a need to organize your thoughts. Perhaps you need to rid yourself of past hurts and failures. When you awake, go back into that attic with Jesus and ask Him to help you clear and clean it out and turn it into a place of light and life. (See also under 'House')

Auction: This indicates that you may have high expectations or you may be overvaluing or undervaluing something or someone in your life. It may also mean that you are ready to let go and move on. If no one is bidding it suggests that your opinion or idea is not appreciated or your suggestions are being ignored. If someone outbids you it suggests that you are being denied something that you want or need.

Audience: Your audience is the world around you and people are watching your performance in life. If you suffer stage fright it suggests fear of not fulfilling the expectations that others have of you, or a dread of having your hidden private thoughts, feelings or actions revealed. If you have no audience it may indicate that you feel that you are not appreciated or your achievements not being acknowledged.

Autopsy: To observe, perform or find yourself being

---
157 Hebrews 12:1 (see also Philippians 2:16, 1 Corinthians 9:24)

dissected suggests that you are analysing or being scrutinized by others and being reviewed or appraising yourself.

Autumn: (see 'Seasons')

Avalanche: Snow is frozen water and water symbolizes life, the higher-self or supra-conscious and emotions. An avalanche is a violent and rapid descent of snow. It is white, cold and suffocating. This dream could therefore represent stifling or crashing emotions, but being cool and white symbolising goodness and purity from the higher-self, so it may mean an overwhelming spiritual onslaught.

Award: To receive an award shows that you feel you deserve some recognition and acknowledgment for what you do. If others are receiving awards and you are not, it indicates a feeling of failure.

Axe: It is used to cleave wood or chop trees and symbolises power and an expression of strength. If the dream was violent you may be experiencing hostility or frustration. If the dream was calm it may be interpreted to symbolise productivity and creative power.

❧ B ☙

Baboon: (See Ape)

Baby: Babies represent our fragile or undeveloped side: That part of us that needs to be cared for, protected, nurtured and brought to maturity.

Adopting a baby – need to adopt new ideas or taking responsibility for what is not of your making; A project that is growing well.

Baby boy – new birth of masculine traits. (see Man)

Baby girl – new birth of feminine traits. (see Woman)

Beautiful healthy baby – New awareness; re-birth of lower self to a higher plane of awareness.

Being given a baby to care for – receiving a new task; a responsibility we carry; position we hold; some project that needs to be nurtured or brought to completion; a new phase in the project.

ABDead baby – failure in responsibilities.

Deformed baby – a project that is going wrong.

Giving birth – A new idea or thought. Something that has come about as a result of the union of intellect and emotions, logic and intuition – a new project being launched.

Looking at, or admiring a baby – viewing a new project, exploring the possibilities or potential.

Several babies – numerous responsibilities.

Sick baby – shirking responsibility.

Twin babies – double responsibility.

Think also: 'Babes in the woods'; 'throw the baby out with the bath water'; 'left holding the baby'; 'that's not my baby' = not my responsibility;

Back: Indicates physical strength, endurance, burden bearing. Turning you back on what is not constructive. Go back to what is unfinished. Backbone = stand firm in the face of opposition; strength or endurance; be decisive.

Back Door: (See under 'House')

Back Yard/Garden: (See under 'House')

Bake: (See Cook)

Bald: Hair represents strength and beauty. As a covering for the head it symbolises thoughts. Lack of hair could indicate lack of clarity of thought.

Bananas: Foods is nourishment and fruit symbolises fertility and fruitfulness. Freud suggested that all such objects are phallic symbols. Over-ripe bruised or rotting fruit often implies bad or bruised relationships.

Bank: This relates to your assets and resources. It could also refer to your treasures or treasured memories. Are you there to make a withdrawal? You could be trying to remember something from the past; drawing on your resources, relying on some asset. Are you making a deposit? You may be adding to your store of valuable knowledge or implanting a treasured memory. Think also: 'don't bank on it.'

Baptism: Signifies a new beginning; dedication or commitment; renewal through the washing away of sin in your life; surrender to God; infilling of the Holy Spirit.

Bar: (See Pub)

Barber: (See Hairdresser)

Bare: (See Naked)

Barefoot: First think of what being barefoot means to you: Freedom; unrestrained; casual approach; standing on holy ground; standing in the presence of God... or is it socially inappropriate in public – insensitivity; non-conformity... or 'tender-footed'; 'feet on the ground'; 'walk/tread softly'; 'built for comfort not speed'; 'on home ground'. (See Naked and Foot/feet)

Barn: The dreamer has a storehouse of untapped potential or power.

Basement: (see House - Cellar)

Bat: Bats are regarded by most people as unpredictable portents of evil. Note your emotional reaction to the dream. What do bats represent to you? Think of the sayings: 'like a bat out of hell'; 'bats in the belfry'; 'blind as a bat.'

Bath: Taking a bath or shower represents cleansing of the outer self. It may indicate a need to wash away those things in your outer life that are disturbing or out of place. It could also indicate a need to get rid of the things that are troubling you or issues from the past or getting rid of bad habits; inappropriate behaviour; corrupt practices; impure thoughts or language; need for spiritual cleansing.

Bathroom: (See under House)

Battlefield: This may indicate hostility and aggression, or impulses that are at war in you; fighting to overcome a strong desire; an overpowering urge like an addiction.

Beach: This could have a vast number of interpretations. To understand the meaning you will need to reflect on the setting, the mood, your feelings and what is happening there.

Bear: Bears are solitary animals associated with being protective; cuddly; warm; playful; smothering; stifling; overbearing; grumpy; Think also of 'bare'; 'bare-faced'; 'bare facts'; "bear-market' (falling prices)

Beard: Beards are a symbol of masculine dignity, strength, age and wisdom. Bearded men usually command respect. Moses, Jesus, Charles Darwin all had beards.

Beauty Salon: (See Hairdresser)

Beaver: Beavers are busy animals gnawing wood to build their homes to protect and isolate themselves. Is something gnawing at you that you cannot ignore? Are you perhaps trying to block out something? Think also of: 'beavering away.'

Bed: This is symbolic of rest; restoration; renewal; relaxation; slumber; recreation; regeneration. It is the bridge between the conscious life and the unknown world of dreams, of the physical world and the mystery of the spirit realm. The quality, order and spotlessness of the bed may indicate the way we feel about ourselves and our relationships. We 'make our own bed and lie in it,' so the dream may be telling us that we have to either change our ways or live with them. Things hiding under the bed may symbolize secrets.

Bees: A symbol of industry. They have good organization skills, are creative and cooperative. Think of the positive and negative associations: 'being a busybody'; 'a sting in the tail.'

Beetles: A symbol of blindness.

Bells: Indicate communication, announcements or reminder. Church bells = a call to worship; wedding bells = celebration; alarm bells = a warning; 'saved by the bell' = end of a fight; 'that rings a bell' = remembering; 'with bells on' = over elaborate.

Belly: (See Stomach)

Bible: This may indicate the need to seek God's guidance; follow God's commands; a reminder of God's promises or standards; study God's Word or God wants to communicate with you through the Word.

Bicycle: Vehicles symbolize our journey through life. As bicycles are our mode of transport in youth it could point to some childlike tendency. It may also indicate that you are doing a balancing act at present; needing to balance time and responsibilities; create a balance in your life. There may be a call for balance between spiritual and physical pursuits. (See also 'Vehicles' in Chapter 11)

Birds: Doves and eagles are strong spiritual symbols. (See Birds in Chapter 12 – Animal Life)

Birth: (see under Baby)

Bite/biting: Who or what is biting? What or who is being bitten? Being aggressive; wounding or being wounded. Think of the various figures of speech: 'bite off more than you can chew' = take on more than you're capable of completing; 'bite someone's head off' = responding snappily to a request; 'bite one's lip' = suppressing emotions (see lip/s); 'bite one's tongue' = remain silent under provocation; 'biting words' = harshness; 'bite the bullet' = endure pain; 'bite the hand that feeds you' = repay kindness with ingratitude; 'bite the dust' = fall down dead.

Black: is not a colour but the absorption of all colour and reflection of none. Black is the symbol of death and the colour of mourning. Spiritually it symbolises not only death but sin, evil, the absence of light and the darkness of hell. 'Black magic'; 'black or white'; 'Black mood'; Black bile'; 'Black-out'; 'Black market' – all convey either ignorance, corruption, deception, evil, renunciation or death as construed by western culture. Black, on the positive side, also conveys a sense of mystery, unknowing, as yet un-revealed profundity; beyond understanding; the unknown and unknowable; obscurity; anonymity and secrecy.

Blanket: Symbolic of warmth, comfort, security; protection; rest. Think of 'blanket of snow'; 'blanket of cloud' = covering; 'wet blanket' = a person whose lack of enthusiasm stifles the fervour of others (a wet blanket quenches a fire). Think also of Linus in the Peanuts cartoon and his 'security blanket' as a symbol of the Holy Spirit.

Blindness: This may suggest that you have a blind spot or are unwilling to see some aspect of your life; unable to see the facts or consequences of an action; groping around in the darkness of ignorance or confusion; not facing reality. Perhaps there is a message trying to surface from your subliminal, preconscious, collective unconscious or supra-conscious level into you conscious mind. If this arouses strong negative emotions, take heart, clarity and inner peace will come as you seek enlightenment. (See also Chapter 13 – Emotional Healing through Meditation and Lucid Dreams)

Blood: A dream with blood in it carries a powerful message. Blood is a symbol of life[158]; bleeding = loss of life-force/vital energy; menstrual flow = absence of potential new life, aborted project. Blood denotes family ties; 'blood on his hands' = destroyer of a scheme, operation or venture. 'hot blooded' = having a temper; 'to make blood boil' = make angry; 'blood run cold' = chilling experience; 'blue blood' = nobility (noble deed).

Blue: This is the colour associated with the sky, heavens, spirituality, water and seas. It promotes peace and contentment. The deeper the colour blue, the stronger the spiritual connotation. (See Chapter 8 – Colours, Gems and Metals).

Bluebird: A symbol of happiness. It could well symbolise a spiritual blessing. (See also 'Birds' in Chapter 12)

Boat: Water symbolises both the spirit realm and the

---
158 Leviticus 17:14

unconscious or subliminal mind. The depths and darkness indicate the intensity of mystery and profundity. Travelling on water or launching out in a boat – entering into spiritual territory and/or the unconscious or subliminal areas of our psyche. Consider the kind of voyage and the type of vessel. As Jesus on occasion preached and taught the crowds on land from the fishing boat on the water it could symbolise for a preacher, the pulpit, or to anyone, a message from God to you in the world. (See 'Vehicles' in Chapter 11 and 'Water' in Chapter 12 – The Four Basic Elements)

Body language: Different gestures need to be interpreted as you read them. What are they telling you?

Body parts: (See individual listings)

Body: The outer shell without the inner life of the soul and spirit. Who we are is held within the wrapping of what we look like and the means of connecting to the world in which we live. Dreaming about your body may refer to your personal identity as relating to the physical world. (See individual body parts)

Bomb: (See Disaster)

Bones: 'Bare bones' = down to essentials; the 'bare bones' of an idea that need to be fleshed out; 'bone idle' = extremely lazy; 'make no bones about it' = candid; 'pick a bone' = discuss and settle an unpleasant issue; 'dry bones' scheme that need to be prayed over, breathed upon or addressed[159].

Books: They are a source of information, a means of gaining knowledge, inspiration and sometimes are life changing. Books in our dreams can represent our ideas, understanding, points of view, facts learned or memories. They can also alert us to the fact that we have something to learn. Note what kind of book you see or are reading.

Boots: Could relate to dismissal – 'get the boot' or a situation reversed – 'boot is on the other foot'; 'these boots are made for walking...' (See Footwear)

Boss: (see Employer)

Brain: This is related to the intellect; abode of the psyche;

---
159 Ezekiel 37:1-14

control centre; 'left brain' = the logical sphere; 'right brain' = creativity; 'brain child' = idea or creative thought; 'brainstorm' = sudden, violent upheaval causing loss of control; 'brain dump' = let one's thoughts, no matter how strange, be freely expressed; 'pick someone's brains.'

Brass: Brass is used in the making of memorial plaques in churches. It is the colour of gold, but tarnishes rapidly, needing to be polished frequently in order to look bright. Brass is a slang term for money. Think of related sayings such as: 'not worth a brass farthing'; 'top brass' = high rank; 'brassed off' = disgruntled; 'as bold as brass' = impudent; 'getting down to brass tacks' = set about a task in earnest.

Bread: This is a positive universal symbol of our basic sustenance. Bread is the 'staff of life' = that which supports life. It is also a profoundly spiritual sign: Jesus referred to himself as 'The Bread of Life'.[160] It is also a religious symbol: 'Bread & Wine' of Holy Communion representing a powerful connection with God and people. 'Breaking bread' means share in a meal together. It could for some refer to money, as the term is used in slang.

Breasts or Breast Feeding: Breasts may have sexual connotations or represent femininity, tenderness, love, nurture or matters of the heart.

Breath: This is associated with spirit and life.[161] (see also Air, Wind)

Bricks: Brick or concrete are man-made earth compounds and therefore symbolise what we make of ourselves – attitudes; opinions; concepts; mindset.

Bridge: Bridges symbolize crossings, links, connections or transitions from one stage to another or from one level of consciousness to another. Note what type of bridge it is and whether it is over water, a railway line or a road and look at references to those symbols. This dream could symbolise rising above your difficulties, subliminal or subconscious drives.

Brother/Sister: The supportive, affirming side of us.

---
160 John 6:35
161 Genesis 2:7

Review your relationship with the dream person. Ask, 'Was there sibling rivalry at that stage in our relationship? Did we share secrets? Was I the elder, responsible or were they? Did I look up to them or did they depend on me?' Ask also, 'Am I my brother's keeper?'

Brown: (See chapter 8 - Colours)

Budgerigar: Caged bird; your spirit is imprisoned or inhibited. What colour is the budgie? (See birds, cage and the colours)

Builder/Construction Worker: Being constructive, productive, creative; edifying; putting all the pieces together. What is the builder doing – laying foundations (get back to basics), building a tower (reaching great heights; aiming high), putting up a wall (creating a barrier)?

Building or repairing a house: (see House)

Bull: This is an archetypical symbol. In Biblical times a bull was a sacrificial sin-offering.[162] It could therefore represent sacrifice. It could also symbolise strength; masculine sexual energy; determination; frankness; stubbornness; tenacity; anger; insincerity; boasting; bullying; someone who is easily enraged – or talking nonsense; 'bull in a china shop' = clumsiness; 'take the bull by the horns' = tackling a difficult issue; 'bull-market' = rising prices.

Bulldog: A symbol of pertinacity; determination.

Bungalow: (See House)

Burial: Dreaming of burying a dead person or a funeral does not necessarily mean a physical death. It could symbolize an ending of a different kind. You may be burying your feelings, an emotion, a grudge or a relationship that has died. It could also indicate that you may be burying emotions that are too difficult to cope with. Burying something that is still alive could indicate the need to deal with it and seek healing in that area. (See also Coffin and Death)

Bus/Train Station: This could symbolise anticipation of change or a new venture.

Bus: This dream is related to our journey in life alongside

---
162 Leviticus 16:3,6

others, known or unknown. Take note though of who is with you on the bus. It indicates primarily the people who are going in the same direction, such as co-workers, colleagues or family members. It could indicate a detached or elevated view of the events which surround you; a weighty problem; difficulty in manoeuvring. Note the other elements in the dream for more clarity. (See also Chapter 11 – Vehicles)

Butcher: A butcher slaughters whereas a surgeon cuts to cure. This is a brutal attack which dismembers the body. What is being hacked? Think in terms of disjointed; cutting; hacking; chopping; mincing your words; slaughtering – all brutal means of dissecting. It may symbolise a desire for greater assertiveness. It could also relate to sacrifice[163]; or a longing for more 'meaty' doctrine - 'As babes in Christ I fed you with milk and not meat.[164]' Cutting off the 'flesh' = carnal nature.

Butler: (See Servant)

Butterfly: A symbol of hedonism, gaiety and transformation through to a higher plain as they go through the cycle of change from egg, through caterpillar and pupa to the beautiful nectar-feeding adult.

Buttons: These could be fastenings on a garment or push buttons. If they are on clothing, note whether they are being done up or undone and thence interpret the meaning for your situation. Unbuttoning generally represents an opening up, being open or new possibilities coming to you. Buttoning-up may indicate a closure of something. Think also of 'button your lip' = keep quiet about something.

---

163 Leviticus 1:11ff
164 1 Corinthians 3:2

∞ C ∞

Cage: This symbolises imprisonment; entrapment; restraint of something which is in nature free. Seeing a caged animal could indicate your constrained spirit or some natural inclination that is being stifled. If it is a dangerous animal, it could indicate that your wild side is restrained. Who holds the keys to the cage or who caged the animal? Are you feeling trapped in a situation or relationship? Do you feel as though you need to restrain your feelings or thoughts?

Cake: To interpret this dream you need to consider what type of cake it is and what it symbolises. Is it a birthday, Christmas, celebratory or fruit cake? What is its shape and size? Note the decorations or lack thereof. How do you interact with the cake? Think too of some familiar sayings: 'To have your cake and eat it'; 'you take the cake'; 'selling like hot cakes'; 'it's a piece of cake'; 'life's not all cakes and ale.'

Calculator: (See Chapter 9 - Numbers in Dreams)

Calf: A symbol of cowardice; being lumpish.

Camel: A beast of burden and symbol of submission. 'Ship of the desert'; barren desires; emotionally dried up; carrying burdens.

Campervan: A relaxed attitude to the situation or venture. (See Vehicles in Chapter 11)

Camping: This is temporary accommodation. It may suggest you get in touch with nature; get back to basics; a more casual lifestyle; need for greater simplicity, a retreat or recreation.

Cancer: This is most likely an anxiety dream. It may also be a warning dream. Is there something eating away at you; growing out of control?

Candle: A symbol of spiritual light, life and enlightenment. Candles are often used as a focal point in meditation. There is something soothing and comforting about a flickering candle flame. Think of some related sayings: 'burning the candle at both ends'; 'where there is light, there is hope'; 'to hold a candle to someone' = give them support; 'light a short candle' = limit the length of the visit. If it is an unlit candle, think of 'being in the dark'

Cannibalism: Living off someone else; destroying another in order to satisfy your own appetite.

Cap: Related to thoughts, intellect or the mind. 'Put on your thinking cap' = give careful consideration before giving an answer; 'cap in hand' = submissive approach; 'to cap it' = make things worse; 'set your cap for him' = (a woman) in order impress or win a man.

Car: (See Vehicles – Chapter 11)

Cards: Shuffling cards signifies indecision; Diamonds symbolize wealth; clubs symbolize work; hearts symbolize love; spades symbolize trouble. Note the numeric value and see the symbolism in the chapter on numbers. Think of a play on words 'on the cards' = it is likely to happen; 'play your cards right' = plan for success; 'play a trump card' = outdo or outsmart someone.

Carnival: Being exposed or involved in deception or lies. Seeing abnormalities at a carnival implies disharmony, disorder in life or a dysfunctional relationship; sorrow in what we expected to bring pleasure. If you are on a ride, it denotes futile pursuits.

Carpet: 'on the carpet' = coming under discipline; 'under the carpet' = covering up something; 'carpet biter' = subject to violent fits of rage. (Note the colour of the carpet)

Carriage: Different way of life; transition; new course of action; wedding carriage = romance; horse drawn carriage – see Horse (See also 'vehicles' - Chapter 11)

Carrousel: (See Merry-go-round)

Carving: Carving meat = hostility or aggression; carving a design in wood or initials in a tree = desire to leave your mark in the world or to make an impression; carving a statue = a desire to be creative. (Note what it is that you are carving)

Castle: Castles symbolise opulence; elegance; security; power; strength; 'building castles in the air' = living in a fantasy world; 'a castle in Spain' (See 'Buildings' Chapter 11)

Casual dress: A relaxed attitude; informality; comfortable to be with; unassuming.

Cat: Positive or negative interpretation depending on how you view cats. It could symbolise deceit; cattiness; nastiness; aloofness; being uncooperative; a gossip; pettiness; stalking its prey; pouncing; a loner; independent... or having 'nine lives' = spiritual progress to completeness (see nine in the chapter on numbers); purring with pleasure; sensuous; 'cool cat'; 'let the cat out of the bag'; 'land on one's feet' = good fortune.

Catastrophe: (see Disaster)

Caterpillar: Larval stage of a flying insect – symbolising earthly, carnal life prior to the sleep of the chrysalis phase for transformation in preparation for the phase in flight – symbolising the spiritual life.

Cathedral: Place of worship (see Church)

Cave: This is an archetypical symbol. It is a symbol of the womb of Great Mother Earth. To dream that you are in a cave signifies refuge, protection, nurture and spiritual growth in preparation for new life. Also a storage place; accommodation; protected area; primitive life; site of mystery; secrecy; hiding; darkness. To dream that you are exploring a dark cave means an examination of your unconscious mind leading to self-discovery. Descent into a cave = a need to explore the depths of the subliminal mind; dread of not being able to find your way out = fear of losing your mind; cave-in = undermining of the body, soul or spirit.

Ceiling: (see under House)

Celebrity: If this is a person that you greatly admire, it could indicate that you wish to emulate the trait that you admire. If it is someone that you dislike, think of what you dislike about them and consider the possibility that you share that weakness or tendency. We often hate those traits in others of which we are ourselves guilty.

Cellar: (See under House)

Cemetery: This may signify a fear of death or anticipation of the demise of someone close to you; the dark corner of your mind where past experiences are buried; something that you would like to forget or which has been forgotten but needs to be revisited to bring inner healing. There is a need to pray for a revelation of what it is and to ask for God's healing touch. (See Chapter 13 – Emotional Healing Through Meditation and Lucid Dreams)

Chain: This indicates restrictions in your life. Think of 'links.' 'A chain is only as strong as its weakest link'; 'missing link'; 'chain letter' – what threat or bribe needs to be broken? What do you feel shackled to/from which you need to be set free?

Chalet: (See House)

Chalice: This is an archetypical symbol. It is a sacramental vessel, the contents of which are believed to have supernatural power, especially for healing. In the Christian church it represents the cup of wine that Jesus shared with his disciples at the last supper and symbolises the blood of Christ.[165]

Chase: Being chased indicates that you are avoiding a situation that you do not believe you are able to overcome. It may be pointing out a feeling of insecurity. Dreaming that you are chased by an animal indicates that you may be projecting your own pent-up anger onto that animal; or you may be running away from a primal urge or fear. If you are chasing someone it might imply that you are attempting to pursue a dream or beat a difficult task. You may also be expressing some aggressive feelings toward someone.

Cheetah: (See Lion)

Chef: Satisfying a spiritual hunger; starving for affection; an emotional emptiness; a desire for fulfilment; longing for gratification; need to be filled. 'You prepare a table before me in the presence of my enemies.[166]' 'Eat that which is good and delight yourself in fatness. Incline your ear and come to me (says the Lord) that your soul may live.[167]' (See also Cook)

Cherub: In art these are depicted as chubby infants with wings. To see these in your dream is a symbol of sentimentality (See Cherubim)

Cherubim: In scripture, the cherubim are 6-winged angelic

---
165 Luke 22:20
166 Psalm 23:5
167 Isaiah 55:1-3

beings of the highest order serving before the throne of God. They have four faces: that of a lion, an ox, a man and an eagle. If these appear to you in a dream, they represent a profound encounter of the highest spiritual significance.

Chest: Looking at your own chest signifies vitality, strength and confidence. Being bare-chested could indicate that you are vulnerable or exposed; or it could be imply that there is something that you need to 'get off your chest'. It is common for those who experience chest pains in waking life, to have a dream of being shot in the chest or feel pressure on the chest. To dream that you are beating your chest indicates triumph and accomplishment.

Chicken: This is a flightless bird. Chickens can represent cowardice; powerlessness; gossiping; fussiness; triviality; garrulousness. Some positive images are the laying of eggs suggesting new life and potential; hatching something. Think of some other related ideas: 'Play chicken'; 'chicken-hearted'; 'chicken-livered' = cowardly; 'Chicken feed' = a trivial amount; 'Don't count your chickens before they are hatched.' (See Birds in Chapter 12 – Animal Life and the Four Basic Elements)

Child/children: Our vulnerability; dependence; innocence; trust; helplessness; defencelessness – Symbol of your inner child or child-like qualities. This refers to the playful; fun-loving; adventurous; emotional; sensitive; easily-hurt; trusting; undeveloped; immature; impressionable; irresponsible; vulnerable; accepting, forgiving side to our nature. Ask, 'What in the above list are dominant in me right now? Am I feeling insecure; dependent; inferior? Am I shirking responsibility?' Remember too, 'Unless you become as a child, you shall not enter the Kingdom of Heaven.' and 'A little child shall lead them.'[168]

Childhood home: (see under House)

Chimpanzee: (See Ape)

Chin: This is associated with talking: 'chinwag'; 'Chin up'= keep going; 'take it on the chin' = not taking offence, not succumbing.

168 Matthew 18:3 & Isaiah 11:6

China: Relates to something valuable. Broken or cracked china can mean that something precious in you is being, or is in danger of being damaged through carelessness.

Choking: If this is not associated with an asthma attack or lung condition, to dream that you are having difficulty breathing may indicate that you experience difficulty in expressing yourself – communicating thoughts, needs, hopes or feelings of anger, fear, love, or any other intense emotion. Alternatively, it may imply that you cannot accept certain situations in your life or are feeling suffocated by a current issue.

Chord: (See Music)

Christ: (See Jesus)

Church: Place of worship; House of God; the soul as the dwelling place of God; the body is the temple of the Holy Spirit[169]; communion with God; a sanctuary; the source of renewal; spiritual life; serenity; peace; blessing; baptism = rebirth; new name = new nature; transformation; dying to self & rising to life in the spirit; spirituality. To dream that you are outside a place of worship indicates that you feel alienated from God; passing a place of worship could indicate that you are avoiding God. Being inside a place of worship is indicative of seeking spiritual direction; divine guidance; a deeper spirituality; or perhaps you are in need of forgiveness and restoration.

Cinema: (See Theatre)

Circle: This is a symbol of completion; wholeness; eternity; perpetuity; infinity and continuity. Circular movement has no beginning or end. Think of: 'What goes around, comes around'; 'Coming full circle'; 'Going around in circles' = getting nowhere, aimlessness; a feeling of frustration and confusion. (See: Mandala and Sphere. See also Zero in Chapter 9 – Numbers in Dreams)

Civil War: Inner conflict of lower nature against higher self and ideals.

Claws: Indicates the power to wound and destroy; our defences.

---
169 1 Corinthians 6:19

Clay: A symbol of our basic humanity. Humanity created from the dust of the earth[170]. Adam = earth. 'Feet of clay' = disappointing weakness of one once held in high regard.

Cliff: This could be a warning of being in danger of a spiritual fall. 'cliff-hanger' = state of affairs producing anxiety.

Climb/climbing: This indicates that you are going up in the world; that you are moving towards a goal or striving to better yourself socially, materially or spiritually. It may be a steep uphill climb meaning that it is difficult but do-able. Think of related ideas: 'Climbing the ladder of success'; 'get on the property ladder'; 'climb on the bandwagon.' If you are looking down on others from a height it may indicate superiority.

Clinic: (see Hospital)

Clock: Carl Jung called all circular images a 'mandala' that represent the spiritual centre of our persona. It symbolises wholeness; unity; completeness; fulfilment. The clock represents the mandala of time marching on to eternity and immortality. If the hands are racing – time is running out; alarm-clock ringing – could be a warning or wake-up call; hands stopped – may mean the end, or death of something.

Clothes: In the theatre of the soul, our form of attire is how we feel we are projecting ourselves to the outside world and relates to our perceived public image or mood. Attire relates to attitude and personality. Note too the colour of your garment. Think of: 'a garment of praise instead of a spirit of heaviness'[171]; 'put off the old nature and put on the new'[172]; 'clothe yourselves with humility.'[173] (See individual listings of garment types)

Clouds: These relate to thoughts. Storm clouds = disturbed or angry thoughts; light, feathery clouds = lack of vision or inspiration. Think of: 'head in the clouds'; 'under a cloud'; 'clouded vision'; 'on cloud nine.'

Clown: In the dream you are identifying with the clown; putting on a false front. The gay bright clothing hides a dull

---
170 Genesis 2:7
171 Isaiah 61:3
172 Colossians 3:9-14
173 1 Peter 5:5

and what we perceive to be a malformed body. (My nose or feet are too big; thin hair; wrong colour) The painted face is masking emotions: Laughing on the outside, crying on the inside. Giving people permission to laugh at the clown in order to cover our pain of real or imagined scorn and ridicule of the real me beneath the facade.

Coat: Protecting the heart (spiritual centre) – Pertaining to the emotions. The coat embraces the body in warmth; security; protection; love. If you are missing a coat in cold or wet weather, you are possibly feeling exposed to trouble; vulnerable; 'Coat of many colours' – under the rainbow of the Father's covenant love and indulgence. Note the colour of your coat.

Cobweb: (See Spider web)

Cock: A symbol of insolence; vigilance; cockiness.

Coffin: There is a need to bury what is no longer viable. It may possibly be a death symbol. Think of the play on the words 'scoffing'; 'coughing' (See also Burial and Death)

College: (see School)

Communion: Relates to a desire to commune with God; a need for spiritual sustenance; feeding the soul. (See elements: Bread and Wine)

Compass: This symbolises our instincts or intuition. It could signify that you are seeking direction in life; guidance in decision making; spiritual wisdom or wanting to follow.

Concrete: Something which is permanent; unyielding; unchangeable; solid; real; tangible.

Conservatory: (see under House)

Constipation: This may symbolise inner tension; non-communicative, being uptight; or lack of expression.

Construction Worker: A need to be more constructive; to build something up; to be edified. 'Let us then pursue what makes for peace and for mutual building up.'[174]

Convict/prisoner: These indicate the awareness of limitations in one's life and the desire to be set free. There may also be anti-social tendencies that need to be restrained.

---
[174] Romans 14:19 (see also 1 Corinthians 14:12)

Do you have any inhibitions or an inability to express your true feelings?

Cook: Preparing a meal/feast... fulfilling a physical, mental, emotional or spiritual hunger for something. What is the Cook doing? Boiling, frying, roasting, beating, mixing, chopping, mashing, stewing, toasting, roasting, mincing, baking, dishing-up... Think of related sayings: 'now you're cooking with gas'; 'something on the back burner'; 'cooking the books'; 'cook one's goose'; 'being half-baked'; 'to be taken with a pinch of salt'; 'a real fruit-cake'; 'being saucy'; 'a tart'; 'crumpet'; 'cheesecake'; 'beef-cake'; 'having a bun in the oven'...

Cord: Think of associations: 'the silver cord' = connection between the physical world and the spiritual realm; the umbilical cord = connecting foetus to placenta or child to mother; 'apron strings'; 'stringing him along'; 'that strikes a chord'; 'being roped in.'

Corn: A symbol of fertility, prosperity and abundance. Think also of something being 'corny'

Corner: This signifies a change of direction; a meeting place of two approaches; the turning point. Think of: 'cutting corners'; 'being cornered'; 'turning the corner'; 'rough corners.'

Cornucopia: A horn overflowing with fruit and flowers is also called the horn of plenty, a symbol of abundance indicating overflowing goodness. (See Horn, Fruit, Flowers)

Corpse: This is the outer shell without the spark of life. It could indicate that something needs to be brought to life, or buried. Something lacking soul or spirit; (see Body and Death)

Costume: This is the clothing we put on when we want to act a part. The type of costume reveals what act we are putting on. It could also be recall of a past life.

Cottage: (See House)

Couch: (See Sofa)

Counsellor: You may be in need of mental or emotional healing; direction; clarity.

Country: This relates to being open; unconfined; free; liberated or natural. If it is a foreign country, it could be referring to something foreign to your thinking or way of life.

Cow: Contented; ruminating; meditate; mull it over; indulgence. In some cultures the cow is a sacred symbol. It may symbolise nourishment; fertility; motherhood; nurture; tranquillity. Think of other related ideas: 'milk & manure'; 'till the cows come home'

Crater: This could be an opening of old wounds; a frightening situation; recalling deep emotions. A prayer for healing will be needed.

Crawl: This indicates immaturity and may be a desire to return to the carefree existence of childhood. Think also of related saying: 'this will make your flesh crawl.'

Crematorium: Something that is 'dead' needs to be laid to rest; dispose of what is no longer needed; dying to self; bury the old to make way for the new - new life to rise from the ashes of what has ended. (See also Cemetery)

Crocodile: This is a cold-blooded animal. Living in the water and on land, the crocodile reveals both spiritual and worldly aspects, the conscious and the collective unconscious areas of our mind. Consider this when seeking to interpret the dream. Reflect also on the context of your dream and what impresses you about the crocodile. Is it the mouth? This could indicate 'a big mouth' = gossip; Snapping jaws = hostile or hurtful accusations; 'Crocodile tears' = a symbol of hypocrisy. Is it the rough hide that you notice? This may be a sign of being thick skinned.

Cross: A cross can be interpreted in several ways. It can be seen as a religious symbol; a cross-roads; a symbol of marking a location on a map; a sign for something being wrong; making one's mark on a ballot paper. What does your dream cross look like and how do you interpret this symbol? As a Christian emblem it is an archetypical symbol for the way of Christ – overcoming worldliness and controlling the lower, animal nature through aligning with the will of God. The horizontal bar symbolises our earthly, human nature and the perpendicular bar our relationship with God: the divine flowing into our being bringing spirituality life and inspiration.

Crow: These are very intelligent birds and a symbol of longevity. Think of various related sayings: 'Something to crow about'; 'she's an old crow'; 'as the crow flies'; 'crow's feet.'

Crowd: This indicates anonymity, being lost in a crowd.

Crown: A Christ symbol – The King of kings; authority; power; eminence. The crown of thorns = martyrdom. It symbolises the highest spiritual centre of the endocrine system relating to the pituitary gland. Think also of the victor's crown and a crown of honour. The circle symbolises eternity and wholeness.

Crucifix: The figure of Jesus on the cross is a symbol of the ultimate sacrifice – giving of his life that we may be spared damnation.

Crying: If you awake crying you may have been dreaming of crying. If not, the dream symbols need to be analysed and dealt with accordingly. It may be a warning of sorrowful consequences of attitudes of actions. Tears are also healing. Think of: 'a crying need'; 'for crying out aloud'; a crying shame'; 'have a good cry'; 'cry wolf'; 'cry your eyes out'; 'crying over spilt milk'; 'crying out for attention'; 'battle cry.'

Crystal: Relates to something valuable and symbolizes wholeness; purity; beauty; something that is crystallizing or taking shape. Examining or looking at crystal could indicate that you are seeking or realizing your purpose in life. Crystal represents the higher self. 'Crystal clear'

Cube: This is a three dimensional form having six sides, eight corners and twenty four angles – symbolising perfection. The Holy of Holies in the Tabernacle, in Solomon's Temple and in the Heavenly Temple are all cubic in form. The Tabernacle 3^3 metres; The Temple 10^3 metre and the Heavenly Jerusalem $2,200^3$ kilometres[175].

Cuckoo: A symbol of cuckoldry

Cup: The cup may signify nurture, rejuvenation, restoration, healing or receptivity (if empty). It could also symbolize transcendence into a realm of higher consciousness. Think –

---
175 Exodus 26; 2 Chronicles 3:8; Revelation 21:16

'Is the cup half-full or half-empty?' = Do you see life from an optimistic or pessimistic point of view? 'Loving cup'; 'my cup runneth over'; a cracked, broken cup or a cup with a broken handle may denote feelings of powerlessness, inadequacy or inability to handle a situation. (See also Chalice and Holy Grail)

Cupboard: These are for the storage of things that we need and use; that we do not use but are reluctant to part with or forgotten items. They can hold precious memories, secrets and valuable thoughts. Consider all of the details in your dream and try to see the message. Do you need to clean out the closet of your soul, come out of the closet or share the things that you have stored in the closet of your heart?

Curlers: Something in your life that 'makes your hair curl'.

Cut: To separate one thing from another. It could indicate a fear of loss. May be indicating the need to detach yourself from something harmful. Think of: 'cut it out'; 'cut down to size'; 'cut you coat according to your cloth.'

D

Dagger: Daggers, knives, and swords could represent feelings of anger. Killing or wounding someone in your dream may be warning against verbal abuse. Think of the injury caused by a sharp tongue. 'Cutting words'; 'piercing remark.' Freud interpreted daggers as phallic symbols.

Dam: Emotions may possibly need to be checked or held back (see Water)

Dance: This is generally a happy dream which suggests that you feel a sense of joy. 'I could have danced all night'; 'dance to another tune' = change of position, allegiance, conduct or views. Depending on other elements in the dream, it may have some sexual connotations. 'Dancing is a vertical expression of a horizontal desire.'

Danger: If in your dream you are aware of being in a dangerous situation you may interpret it as a sign from your conscience. Are you involved in something that can harm you emotionally, physically, or spiritually in your relationship with God or others? If you faced the danger and overcame or subdued it, it may be a sign that you will overcome your obstacles.

Dawn: This symbolises a new beginning; a bright idea; enlightenment. Think of associations with sunrise – Easter and the risen Son of God/Son of man; 'it dawned on me...'

Deaf: Not wanting to know what is going on around you; a fear of hearing something that may cause distress. 'Turn a deaf ear'; 'none so deaf as those who do not wish to hear.'

Death: It is common to dream of death or dying. Dreaming of death is usually a positive sign. It is generally a symbol of some type of closure, implying an end to something in preparation for beginning something new. If you dream that you are dead, it could mean that you would like to leave your troubles behind and begin anew. Dreaming of the death of someone close to you may reveal your fear of losing them. Dreaming about a person who has died is thought by some to be a real encounter with that person coming to us while we are in our unconscious dream state. It is normal and understandable that we miss and long for communication with loved ones who have passed on and it is therefore not surprising that they are not only in our waking thoughts but in our dreams. It could better be interpreted by thinking of what that person represented to you in life. (See the section on Dream Characters). Other death symbols are: a stopped clock; a card or letter edged in black; an hour glass running to its end; a curtain falling at the end of a play; a fallen mirror; crossing a river; attending a funeral; a coffin.

Decapitation: In a decapitation the head is separated from the body, so this dream suggests that you are losing control, as the brain governs the whole body. It may also suggest that you may have become detached from rational thinking and feelings. You may be disassociating yourself from some behaviour or issues in life. 'I was out of my mind with worry'; 'don't lose your head.'

Deceased Person: It is common for someone who has been recently bereaved to dream of the deceased. It might be a visitation from that person, but is more likely a message of consolation at this time, or comfort flowing between different aspects of one's persona. If you are not presently grieving, it may indicate that something in you had apparently died and needs to be resurrected, or finally laid to rest.

Deer: This may symbolise the soul (hart/heart). One that is gentle; easily startled; sensitive; meek; tender; graceful.

Defecating: (See Excrement)

Deformity: This could symbolise something that has not been able to grow to its natural beauty, through fear, repression or trauma.

Deluge: (see Flood)

Demons: (see Devil/s)

Den: (See Cave; or Room under 'House')

Dental Surgery: Teeth relate to speech. Dental work is being done – review your communication style. Rotten teeth – foul language; swearing; unclean talk; corrupt destructive speech; loose teeth – loose talk; scandal; gossip; rumours; teeth falling out – verbosity; being long-winded; over talkative; complaining; false teeth – lying; insincerity; dishonesty; braces – control your language; sharp or pointed teeth – anger; condemnation; belittling; criticism; accusation.

Desert: This usually symbolizes the unconscious mind and has a sense of detachment from the conscious thoughts. Deserts are dry and barren with little vegetation or animal life. The desert in your dreams could be bringing up issues of little or no spiritual growth or accomplishment in your life. A desert could also indicate a feeling of loneliness and isolation. However, it is a place of solitude for meditation and getting in touch with your innermost being, free of the distractions of the world and demands of daily life. What is your dream desert calling you to do?

Detective: Something needs to be investigated; a problem to be worked out; a mystery solved. Perhaps it is a warning about being nosy, inquisitive or interfering.

Devil: This is an archetypical symbol. Dreaming about the devil or demons is a very frightening experience and you may wake in fear. Such dreams usually symbolize elements in our lower nature that resist being led by our higher nature: Inner conflict; opposition to the will of God; being tempted; straying from the truth… It may be that part of you is caught up in something destructive but not without being aware of the effect it is having on your soul. You may think that it is only an innocent indulgence, but take heed and be warned. According to Carl Jung, the devils in our dreams represents what he calls our 'shadow' self. There is no such thing as a bad dream. All dreams are good dreams in that they bring unconscious issues to the conscious level of the mind and destructive elements in us into the light of truth so that we can deal with them.

Diamond: Diamonds are precious, timeless and exceptionally beautiful. They capture the light and reflect it in sparkles of bright rainbow colours. Dreaming about diamonds may represent spiritual enlightenment, truth, clarity and ultimate in purity. This dream may help you to interpret what is most valuable or precious to you and then to acquire it.

Dice: This relates to gambling; games of chance. Think of related concepts: 'dice with death' = facing danger/being rash; 'dicey' = speculative/casual;

Digging: This indicates a desire to discover the true facts in a relationship or something that you are unsure of, or it could relate to a fear that something you have been hiding may be discovered – 'dig up the dirt.' Alternatively, you may be digging in order to plant something. Note what kind of soil it is that you are digging in. Is it rich, fertile soil or rocky? (See Earth)

Dinosaur: These are extinct, dead and gone; old fossils but still holding our interest. They are alive only in the imagination. This dream could therefore possibly be related to some outdated ideas or outlook. They may represent old issues that have not been properly addressed and that continue to have the power to affect our life in the present.

Diploma: This signifies an award, reward or acknowledgement for having achieved something; it comes through hard work and discipline.

Dirt: Basically, dirt is matter out of place. Dreaming that something is dirty could relate to inappropriate behaviour, our state of mind, a situation from our daily life that is out of place. It could symbolize a relationship, a business venture, or any other part of our life where someone (self or another) has been dishonourable or less than honest. Dirt in our dreams could also represent our unwholesome attitudes and a devious state of mind. This dream may be encouraging you to 'clean up your act'; 'come clean.'

Dirty clothing: This is indicative of an impurity; sin; inappropriate behaviour or attitude; being judgemental; iniquity.[176] (see Clothes)

Disabled Person: This may indicate something in you which is perverse, warped, twisted, crippled or not functioning perfectly.

Disaster: This could signify a big change in your life or

---
176 Zechariah 3:4

may indicate a need for a change in attitude or behaviour. Change is not easy, but it can open new opportunities for growth and enrichment. Note the element. Is it an earthquake; fire; tornado or flood? (See Earth, Fire, Wind and Water) Note also the source of the disaster: Is it an act of God or due to human error or intention?

Disease: The word disease means dis-ease. The body, mind or spirit out of syncrinisation with natural rhythm of wellbeing. You may need to check your health or think of what is causing mental or spiritual disturbance.

Dishevelled attire: Implies a disorderly nature or attitude; rebellious thoughts or confusion; having a rough time; poverty of spirit (see Clothes)

Dismembering: Removal of a limb or branch of a tree or any outgrowth from a larger body may indicate loss of something or someone close, loss of virginity, fear of castration, circumcision or any imminent surgery.

Distress: To dream of a person or animal in distress could indicate that whatever the stressed creature symbolises for you is in danger of being in trouble, tension or pressure.

Diving: Water is a symbol of the subliminal mind. To dream of diving suggests that you are trying to 'get to the bottom' of an issue or situation or that you may be delving into the subliminal depths of your psyche to discover the mysteries of who you are or are meant to be = your purpose in life. (See: Chapter 3. A Scientific Perspective on Dreams) Sigmund Freud thought that diving is a symbol for sexual intercourse. Viewed from this angle, it may signify a plunge into deeper spirituality and fulfilment. (See: Chapter 7. Philosophy of Dream Interpretation - Sexual Acts in Your Dreams)

Divorce: Everything in creation God affirmed as being 'good' or 'very good'. The first statement of something being 'not good' was that Adam had no mate.[177] Eve was created to complete the man. Man and woman together reflect the image of God as God created them. Divorce therefore is an amputation of one's other half. Of course, if a limb is gangrenous it is better

177 Genesis 1:4,10,12,18,21,25,31 & 2:18

for the body to be rid of it rather than for the whole being to be poisoned, but divorce is still painful and robs each of something that was potentially enriching. To dream of divorce, if you are not already contemplating divorce or in fear of its possibility, symbolises the loss of the other half of the male/female bond which makes us complete beings in ourselves. Of the mind, it is the separation of intellect from emotions; of intuition from logic; intellect from will. To dream of divorce may be encouraging you to work at harmonising or balancing your male/female qualities to find greater fulfilment.

Doctor: What is the doctor doing? Is he examining you? If so, what kind of examination is it? This may indicate the need to undergo a medical check-up. Is she writing out a prescription? What is being prescribed? Perhaps there is a need for inner healing. 'Physician, heal thyself.' Perhaps something, a relationship or attitude, needs healing or to be removed. It may be that God, the Great Physician, is at work in you or telling you of a disease of the soul; the need for a 'heart-transplant' = change of heart; blood transfusion = new lifestyle (the life of the body is in the blood).

Document: (See Letter)

Dog: Depending on what you feel about dogs in general, it could symbolise loyalty; obedience; faithfulness; protection; companionship; 'man's best friend'; domestic care; sniffing out potential problems; instinctive behaviour; or destructive behaviour; ferocious; growl; snarl; snap. Think of associations like 'lap-dog' = indulgence; "dog's dinner'; 'bite the hand that feeds you'; 'in the dog house'; 'let sleeping dogs lie'; 'can't teach an old dog new tricks'; 'every dog has his day'; 'my dogs are barking' – my feet hurt. Note the breed and behaviour of the animal in your dream: St Bernard – rescuer; Alsatian – protector; Guide-dog – insight; Hound – pursuit.

Doll: It is important to first establish what kind of doll it is. Is it a baby doll or a doll in national dress? Is it a doll that you loved as a child or disliked? What happened to that doll? The answers to these questions could help you to interpret the meaning of your dream. A doll is a substitute figure for a baby or child; but it could represent a souvenir or a holiday reminder. Whatever they represent to you, they are lifeless images of people and suggest that someone is not genuine, not expressing feelings. Most dreams are about us and not other people, so what is this telling you about yourself? Perhaps there is something within you that needs to be brought to life.

Dolphins: These are water dwelling mammals. Water represents our subliminal mind, so to dream of dolphins could indicate a journey into the subliminal arena of our psyche. They are playful animals and in our dream they may represent our joyful frolicking between the conscious and the subliminal depths of our being and may represent the connection between our conscious mind and the mystery of the subliminal parts of our psyche.

Donkey: It is docile, passive, compliant, unassuming, humble, carrier of burdens, a symbol of meekness, humility, loyalty, endurance, ruggedness or alternatively, stupidity, obstinacy, stubbornness. It may indicate one of the above traits in your nature or present circumstances, or it may represent the heavy burden you are carrying.

Door: These represent means of access from one plane of consciousness to another. Locked or closed doors may symbolize obstacles or blocked opportunities that are not available to you or not the best choice for personal enrichment or fulfilment. Many doors may indicate that there are several choices or options open to you. (See also House and Rooms)

Dove: A symbol of gentleness; innocence; peace; love and the Holy Spirit. Note where the dove is and what it is doing. It is a messenger of peace.

Dragon: A dragon may symbolize the power in your unconscious mind. It could represent both negative and positive forces. On the negative side, it could symbolise Satan, the adversary, evil power, an authoritarian figure, a hostile force, the inner rebel, an antagonist, dictator, strict person, destructive energy, threatening devastation by fire. On the positive side, it may represent a time approaching when you will confront your fears and be empowered to cope effectively with negative emotions, potentially destructive elements or issues and be able to gain freedom.

Dress: This represents how we present ourselves to others. Note the colour, style and how you feel in relation to what you are wearing.

Drinking: Indicates a spiritual or emotional thirst. Note what it is that you are drinking and what the drink symbolises for you. Note also the nature of the vessel. It could be a symbol of mystical communion with God. Think of some related phrases: 'drinking in the scenery'; 'thirst for knowledge'; 'in the drink'; 'drink of the water of life' (See: Isaiah 55:1 & John 4:10,11)

Driving: (See Vehicles in Chapter 11)

Drowning: This type of dream could manifest itself in a person with a lung condition like pneumonia or emphysema. It could also indicate an overwhelming predicament which is causing you to feel as though you are being swamped or going under.

Drum: What kind of drum is it – a container? a percussion instrument? or the action of drumming one's fingers signifying impatience? What do drums or drumming suggest to you? It could symbolise many things: the beat of a military band, a drum-roll heralding a performance, the sound of a beating heart. Depending on your association with it, dreaming of drums or drumbeat could be comforting or disturbing. The sound of mother's heartbeat is the sound that gives comfort to a foetus in the womb for the first nine months of life. As a drum-roll, could it be heralding your performance of a lifetime, could it be the war drums of primitive tribes, or could it mark time as you march on parade?

Drunk: (See Intoxication)

Dry Cleaners: (See Launderette)

Duck: This bird swims, walks, and flies and is perfectly at home on land, in the water and in the air. As earth represents our conscious mind, water the subliminal and air, the supra-conscious – dreaming of ducks indicates a connection between these three areas of our psyche. To enable you to interpret the area of your mind that is indicated, ask: Is it in the water, flying or on land?

Dung beetle: A warning against gathering dirt; hoarding garbage or storing other's offences in order to gossip or expose them?

Dusk: This could signify the end of a phase or project, the closing of a chapter in your life. It need not cause anxiety although we do not generally like to see the end of something we have enjoyed, but an ending also anticipates the beginning of something new, perhaps after a period of rest for renewal of energy and preparation for the task.

Dwarf: Implies traits of the lower self that are stunting spiritual growth. What is stunting your spiritual, emotional or intellectual growth? Think of: challenges in life; characteristics of your disability, inability or limitations. Think of Snow White's seven dwarfs – Dopey, Bashful, Grumpy, Happy, Sneezy, Sleepy, Doc - and what their names suggest: (dim, shy or timid, a crabby disposition, carefree or careless, scoffing/sensitive/ill-health, slothful, bossy or superior).

৪০ E ৫৩

Eagle: A symbol of majesty; inspiration, courage and immortality. In mythology the eagle represents the sun and in Christian art it is the symbol of St John. This bird is a profound spiritual icon. It can fly higher than any other bird, is able to see a mouse from a height when we, from the ground, can no longer see the eagle with our naked eye. Cherubim, the angels that surround the throne of God have the face of an eagle on one of their four faces.[178] Which of the above images strikes you as giving insight into the meaning of your dream? Note too that the eagle is a bird of prey. Think of 'eagle eye'; 'rise up with wings of an eagle.'

Earrings: Drawing added attention to the ear or hearing. Earrings are jewellery enhancing the appearance so this underlines the need to listen and hear the message.

Ears: Listening; hearing. It may indicate a need to be more attentive and sensitive to the inner voice of conscience or the still small voice of God. 'Now hear this'; 'listen up!'; 'lend me an ear/your ears'; 'hear no evil'; 'are you listening?'

Earth: One of the four basic elements, that relates to the conscious area of the psyche that interacts with the world around us during waking hours. Dreaming about earth and soil generally symbolizes fertility in the conscious arena of the mind and your potential to influence mental growth. Rich soil may indicate that within your conscious mind where there is great potential. Dreaming about dry, barren soil may be indicative of negativity or fruitlessness coming out of feelings of lack of purpose and despair or failure to nurture productivity[179].

Earthquake: (see Disaster)

Eating: Food is one of the basic necessities for life and eating can be for nourishment, pleasure, comfort – or it can be problematic. It may symbolise essentials or luxuries depending on the type of food being eaten. To dream of eating could also indicate an emotional, physical, psychological or spiritual hunger or need.

---

178 Ezekiel 1:10, Revelation 4:7
179 Luke 8:4-15

Eggs: The egg represents life and development in its earliest form. It can also indicate captivity; reserve; detachment; reticence. Think of some related sayings: 'Come out of your shell'; 'teaching grandma to suck eggs'; 'walking on eggshells'; 'don't put all your eggs in one basket'; 'egg on one's face.'

Elephant: A symbol of wisdom, power, forcefulness, resilience, determination, long memory, commanding, ponderousness, lumbering or thick-skinned – insensitive.

Elevator: (see Lift)

Elves/Imps: Elusive spirits having mischievous, mysterious, or irritating habits – envoys for good or evil. Symbol of your teasing or vexing habits, frustrations, irritations – whichever way you see the imp within you.

Embrace: (See Hug)

Employee: A need for greater assertiveness; feeling subordinate; dependence; being controlled.

Employer: Are you or someone in your life being too bossy? An employer suggests power or control. It may be a call for you to be more assertive or decisive. It may also be a warning against being too bossy, having, or wanting power and control, being manipulative, needing to take control of the situation.

Entertainment Centre: (See Theatre)

Envelope: This usually indicates receiving news, information, a message from afar. Take note of your feelings in the dream. Are you anticipating good news or bad, demands or affirmations? An unopened letter could indicate a missed opportunity.

Eraser: Is there something that you need to obliterate, eliminate or get rid of?

Escalator: Note whether you are ascending or descending. This indicated either that you are on the right track and succeeding in what you are doing, or on the wrong track and heading for failure. Rethink your actions and intensions.

Escape: This indicates a need or desire to be free of physical, emotional or psychological forces, burdens or ties that restrain or inhibit your ability to express or be yourself.

Ewe: (See Sheep)

Examination: If this is not related to a forthcoming event in your waking life, it could symbolise a time of physical, emotional or spiritual trial or testing. It would be well to be prepared and understand that trials often lead to gaining strength in some area.

Excavation: To dream that you are digging into the earth, mining for precious gems, metals or minerals or hidden treasure indicates that you are unearthing your hidden potential, discovering hidden talents or realising spiritual gifts.

Excrement: Dreams related to excretory functions generally represent emotional release and cleansing. Being purged of guilt or some burden you have been carrying, or physical cleansing of your body of drugs, alcohol or tobacco dependence. It may indicate that you are eliminating unnecessary, harmful or hurtful attitudes, ideas and emotions. Look at all of the details of the dream in order to extract meaning. Think of what emotions you need to let go of: fear; anxiety; anger; hostility; annoyance; resentment.

Explosion: (see Disaster)

Exposed: (see Naked)

Eyes: Vision; observing or being observed; your view of things or a situation; personal outlook; perceptiveness; curiosity; awareness; involvement. The eyes are the windows of the soul; 'apple of my eye' = most loved; 'look down one's nose' = behave in a superior manner. Closed eyes indicate fear; spiritual blindness; detachment; unwillingness to get involved – 'see no evil.'

∞ F ∞

Faces: Consider the facial expressions and what they communicate. The faces of strangers may possibly represent different facets of your personality or psyche. A comical face may indicate that you are contemptuous of convention. A featureless face suggests that you may be feeling unappreciated or ignored. A smiling faces indicates positive feelings or a favourable outcome.

Factory: This indicates resourcefulness, innovation, inspiration, motivation or creative potential. Also tedium, repetition, wage-slavery or inter-dependence.

Faeces: (see Excrement)

Fairies: (see Elves)

Falling: The feeling of falling as you drop off to sleep is simply a spontaneous relaxing of your muscles. Dreaming of falling could be that you fear a plunge in a situation that is not under control.

Fancy Dress: (See Stage Costumes)

Farmer: Something in your life is being, or needs to be cultivated or transformed from the 'earthly' (worldly) lower-being into the more spiritual higher-being; to become spiritually fruitful.[180] Note what the farmer is doing. Is he ploughing, sowing seeds, fertilizing, reaping, milking cows or tending livestock?

Fat: Think of what this means for you, personally. Consider also various related sayings: 'Fat chance'; 'fat cat'; 'chewing the fat'; 'the fat of the land'; 'the fat is in the fire'; 'it's not over untill the fat lady sings'

Father: This is an archetypical symbol. At its most intense level, this is the symbol of the God-figure: Creator, initiator, author, protector, provider, disciplinarian, influential, all-knowing, all-powerful, wise, or a symbol of the leading, dominant, authoritative side of our nature; the controlling, decision-making side of self. It could relate to old attitudes (male dreamer). If it is a dream about your own father, reflect

---
[180] Galatians 5:16-24

on your relationship with him and ask, 'What in me is like him?' 'What must I do about it?'

Fear: Nightmares are positive signs as your subliminal mind is clamouring for your attention. There may be repressed issues coming to the surface. Contemplate the nature and source of the fear, then face it, deal with it and take control.

Feather: This is a symbol of comfort; success; confusion; cowardice; acquisition; transitions. Think of related sayings: 'a feather in one's cap' = achievment; 'flying feathers'; 'to show the white feather'; 'to feather your nest.'

Feet/foot: This relates to your standing, or what you stand for. It could relate to your balance; or how well-grounded you are. Both feet will double the intensity of meaning. One foot – which one is it? Are you in danger of being unbalanced? 'Finding you feet' = get acquainted with a situation; 'Get off on the right (or wrong) foot' 'Best foot forward'; 'put your foot in it'= make a blunder; 'land on one's feet' = a stroke of luck; 'put you foot down' = refusing to do something; 'get your foot in the door'; 'feet of clay' = disappointment with or failure of a person once held in high regard.

Female: (See Woman)

Fence: The outer perimeter of a private garden is that which marks out our territory and separates us from others. This symbolises the barriers and dividers in our life demanding privacy. Note what the fence is made of – wire or metal; brick or stone; wood or live hedging. Think of related concepts: 'sitting on the fence'; 'don't fence me in'; 'mending one's fences'; a 'fence' is also a dealer in stolen property.

Field: This indicates wide open spaces; freedom; expansion; prosperity; opportunity. Think also of 'playing the field'; 'having a field-day'; 'out in the open.'

Fighting: This usually indicates an inner conflict. This could be the result of confusion or indecision. Fighting with a person you know may relate to your present relationship with that person or a struggle with whatever that person represents to you of your own nature.

Finding money, treasure or valuables: This may suggest that you are or will be rewarded in some way, for simply being in the right place at the right time; your search for fulfilment will be rewarded. Reflect on the context of the dream for greater clarity.

Finger: Which finger is it? Is it the index finger; middle finger; ring finger or little finger? Think of what that finger signifies for you. Is it on the left or the right hand, your dominant or weaker hand? Take note of what the finger is doing. Is it giving direction; chastising; accusing; beckoning; caressing...Think of some related sayings: 'I can't put my finger on it'; 'to snap one's fingers'; 'to slip through your fingers'; 'to have a finger in the pie'; 'having a green finger/or green thumb'; also 'being all thumbs'; 'thumbs up'

Fire engine: The resources available or the need to quench that which is likely to rage out of control.

Fire station: Uncontrolled passion or anger which needs to be dampened. Devotional or missionary zeal is being stifled.

Fire: This is an archetypical symbol. One of earth's four basic elements; it is related to the preconscious area of the mind which is the memory-bank where information is stored for possible use in the future – 'on the back burner'. Memories enlighten our understanding; warn us of dangerous practices and generate warm feelings. Fire purges, warms and gives light. It is a symbol of the Holy Spirit. It is also associated with fever; sacrifice; cleansing; refining; rebirth; purging; kindling the flame of devout passion, 'fire in the belly', or something which is destructive. It may be a warning to 'fire him/her/it' = get rid of some useless element. Think of other related ideas: 'The phoenix rising from the ashes'; 'being fired up'; 'on fire'; 'in the firing line'; 'fireworks'; 'he's burning up with a fever'; 'a baptism of fire'; God's presence: 'He is like a refiner's fire'; 'pillar of fire by night'; 'Moses at the burning bush'[181]

Fireman: Some destructive force may need to be controlled; a fiery emotion may need to be quenched. Put out the flames of passion, anger, lust, temper, jealousy, vengeance. The

[181] Malachi 3:2,3 Zechariah 13:9 Luke 12:49 Exodus 3:3-6 14:24

opposite may be true. Is someone trying to quench your 'fire' of spiritual zeal or enthusiasm? Are you quenching the fire of God's Spirit?

Fireplace: This, for most people, is a symbol of comfort; warmth; security; peace and tranquillity.

Fireworks: Symbolise celebration; excitement; emotional release…

Fish: (See chapter 12 – Animal Life and the Four Basic Elements)

Fitness: (See Gym)

Flag: An ensign; banner; device for signalling; warning; a standard; symbol of patriotism; identification of allegiance; also 'to wilt'. Reflect on what this symbolises for you.

Flame: (See Fire)

Flat: (See House)

Floating: Floating indicates inner peace, tranquillity or freedom. It may also be interpreted as detachment, aloofness, being disconnected or rising above the situation in which we find ourselves. (See Water) Floating through the air (See Flying)

Flood: This indicates an overwhelming release of emotions as is experienced in severe shock. The flood in Noah's time[182] purged the earth of sin and corruption. Think also of: 'flood of tears' – tears can be cleansing and healing. (See Water and Disaster)

Flowers: These represent beauty; fulfilment; hope; growth; simplicity; innocence; femininity and virginity. The circular or spiral whorls formed within most flowers indicate harmony, wholeness and completeness. Note the colour and type of flower, and what significance that particular bloom has for you. (See also The Great Outdoors in Chapter 11)

Fly: A symbol of feebleness; insignificance. These insects are irritating and detract from the enjoyment of life. They could symbolize people or things that get in your way or may point towards your present frustrations or annoyances. Consider whether you are successful in getting rid of them or if they are getting the upper hand. This may give you a clue as to

---
182 Genesis chapters 6 to 8

how well you are coping with distraction and frustration. (See Insects in Chapter 12 – Animal Life)

Flying: This suggests that you are rising above the problem or a wish to escape the pull of the natural limitations or the world's influence. Think also of 'flights of fancy'; 'being left in suspense' = uncertainty; or 'get your feet on the ground' (See Air in The Four Basic Elements – Chapter 12)

Fog: This could indicate a hazy view or obscured vision creating confusion or uncertainty. It may represent a journey into the subliminal or subconscious mind where things are obscure and mysterious. If the fog causes you fear, try to analyse what is causing fear in the dream and what in your waking life is fearful. Think also of the saying: 'I don't have the foggiest notion.'

Food: Think of what kind of food it is. Is it meat? Flesh symbolises lust; carnality; the body without soul or spirit; sex without commitment, obligation, loyalty or caring. Consider what animal the meat is from, and then see listings. Is it vegetables, fruit, pastries, bread? (See individual listings) If you are serving food to others this may indicate that you are providing physical, emotional or spiritual nurture and nourishment.

Footwear: Protecting the feet; our journey through life; our standing; understanding; what we stand for; stand up to; stand against; take a stand; walking tall; your foundations. Clean/shiny footwear indicates a walk in the paths of righteousness; dirty footwear symbolises a walk in the way of sin. Bare feet relates to your spiritual stance; sole (soul); 'take off your shoes for you are standing on holy ground[183]'; standing naked before God, without protective covering; 'Don't criticise your brother until you've walked a mile in his moccasins'; 'If the shoe fits, wear it'; 'Who'll fill his shoes?'

Forehead: This is a symbol of wisdom; vision; lofty thoughts; superior intelligence; insight.

Foreigner: This may indicate that you have or are in danger of alienating yourself from others.

---
183 Exodus 3:5

Forest: This could represent the inner darkness of your subliminal mind or subconscious thoughts; confusion; lack of direction; being or feeling lost; the darkness within. If it is a pleasant experience, you may be enjoying exploring the dark and unfamiliar areas of the psyche.

Fork: This could symbolise prongs; division. Think also of 'fork out' = give; 'fork in the road' – a choice of direction; 'forked tongue.'

Formal dress: This can symbolise discipline; being presumptuous; auspicious; high standards and demands; strict; reserved; wanting to make a good impression (see Clothes)

Fort: This might symbolise a defensive attitude or warring.

Fountain: (See Water)

Fox: A symbol of cunning; deception; slyness; craftiness; deviousness; shrewdness; subtlety; furtiveness. Jesus called Herod, 'that fox'.[184] Think also of 'foxed' = baffled or bewildered.

Friends: It is common to dream about friends. They are people who are valuable to us on an emotional level, and we learn a lot about ourselves through them. This dream is most probably bringing to your attention prickly issues or feelings that you may have about yourself or others.

Frog: A symbol of inspiration, subliminal consciousness or the spiritual life as they are air breathing water creatures. Frogs also represent positive transformation.

Frost: (See Ice)

Fruit: This is a symbol of abundance; prosperity; productivity; satisfaction; accomplishment; fruitfulness. Fruit follows bud and blossom – the final phase and fulfilment of the purpose of the plant – indicating full maturity. The fruit carries the seed for new growth. It may indicate new life for you. Consider whether the fruit is still unripe, ripened, over-ripe or rotting for more clarity. Note also what that particular type of fruit means to you.

Funeral/Funeral Parlour: (See Burial and Crematorium)

---

184 Luke 13:32

ଊ G ଓ

Gale: (See Storm)

Gambling: This could be a warning that you are taking a chance in life, in a business venture or in a relationship.

Game: To interpret the dream you need to consider what game it is that you are playing or if you are watching others playing. Reflect on its context and your emotional reactions in it. Consider too, your interactions with other players and the role that each plays. It may represent the challenges in your life, your competitive nature, or your inner child at play. Is it indicating a goal or ambition?

Gangster: This indicates a self-indulgent, hostile force which is blocking the freedom and/or growth of yourself or of another.

Garage: The parked car may represent apathy or uncertainty in your life. It could be urging you to get going. Another interpretation may be that the parked car symbolises a reflective period or mood; a need to rest, relax or think things over.

Garbage: This may be a hint that it is time to throw out unnecessary things in your life; let go of clutter in order to free the mind. It could also represent the things in your life or from your past that is not worth keeping or simply worthless. Preventing rubbish from entering our body, mind or spirit is vital to our well-being and so too is it necessary to remove garbage that has lodged in the body, mind or spirit. Dreamwork accomplishes this.

Garden of Remembrance: Something lost and forgotten which needs to be recalled to experience a healing of the memories. (See Cemetery)

Garden: *Front garden* – Projected presence; being out in the open; 'up-front'; *Back garden* – this relates to your private space, place of personal growth; *Roof garden* – intellectual or spiritual growth and fruitfulness. (See Chapter 11 – The Great Outdoors)

Gardener: This could indicate a need to cultivate the productive or fruitful aspect of your life. Jesus said, 'I am the vine and my Father is the gardener.'[185] What is the gardener doing? What is the state of the 'ground' in which you are growing? What 'weeds' are choking your growth? What in your life needs to be pruned, weeded out, cut back, nurtured and cultivated to increase your fruitfulness?[186]

Gate: Where does the gate lead out from or in to? Gates symbolise access to the pre-conscious or subliminal psyche. A garden gate may indicate access to Paradise as in the Garden of Eden or the 'Pearly Gates' to heaven. This is a place of peace and tranquillity, security and communion with God. Note that hell also has gates[187] but not giving access to peace.

Genitals: This may be, though not necessarily a dream with sexual connotations. If so, you will be able to relate it to your own situation or recent events in your life. If not, dreaming of genitals may symbolise creative power or generative influences. Consider the state of development of the genitalia: is it mature or immature; deformed, malformed or well-formed; undersized or oversized? Female genitals generally represent receptivity whereas male genitals, giving, projecting or hostility, depending on how you interpret it. Other related symbols are keys and locks; hooks and eyes; snakes and holes; arrows or guns and targets; mice and nests...

Giraffe: Head in the clouds; out of touch with what's happening 'on the ground'; rubber-necking; nosy; rising above circumstances.

Glacier: This is a river of ice, so as water indicates the collective unconscious area of the mind so a glacier may symbolise the frozen areas of the unconscious mind. (See: Ice, and Water in Chapter 12 – The Four Basic Elements)

Glands: (See: The Endocrine System in Chapter 8)

Glass: Indicates transparency; openness; clarity of thought; fragility; vulnerability. If the glass is opaque it could indicate that something is not clear; if shattered it may represent shattered hopes or dreams.

---

185 John 15:1-11
186 Galatians 5:22
187 Matthew 16:18

Glitter: This is related to celebrations and may indicate revelry; signify the adding of sparkle to life or things will brighten up. Think also of: 'all that glisters is not gold.'

Gloves: Protecting the hands they pertain to will, determination and service. Reflect on what it may suggest your hands ought to be doing. Pray; serve; heal; care; reach out; feed; caress. Think also of various related sayings: 'handle with kid gloves' = treat with great care; 'throw down the glove' = challenge; 'hand in glove' = close association; 'fight with gloves on' = dispute without animosity; 'the gloves are off' = oppose without restraint.

Goat: They are sturdy, tenacious, sure-footed and able to scale rocky peaks. This indicates high aspirations; an ambitious nature; butting; confrontative; argumentative; annoying; frustrating; Think also of: 'scapegoat'; 'old goat'.

Ghost: Ideas that have no substance; insubstantial evidence; something 'haunting' you; something that is unclear or that you do not understand. It is important to note your reaction to the ghost. If it frightened you, this could mean that others are trying to impose their will on you, and you need to resist.

Giant: The adversary or strong opponent. In children, this could symbolise an adult of whom they are wary. It is a symbol of something larger than you can handle or someone who is intimidating. You may be feeling overwhelmed, or will become great in the task set before you.

Gift: Giving or receiving gifts may be a reflection on positive exchanges that are occurring in your life. Gifts are not earned or purchased by the recipient and symbolise something unexpected that you need to use in order to fulfil your purpose. The gifts that the Magi brought to the infant Jesus were gold, honouring him as King of kings; frankincense for his role as Great High Priest; and myrrh for his sacrificial offering as Saviour. These relate to body, spirit and soul. With the coming of the Holy Spirit at Pentecost and into our lives, God comes imparting spiritual gifts.[188] What do the gifts of your dream symbolise for you?

---
188 1 Corinthians 12:1-11 Ephesians 4:11-12 Romans 12:6-8 1 Peter 4:10-11

Goblet: (see Chalice and Holy Grail)

Goblins: (see Elves)

God: The symbolism depends on the dreamer and your relationship with God or your perception of God. This is considered a positive and affirming sign. The three primary facets of God's nature are holiness, justice and love.[189] God therefore represents purity, truth and mercy; requiring of us to 'act justly, love mercy and walk humbly with God'.[190] It also represents the creative energy in us. For some people God may represent punishment or damnation, and invoke fear or guilt. Dreams do connect us with the spiritual realm or with our own spirituality, so this dream needs to be taken seriously and followed through.

Gold: It is the most precious and beautiful of metals. Gold symbolises wealth; prosperity; high rank; highest honour (gold medal) status; spirituality and the Holiness of God. (See under 'Metals' in Chapter 8)

Goose: A symbol of conceit; folly; or a simpleton.

Gorge: This is a narrow and deep passageway between two mountains or plateaux and may represent such passageways in our bodies. It can then indicate the abuse of your body via any of the bodily passages with gluttony; alcohol; drugs; smoking; sexual promiscuity; speech; listening to or watching what is harmful to the soul.[191] Think also of gorging as overindulgence.

Gorilla: (See Ape)

Grain: A symbol of fertility, prosperity, abundance and sustenance.

Grand-parent: Infinite wisdom and experience; the awesome, all-knowing God-figure; a symbol of your inner wisdom or collective unconscious. This could relate to old attitudes; the higher-identity symbol; superior father or mother identity – grand parent (See 'Father' or 'Mother'). It could also relate to how you view that grand-parent – frail, wise, caring, indulgent.

---

189 Deuteronomy 10:17,18
190 Micah 6:8
191 Matthew 12:33-37 Colossians 3:5-9

Grasshopper: A destructive creature, annoying, devouring and a symbol of old age.

Grave: Something solemn or serious needing to be looked into.

Graveyard: (see Cemetery)

Green: In nature it is the colour of leafy trees, grasses and growing healthy plants. It is therefore the colour of growth and healing. It can also symbolise jealousy or money. (See Chapter 8 – Colours)

Gremlins: (see Elves)

Grey: Could symbolise a lack of clarity or limited vision. (See Chapter 8 – Colours)

Gull: A symbol of gullibility; wandering; restlessness.

Guns: This is commonly thought to symbolize the male sex organ so the dream may have sexual connotations. It is also associated with aggression, attack and hostility. It could also indicate a need to protect yourself physically or emotionally; or to take aim. If the gun has hurt or killed you or someone else, consider your hostile feelings, thoughts, words or actions and interpret it as a warning. Think also of some related sayings: 'stick to you guns'; 'to jump the gun' = start before time; 'shot down in flames' = to have a position refuted devastatingly; 'shoot' = go ahead; 'shoot a line' = exaggerate; 'shoot oneself in the foot' = spoil one's own chances.

Gut: (See Stomach)

Gym: There may be a need to exercise your brainpower; stretch your imagination; bend to authority; carrying a burden; exercise more or could indicate a weight on your mind.

Gypsies: (See Dream Characters – Chapter 10)

≈ H ≈

Hades: (See Hell)

Hail: This is frozen rain so it would probably indicate hardness or coldness in what rain symbolises for you. (See Rain)

Hair: As covering the head, like a hat, it represents thoughts. White hair – wisdom; Black hair – negative or mystifying thoughts; Golden hair – spiritual, mystical thought, prayerfulness; Dishevelled hair – mental confusion; Kinky or curly hair – kinky thoughts 'makes your hair curl'; Change a hairstyle – change ideas; Haircut – stop that line of thinking; Dyeing one's hair – change of mind; New hairstyle – new approach or ideas; Wig – judgemental; false belief; prejudice. Hair may also represent vanity; security; sexual appeal; sensuality; virility; physical or spiritual strength, depending on your own interpretation.

Hairdresser: Change of mind; new ideas. (See also Persona in Chapter 10 – Dream Characters.)

Halo: This is a mandala indicating a holy aura or saintliness. (See Mandala)

Hand/s: These represent self-expression and service or creativity. They reveal a person's emotions, intentions, and actions. What the hand or hands are doing will help you to interpret the meaning. Think also of various related expressions: 'Put your hand in your pocket' = give freely; 'put your hand to the plough' = to undertake a task; 'Hands on' = get to work; 'wash one's hands of something' = relinquish control and responsibility; 'rubbing hands' = eagerly anticipating; 'clean hands' = innocent; 'caught red-handed' = caught in the act of impropriety; 'right-hand man' = indispensable assistant; 'right hand of fellowship' = welcome with a handshake. Think also of 'the job in hand'.

Handbag: This is a symbol of a person's personal identity. A handbag carries that which is valuable; car, house, office, safe keys; mobile-phone; money and credit/debit cards; grooming kit; precious mementoes. Think about what is in your handbag and that may give a clue to the message.

Hare: A symbol of timidity and speed of flight. (See Rabbit)

Harp: Associated with the music of the angels or heavenly music. (See Music) It may also indicate persistence: 'harping on' something.

Harvest: Gathering of information or a plan may be ready to harvest; a time to celebrate fruitfulness.

Hat: These are symbols of power and authority, and indicate the role of the wearer. Covering the head is a sign of coming under (God's) authority. Worn on the head, hats also relate to the mind; thoughts; intellect. Black hat may signify devious or mysterious thoughts; Fur hat could indicate fuzzy thinking. Think of various related sayings: 'Keep it under your hat' = keep it secret; 'Cap in hand' - begging; 'Wearing many hats' = many and varied tasks; 'Hang up your hat' = resign or retire; 'Put on the helmet of salvation' = protection against spiritual doubt and despair; 'Put on your thinking cap'; 'Dunces cap.'

Hawk: A symbol of acquisitiveness. Think also of the saying: 'Watch like a hawk.'

Head: This is the centre of the intellect so it represents thoughts, ideas and decisions. A bodiless head or a headless body could be saying, 'don't lose your head' over a situation. 'Head off' = to intercept or get ahead of something or needing to turn back; A bald head could indicate that there are no thoughts on a matter; being blunt, frank or direct. Reflect also on the expressions: 'big-headed' = boasting; 'pig-headed' = stubborn; 'head-over-heels' = bowled over; 'it's doing my head in' = confusing; 'a head start'; 'turning one's head'; keep your head up'; 'head above the parapet'; 'head above water'; 'coming to a head'; 'way over your head'; 'Running ahead of oneself'

Health Centre: (See Hospital)

Hearse: That which is dead needs to be carried away and disposed of; a pursuit that is futile; a possible death symbol.

Heart: This is the centre of love, feelings and inspiration; 'the heart of the matter' = central or core issue; Heart ruling the head' = emotions governing logic; 'from the bottom of my heart' = deepest sentiments; 'a heavy heart' = sad; 'a girl/boy/man after my own heart' = I love what you are/do; 'broken-hearted' = deep sorrow; 'have a heart' = have pity; 'change of heart' = feelings have changed; 'my heart was in my mouth' = apprehension or fear.

Heaven: It represents all of the things for which we hope. It may mean happiness; peace; fulfilment; rest; love; reunion with loved ones now deceased; harmony between people; union with God; and many other positive things. Whatever your belief or dream experience, this dream is joyous and energising.

Hedge: (See Fence)

Hell: This is not necessarily a bad dream, though it may have caused fear. Hell or Hades was believed to be the kingdom of the dead beneath the earth. It was thought the holding place for the eternally-damned. Under-ground is the place where seeds germinate and the transition from apparent death to life takes place. Also symbolic of metamorphosis where carbon is transformed into diamond and all mineral wealth is held. Gold is purified in a furnace. This sinister part of the psyche may also hold the greatest amount of transforming energy. It may symbolise the holding place of the darkest secrets or most disturbing elements of your soul, the most destructive emotions and greatest fears. (See Chapter 13 – Emotional Healing through Meditition and Lucid Dreams)

Hen: A symbol of maternal care.

Hermaphrodite or androgynous being: Genderless or bi-sexual symbol of perfect balance between masculine and feminine qualities – a woman's masculine and a man's feminine side. Symbol of the strength of the opposite gender of your natural being.

Hiding: We hide from things that we fear, don't want to face or deal with. If it is fear, consider the things in your life that pose a threat to you. If not, what is it that you do not want to face or deal with? Are you perhaps hiding your feelings?

Something might need to be hidden or brought into the open. This dream may call for an honest reflection on personal conduct. It could also relate to a wish to retreat to the security of the womb.

Hill: Going uphill may indicate a difficult task ahead, making progress, success or a rise in status – 'going up in the world.' Going downhill could imply an easy project, difficulties soon to be overcome; degeneration; slipping morally.

Hog: A symbol of impurity; gluttony; over-indulgence; greed; selfishness. Think of various related sayings: 'the whole hog'; 'hogging the show'; 'making a hog of oneself.'

Hole: To enable you to interpret the meaning of this dream symbol, you need to note what type of hole it is. Is it a hole in clothing that can be mended? What the garment is or where it is worn is significant, e.g. a hole on the sole of the shoe – you may want to think of 'soul' and 'whole' or 'holy'; you would know when you hit on the right interpretation. Alternatively, there may be something that needs to be repaired. Is it a hole in a wall or in the ground – what does that make you think of? Dark holes could symbolise evil beyond or the mysterious unknown. This is where feelings need to be taken into consideration. Does the hole need to be repaired or filled, or does it give access to what is beyond? Think of other related ideas: a hole in the sock = 'potato'; 'hole in one'; 'hole in the wall' = dingy place; 'burn a hole in his pocket' = quickly spent.

Holy Grail: This is the vessel for the blood of Christ; a receptacle for the divine within. A quest for the Holy Grail is a search to realise the higher self. The lower nature may be in search of the higher nature. This can relate to God's offer to you of cleansing; healing; redemption; restoration; wholeness; sanctification; or new life which needs to be accepted. (See Chalice and Blood)

Holy Land: Holy condition; a state of blessedness; position of God's choosing.

Home: If this refers to 'back home' or where you used to live it usually symbolises something left behind. (See the various symbols under - House)

Homosexuality: Sex in a dream does not necessarily have a sexual interpretation. It could be about power, control, acceptance, identity, unity, submission or fulfilment. For a heterosexual to dream of having a homosexual encounter may indicate that you want, or need to embrace your femininity (masculinity), or love yourself for who and what you are. (See also Sexual Acts in Your Dreams - Chapter 7 – Philosophy of Dream Interpretation)

Honey: You may be experiencing or looking forward to good health and pleasant experiences in your life.

Hoodlum: (See Gangster)

Hooligan: This is linked to vandalism and violence. There may be a destructive element in your life or it could be indicating insensitivity and lack of concern for the needs or feelings of others.

Horn: Deer horns symbolise strength and dominance. Horns protrude from the head and relate to thoughts – inspiration; insight; musing. Think also of related ideas: 'to lock horns' = clash; 'blow one's own horn' = bragging; 'Horns of a dilemma' = two choices, both of which are equally distasteful; 'horny' = sexually excited; 'horn of plenty' (See Cornucopia)

Hornet: This relates to an unpleasant experience. 'Stir up a hornet's nest'; 'mad as a hornet.'

Horse: A symbol of speed; grace; intelligence; tempestuousness; hard-working; self-assurance; 'horse and rider' = a message from God; Apocalyptic; Prince Charming on a white horse = spiritual energies rising to the highest level (sweeping the maiden off her feet to become his bride). Consider also the meanings of: 'a horse of a different colour'; 'hold your horses'; 'you can lead a horse to water but you can't make it drink'; 'having horse-sense'; 'to eat like a horse" 'don't get on your high horse'; 'you're flogging a dead horse'; 'don't look a gift horse in the mouth'; 'straight from the horse's mouth'; 'back the wrong horse.'

Hospital: The interpretation depends on whether you are

employed there, a patient or visiting. Consider the reason for you being there. This is a place of healing. It may be indicating sickness in body, mind or spirit. Disease could signify dis-ease. Where are you 'ill-at-ease'? Sorrow is sickness of the soul. Sin is sickness of the spirit. It is also a place to be born and a place to die. Birth indicates some new responsibility or project. Death symbolises the end of something in preparation for a new venture.

Hostage: Being a hostage suggests that you could feel powerless, that you are trapped or ensnared in a relationship or in a financial situation. It could also indicate an inability to express yourself or that your creativity, intellect or freedom is restricted.

Hotel: This is related to travel or a state of transition. It symbolises a temporary situation; a place of change or need for adjustment; a detachment from responsibilities; a need for recreation; retreat or escape.

Hour-glass: A symbol of time running out. It could be a reminder of deadlines or a prompt to get on with a project; or it may be a death symbol – time to quit the old and address something new.

House: This is the most common dream-structure and generally represents your being. The different parts of the house represent the different parts that make up who you are in body, soul and spirit, but especially your mind, or conscious state. (See alphabetical listings also, for more detail. See also 'Buildings' in Chapter 11)

Attic – This is connected to the higher self – a symbol of our spirituality. It also relates to the mind and stored memories.

Back-door – could relate to wicked, secretive or hidden part of your nature.

Back-yard – This probably relates to something at the back of your mind; private thoughts; secret opinions; hidden pursuits; what goes unnoticed; or your background.

Bathroom – Cleansing; confession; forgiveness; elimination of impure thoughts, emotional or psychological baggage. It would suggest making an effort to cleanse the mind and spirit by putting useless thoughts and feeling behind one.

Beautiful furnishings – This indicates a positive outlook on life; beauty in the spiritual life. 'Beauty for ashes[192]' Beatitudes[193] = beautiful attitudes.

Bedrooms – Rest; restoration; knowing; realisation; intimacy; conception; reproduction; extension; spiritual union; actualisation; fulfilment.

Building or repairing a house – Working on family rifts; getting thoughts in order; building/repairing relationships; making decisions; organising ideas.

Ceiling – Intellectual heights; mental limits.

Cellar – Symbolises the subconscious; forgotten events or memories; hidden depths of the mind; subliminal impressions; ideas that need to be brought to the surface; base attitudes and emotions; foundation concepts.

Childhood home – Regression to a previous emotional state; old attitudes; helplessness; avoidance of problems or responsibility; past hurts; inadequacy.

Closed door – This signifies pursuit not to be entered into; opportunities not to be taken; not expedient.

Conservatory/porch/patio – Extension of inner being; enlightenment; clarity; inspiration.

Curtains/blinds – obscured view; privacy; the end/beginning; death – 'it was 'curtains' for him'

Dilapidated house – Body or mind in need of attention. Mend your ways; renovate, restore, refurbish attitudes, 'be transformed by the renewal of your mind.'[194]

Dining room – This is a place where we receive nourishment, indicating the nurture of the soul; spiritual feeding; pure milk of the word; need for solid teaching[195].

Doors – Admission to or exit from the inner sanctuary of the soul.[196] Going out = escape or gaining a wider perspective.

---

192 Isaiah 61:3
193 Matthew 5:3-12
194 Romans 12:2
195 Hebrews 5:12-14
196 Matthew 12:35, 15:18 James 3:5-10

Going in = seeking protection, security or confinement. Take note of where or whence the door leads.

Down-stairs may signify an effortless way or negative approach. It could also relate to the tedious, basic or menial aspects of our being.

Empty rooms could indicate a need for intellectual development; mental expansion or spiritual growth.

Exterior – may represent our façade; how we appear or present ourselves to others.

Finding new rooms – Indicates that you may be finding latent talents; discovering untapped potential; developing your spiritual gifts; discovering new abilities.

Fire-escape – may symbolise an escape from judgement or a potentially harmful situation.

Flooded house – could signify being over-emotional (flood of tears); feeling swamped or overwhelmed.

Floor – symbolises our stance; support; basis for understanding.

Foundations – may signify the basis on which you build your life; underpinning of your dreams; that on which you build your future; groundwork for a project or ancestry.

Front door – is the primary port of entry symbolising the most visible, primary, superior or godly access.

Front garden – signifies our visible and projected presence: 'up-front'; 'out in the open'

Garbage/refuse/rats at the door – Indicative of bad attitudes 'sin lies at the door.'[197]

Going into the next room – is a possible death symbol or, more likely, entering a new level of consciousness or discovering new possibilities.

Ground floor – symbolises the conscious mind.

Interior – of the house could represent your mind in which the will, intellect and emotion dwell; the soul accommodating many characteristics at different stages of our development or different personalities in different situations and varying relationships.

---
197 Genesis 4:7

Kitchen – This is a place of warmth, preparation for physical, emotional and intellectual nourishment. Note the conditions of your dream kitchen to become aware of possible emotional needs in yourself or others.

Large house – indicates a desire to expand the mind; a broader knowledge of self or greater understanding of things.

Large or beautiful rooms – reveal an increasing state of consciousness; growth in spiritual maturity.

Lavatory – This may signify a need to let go of something that is burdensome, hindering progress or not essential. There may be a desire to be relieved of responsibilities which are irksome, to be purged of guilt or to be liberated.

Living room – This relates to thoughts or activities in inter-personal relationships; generally the place in which we exchange thoughts, opinions and ideas with others.

Lower Floor – This indicates the routine or daily activities of the mind.

Open door – Welcoming new opportunities; receiving new understanding; being open-minded; awareness; in transition; entering a new phase.

Outer perimeter wall/fence/hedge/moat – This indicates our need for privacy; seclusion; separation; solitude; isolation; creating a barrier; division; protection. Think also of: 'Sitting on the fence'; 'mending fences'; 'being fenced-in.'

Playroom – A place of relaxation; recreation; setting the inner-child free; enjoyment; letting go of responsibilities.

Re-arranging furniture – Disorderly thinking; confusion; a change of mind; taking another viewpoint.

Roof – This is our protection. It is also what is uppermost in the mind; high ideals.

Small house – restricted existence; cramped mind-set; narrow-minded.

Stairs – are ascending/descending; spiritual awareness/down to earth; reaching for a higher consciousness/delving into the subconscious. Think also of 'Jacob's ladder'.[198]

Study – is a place of mental activity; learning; research;

---

198 Genesis 28:12

problem-solving; dilemmas; decision-making.

Underground passages/cellar/dungeons/caverns – The subliminal mind; subconscious; buried treasure or gloomy thoughts; depression; sorrow; despair; despondency; melancholia – depending on the mood and light or darkness of the area.

Unfinished house – may indicate a deficiency in understanding; lack of wisdom; inadequate knowledge; insufficient warmth, love, faith.

Up-stairs – This could point to being upwardly mobile; 'going up in the world' demanding; challenging.

Upper floor – symbolises the supra-conscious. Higher thoughts; high ideals; positive stance or planning.

Wandering from room to room – process of self examination; looking within; discovering potential.

Windows – This relates to your outlook on life; point of view; perception; vision; insight. Eyes are the windows of the soul. Note whether you are looking in from the outside or out from the inside.

Housekeeper: (See Servant)

Hug: A hug suggests acceptance, love and tenderness. It also symbolises comfort and protection. If you are hugging or being hugged by a hostile or wicked person it is a warning to beware of embracing evil.

Hurricane: (See Storm and Air)

Husband & Wife: This is a symbol of balance - a uniting which is creative, fruitful and productive or complementary and fulfilling. It could indicate a need for balance between masculine/feminine, thinking/feeling, intellect/emotions or that this is being achieved in you. It may also represent clashing and conflict between these opposites depending on your experience of marriage.

Husband: The 'Head' or 'masculine' facet of our nature – mind; intellect; logical; thinking; forceful; directing part of our psyche. It can also relate to the projecting, planning, controlling, managing, or protecting and providing side of our nature. Review your relationship with your spouse.

೫ I ೧೩

Ice: This is frozen water. Water is related to the collective unconscious area of the mind: the shared experiences of our ancestors, and common to the whole human race. Think of concepts associated with ice or cold: 'put on ice'; 'break the ice' or 'ice-breaker'; 'skating on thin ice'; 'icy stare'; 'icy fingers up and down my spine'; 'cold comfort'; 'in cold blood'; 'to pour cold water on it'; 'left out in the cold'; 'cold calling'; 'cold feet'; 'cold fish'; 'cold shoulder'; 'cold sweat'; 'cold turkey'; 'cold war'; (See Water under The Four Basic Elements – Chapter 12)

Illness: Occasionally the subliminal mind is aware of physical or mental disease before symptoms manifest themselves. It may be wise to check on your health. Alternatively, illness indicates dis-ease or being ill-at-ease about something: 'you make me sick.'

Imprisonment: (See Prison or Prisoner).

Imps: (see Elves).

Inappropriate dress for the occasion: Not equipped for the task or unacceptable conduct (see Clothes).

Incest: This does not necessarily have anything to do with sex. It is most likely a desire to connect with your alter ego (the inner child/parent or male/female side to your personality, depending on who is the other party in the dream act. Remember that most of the 'actors' in our dreams are simply other facets of our own nature.

Indigo: (See under Colours – Chapter 8)

Infections: This may indicate that there is something festering within.

Infidelity: Dreaming about being unfaithful may have come out of feelings of inadequacy or dissatisfaction. This suggests that you take a good look at your present relationships. What was the person in your dream giving you (physically or emotionally) that your spouse does not? You may need to communicate your needs and seek to understand the needs of your spouse. Taking this dream seriously and working at weaknesses in your personal relationships may well lead to a deepening of relationships that you never thought possible. If the partner in your dream was a stranger, it may indicate that you are struggling with a poor self-image.

Injury: This may indicate hurt feelings or guilt. Reflect on whether or not you have caused injury or been injured by someone, and decide what needs to be done about it to bring healing.

Ink: This could indicate the need to write, record or communicate with someone.

Insects: (See Insects in Chapter 12 – Animal Life and individual listings).

Intercourse: (See Sexual Acts in Your Dreams - Chapter 7 – Philosophy of Dream Interpretation).

Intoxication: If you do not have a drink problem, it could relate to a stupefying of the carnal mind or lower nature by an overwhelming rush of energy from the spirit.[199]

Intruder: If you have had a fearful real-life experience with an intruder, this dream may be reliving that experience and working a healing process in you. Alternatively, the intruder may symbolise negative influences that are breaking into your thoughts to rob you of your peace or security.

Island: This may indicate a feeling of isolation, loneliness or being too independent. 'No man is an island.' Being on an island also involves symbols of both land and sea – earth and water. Analysing your feelings in this dream and on waking will lead to different interpretations and greater clarity. It could indicate that you are receiving rest and renewal or that you are experiencing isolation and alienation in your present situation. (See too the significance of Earth and Water in Chapter 12 – The Four Basic Elements)

Ivory: As ivory comes from elephants tusks, it is a symbol of strength and power. It also signifies purity and beauty. Think too on related concepts: 'tinkle the ivories' = playing the piano; 'living in an ivory tower' = detached.

---

[199] Acts 2:12-17

ஐ J ⊗

Jackdaw: A symbol of vanity; conceit.

Jacket: This is our outer protective covering that identifies who we 'are' or what we want to project. Note the details of the jacket, whether it is smart or shabby, appropriate or inappropriate to the occasion.

Jail: (See prison)

Jay: A symbol of garrulousness.

Jealousy: This may be indicating that you feel insecure or inadequate in your present relationship or position.

Jelly: Shaky situation; instability; fear. Think of various related sayings: 'It must be jelly, 'cause jam don't shake like that' = obesity; laughter; 'my legs turned to jelly.'

Jellyfish: Relates to having no backbone.

Jerusalem: The meaning of the name is: 'There is Peace' signifying inner peace; the heart of the Holy Land; the centre of spirituality.

Jesus: As a man, Jesus represents our model of human perfection. Human beings were created in the image of the triune God.[200] That image was distorted through rebellion and disobedience.[201] Jesus is the image of both God[202] and human perfection. God's purpose is to transform us by His Spirit that we may reflect the image of Christ.[203] Seeing Jesus in a dream would therefore probably signify that God is calling you to fullness of life and spiritual perfection irrespective of your beliefs. (See also God).

Jeweller: The outlet for jewellery manufactured from precious metals, jewels and gemstones. These commodities are minerals from the earth and symbolise God's gifts to humanity. Dreaming of a jeweller signifies the desire for, or receiving of spiritual gifts or blessings. (See Chapter 8 – Gems and Metals for listings of various jewels and precious metals)

Jewellery: Note whether the jewellery is of genuine

---

200 Genesis 1:26,27
201 Genesis 3
202 John 14:9
203 1 Corinthians 3:16

gemstones and precious metals or costume jewellery in order to interpret the dream accurately. How did you react to the jewellery?

Journey: (See under Vehicles - Chapter 11)

Judge: This could be a warning that you may be being judged by others. Or could it indicate that you are being judgemental? 'Judge not, that ye be not judged.'[204] Satan our accuser; Jesus defence council; Holy Spirit our advocate; God is our supreme and one true Judge.

Jungle: A dense, overgrown jungle could represent confusion or being overwhelmed and anxious. If you are enjoying exploring the jungle, it indicates the anticipation of an exciting new venture or discovering unexplored areas of your psyche.

---

204 Matthew 7:1

ಬ K ಞ

Key: To understand this you will need to reflect on other aspects of the dream. What kind of a key is it? Are you trying to, or did you plan to lock or unlock? How is the key related to your waking life at present? Do you wish to hide something? Are you trying to figure something out and 'unlock' a memory or a puzzling issue? A key in a lock may also have sexual implications. Metaphorically, the key is that which explains or is a solution to a problem. Think of some related concepts: 'Keys of the kingdom';[205] 'key issue'; 'being keyed-up'; 'key position'; 'Key of the door' = independence.

Kidnapping: (See Abduction)

Killing: It is important first to note the mood of the dream and your feelings. If the mood is sombre and you are fearful, it may suggest that you are afraid of losing something that you value. If you are angry, it could symbolise a desire to rid yourself of some hindrance to experiencing fullness of life. If you are in high spirits, indicates that something of an obstacle is being overcome. Note too: Who or what is killing what or whom? Look up the various symbols for greater clarity. Think also of related sayings: 'killing with kindness'; 'in for the kill'; 'make a killing'; 'killing time'; 'kill two birds with one stone'; 'kill the fatted calf'; 'kill the goose that lays the golden eggs.'

King: This is the highest spiritual force that overcomes the animal nature in us. Self-discipline; self-mastery; 'king of the castle'; 'king of the beasts'; 'kingpin'; 'the king can do no wrong.'

Kissing: This signifies joy; affection; acceptance; comfort; warmth; happiness. Note who is kissing whom and relate this to acceptance of that facet of your nature or a bonding between the two. (See Chapter 10 – Dream Characters)

Kitchen: (See under House)

Kite: Is this the bird or the play-thing? Kites fly high in the atmosphere and symbolise lofty spiritual contemplations;

---

205 Matthew 16:19

elevated thoughts or soaring aspiration. (See 'Air' in Chapter 12 – Four Basic Elements)

Kitten: A symbol of playfulness.

Knee: This is a possible symbol for weakness. Think of related sayings: 'knee-high to a grasshopper' = little; 'knee-deep in...'; 'weak in the knees'; 'bring him to his knees'; 'bend the knee' = bowing in submission or prayer.

Knife: It is important to note what kind of a knife it is and how it is being used. There are many uses for a knife. It is generally used for cutting so this could symbolise the cutting loose of ties that bind. It is also regarded by some as a sex or phallic symbol. Think of related sayings: 'Cut to the quick'; 'cut it out'; 'cut loose'; 'under the knife'; 'a knife in the back.'

Knock: This may indicate expectation or unexpected opportunities. Think also of: 'Behold I stand at the door and knock...'[206] = Christ's calling; 'knock and the door shall be opened to you[207]' = promise of answered prayer; 'knock it off' = stop doing that; 'knock about' = travel; 'knock down' = disposed of; 'knocking-shop' = brothel; 'knocking-off' = stopping work.

---

206 Revelation 3:20
207 Luke 11:9-10

ಬಿ L ೞ

Ladder: This indicates the movement towards a goal. Ascending is more positive than descending, though descending may indicate a delving into the subliminal areas of the psyche and ascending may indicate lofty ideals. Climbing a ladder is suggestive of work rather than ascending stairs to an upper floor. Missing rungs may symbolize missing elements or handicaps that you may be encountering. 'Jacob's Ladder' was where Jacob encountered God.[208] Think also of: 'ladder of success'; 'get onto the property-ladder' (See Climbing)

Lake: (See Water and Chapter 12 – The Four Basic Elements)

Lamb: A symbol of innocence; self-sacrifice; gentleness; meekness; purity 'a lamb without spot or blemish'; sacrifice 'lamb to the slaughter'; depiction of Jesus – the Lamb of God; Pascal Lamb; atonement. Think also of: 'silence of the lambs'; 'feed my lambs'[209] = nurture to spiritual maturity.

Lamp: This is a symbol of enlightenment, guidance; wisdom; understanding; truth; 'put light on the subject'; 'bring to light'. (See Light)

Lark: A symbol of cheerfulness. 'Happy as a lark'; 'having a lark'

Lateness: Arriving late suggests that you may be feeling unprepared and distracted in a particular situation in waking life or in regard to long-term goals. Think of: 'It's later than you think'; 'my late father' = deceased.

Laughter: This indicates joy; positive outlook; amusement; the bright side of an issue; carefree. Think also of: 'laughing on the outside, crying on the inside'; 'laugh up your sleeve'; 'laugh on the other side of your face'; 'no laughing matter'; 'he had the last laugh'; 'laughter is the best medicine'.

Launderette: Being a place where clothes are cleaned, a launderette symbolises the need to clear your name; clean-up a soiled image; may indicate impure thoughts; unholy living; inappropriate behaviour; a need to iron-out difficulties.

---

208 Genesis 28:10-15
209 John 21:15

Lavatory: Need to let go; to be delivered of responsibilities which are irksome or not essential; purged of guilt; being liberated; dump baggage.

Law Court: Being judged or judgemental; coming under conviction; accusation; condemnation; feeling a need to justify your motives or actions.

Lawyer: This is a person who advises on the law. It could be a warning that you are in danger of breaking the laws of nature, of society or of God. (See Judge)

Leak: Any type of leak is usually a waste of something. If you are dreaming about leaks, you may want to consider where you are wasting energy and resources. Alternatively, it may indicate the 'leaking' of information from the preconscious or subliminal to the conscious. Water leaking may represent spiritual insights filtering through to your conscious mind.

Leaping: Are you jumping over a hurdle, up onto or down from something? What is the hurdle or object, if there is one? How high am I jumping? Do I clear it or not?

Leaves: These are the lungs of the earth absorbing carbon dioxide and releasing oxygen into the air. Reflect on the state of the leaves – are they fresh new shoots of spring; summer vibrancy; autumn splendour or lethargy; winter sleep, decomposing or dead? Think also of the play on the word – 'leave me be'; 'leave off'; 'I'm on long-leave'

Lecturer: (See Teacher)

Leech: Leeches are blood-sucking parasites that drain life. Think about what may be draining energy and resources.

Left: The left side of the body is governed by the right brain, which is associated with being creative, imaginative, intuitive, having vision, ingenuity and inspiration. It is related to feminine, receptive energy. It may also signify a liberal attitude. Taking a left turn could indicate all or any of the above regarding your present circumstances. It may also imply that you are not going in the right direction. Think also of left as the past tense of leave: 'left behind'; 'left holding the baby'; 'left in the basket' = neglected or abandoned.

Legs: They are your foundations, support and means of progress on your journey or path in life. Reflect on what path you are following: where are you heading? is it easy or hard going? Think also of various sayings: 'Legless' = very drunk or unable to stand on your own two feet; 'to find one's legs' = being secure; 'shake a leg' = get active; 'you're pulling my leg' = you're joking; 'give a leg-up' = helping over a hurdle; 'on its last legs' = moribund; obsolete; about to collapse or cease functioning.

Leisure Centre: (See Gym)

Leopard: This is thought by many to be a symbol of sin. (Alternatively, see Lion)

Letter: This signifies the conveyance or receiving of news, information, or messages to or from someone specific, from the world at large or from your subliminal or preconscious mind. Depending on your feelings in the dream, this could signify good news, a reminder or a warning. You may be getting to the truth of something; coming into greater awareness about some aspect of your life; receiving a revelation; having new realizations; increased understanding of yourself or of things concerning you.

Library: A search for truth; information; wisdom or knowledge; a need to understand the situation; looking for answers. It may suggest that you are close to solving a problem or discovering something new and exciting.

Lift: Going up and down in a lift may indicate the raising or deepening of your consciousness. Going up would possibly be rising to a level of the supra-conscious, and going down may indicate entry into the subliminal area of you mind. The lift may also represent the 'ups and downs' of life. If you are ascending, then you may perceive your current situation as optimistic and moving upward. If you are descending, you may be experiencing some negativity or helplessness. This is a quicker and easier movement than using the stairs.

Light: This is an archetypical symbol. It represents enlightenment; understanding; knowledge; clarity; openness;

truth; the dispersal of darkness and shadows. Spiritually, the light may represent God's presence: loving; purifying; healing; inspiring or empowering for service. A burned-out light bulb could indicate failure to keep the light of the spirit within kindled. Alternatively, it may indicate a solution to a problem. Think of some related sayings: 'out like a light'; 'make light of the situation'; 'light at the end of the tunnel'; 'see the light of day'; 'shed light on the matter'; 'speed of light.'

Lighthouse: This is a symbol warning of entering an area of potential danger. It signifies that there is hidden danger.

Lightning: This is a charging energy and may symbolise God's powerful presence; sudden illumination; sudden and startling occurrence; a shift in awareness; startling news or a warning of adversity.

Lily: A symbol of purity and spirituality.

Line: A vertical line is positive; active; between heaven and earth, God and humankind; masculine. A horizontal line is submissive; human-to-human; grounded; feminine. A wavy line indicates indecisiveness. Think also of 'Lay it on the line'; 'read between the lines'; 'drop me a line'; 'draw a line under it'; 'draw the line'; 'being sidelined'; 'line one's pocket.'

Lion: This is an archetypical symbol. It symbolises courage; social distinction; dignity; leadership, which relates to all the big cats, but especially the lion as supreme predator. It is regal, noble, majestic, proud (pride of lions); boastful; confident. Think also of: 'Lion-hearted'; 'Lion King'; 'Lion of Judah' = Christ symbol; 'roar like a lion'; 'raging lion'; 'take the lion's share'; 'fight like a tiger.' Alternatively, if fear is attached to the image, it could symbolise your wild untamed animal nature or feelings that you are not ready to deal with.

Lips: This is usually related to speech. What did you observe about the shape of the lips and what does this communicate to you? Are the lips smiling; smirking; whistling; whispering; pursed; puckered? Think also of 'Being tight-lipped'; 'hot-lips'; 'my lips are sealed'; 'button your lip'; 'keep a stiff upper lip'.

Lock: Consider the feelings in your dream. Were you

at peace or feeling frustrated? It could denote security or something that is inaccessible; hidden; an unattainable goal or a blocked opportunity. Alternatively, this may indicate that you are secretive, closed, locking others out. Consider also the sexual connotations.

Locust: A symbol of old age.

Losing valuables: This may imply a danger of losing spiritual direction or contact; losing moral values; warning of theft; not keeping watch on what is important in life. Note what is lost and consider the symbolism for that.

Lotus: A symbol of passivity or distaste for an active life; meditative and receptive posture. It represents the perfection of the higher self rising out of the stagnant water of our lower self. It is an archetypical symbol.

Love: To love and be loved is the basic need in all of us. It is vital to healthy growth and development, important to our emotional, psychological and spiritual well-being. Meditate on and continue to nurture the image from your dream.

Lovebird: This may relate to a love relationship that is caged and needing to be liberated. (See Birds in Chapter 12)

Lynx: A symbol of acuity; vigilance.

ꙮ M ꙮ

Magpie: A symbol of talkativeness.

Maid: (See Servant)

Male/Man: If he is unknown to you it would be related to your male qualities, even if you are a woman. Each of us has a masculine and feminine side to our nature, varying in intensity. Male qualities are: dominance; managing; controlling; down-to-earth; logical; thinking; intellectual; reasoning and the analytical side to us. If he is known to you, think of the similar traits of that person in you or his role, e.g. your boss could indicate the bossy side to your nature. (See Chapter 10 – Dream Characters)

Mandala: Carl Jung called all circular formations a mandala and said that they hold valuable meaning for the dreamer. The mandala is an archetypical symbol. All rounded forms, such as a ring; a bowl; a spiral; whirlpool; fairy circles; haloes; growth rings in the cross section of a tree trunk; the grooves in a record; any symbol or picture within a circle or circular frame symbolises harmony and wholeness. However, a cobweb or maze within a mandala may indicate confusion or disorder.

Manna: This is a symbol of our spiritual sustenance, the miraculous provision for our nourishment as we wander through the desserts of life as the Israelites did and were fed in their forty-year wilderness wanderings.[210] 'Give us this day our daily bread' of the Lord's Prayer and Jesus' reference to: 'I have bread that you do not know about.'[211]

Map: This indicates a detailed guide to a desired destination; your plans for the future. Consider whether the map is clear or confusing. Following a clear map suggest that you are confident in your current path and pursuits. Confusion may indicate that you lack a clear sense of direction.

Marriage: This is an archetypical symbol. It is a symbol of commitment or the coming together of various parts of your nature e.g. your feminine and masculine qualities; supra-

---

210 Exodus 16:4, 14-26 Joshua 5:11-12
211 John 4:31-32 6:26,27

conscious and conscious in harmony or your spiritual and secular in balance. The commitment could be to your work, to yourself or to your partner. (See also Wedding)

Masks: (See Stage Costumes)

Maze: Being trapped in a maze and having difficulty getting out suggests that you may be facing many hard decisions and are unsure of which way to turn. At times we are all confused or disorganized, and acknowleging that this is a step towards finding our way through. Think also on the play on the words: a maze – and amazed or amazement.

Meat: This may indicate carnality; a meaty matter; something to get your teeth into.

Medal: This symbolises the recognition of achievement (See also Metal and Metals in Chapter 8)

Medicine: Taking medication indicates an attempt to restore physical, psychological or spiritual health and well-being.

Melody: (See Music)

Merry-go-round: This could indicate that you are going around in circles. It may also be a sign of pleasure; being more care-free; setting the inner child free.

Metal: This suggests strength and durability. (See specific metals in Chapter 8)

Milk: This symbolises primary nourishment for infants. It suggests that you are giving or receiving an adequate amount of nurture, support and consideration for your growth and well-being. Think also of related sayings: 'milk of human kindness'; 'milk him dry'; 'crying over spilt milk.'

Minister: Are you that minister? If so it could be indicating a need for you to minister, counsel, forgive or care for someone or for others in general. If a minister enters your dream, it could indicate a need for you to be ministered to, to take counsel, seek care or forgiveness. Think also of related thoughts: 'Practice what you preach.'

Mirror: You may be concerned about your image and the way you present yourself to the world or calling for self-examination as identity is very much connected to appearance.

Broken mirrors indicate a distorted image or, if you are superstitious – seven years bad luck.

Mobility Scooter: Slow, but steady progress; proceed cautiously; limited energy; being battery operated it could indicate the need to recharge your inner resources.

Mockingbird: Think of the implications on the word 'mocking.'

Mole: As an animal, a symbol of blindness; obtuseness. As a skin blemish, how do you interpret it? Is it a beauty spot or a bleminsh, and on what part of the body does it appear?

Money: This is symbolic of power, status and wealth. We often judge ourselves and others on the ability to make, save and spend it. Consider your own relationship with money and your current financial situation. This could be an anxiety or a wish-fulfilment dream. Money may not necessarily represent cash, but those things that you value most. Think of related sayings: 'Mr money-bags'; 'money is the root of all evil'; 'get your money's worth'; 'money for jam'; 'in the money'; 'in the pound seats'; 'in for a penny, in for a pound'; 'penny wise, pound foolish.'

Monk: This is a symbol of the sacred vows of poverty, celebacy and obedience. It may be a warning that you are too interested in money, sex or pleasure. It could also indicate a need for spiritual guidance or direction; a need to devote yourself more to spiritual matters; develop a higher spirituality; hear or make a confession; offer forgiveness; self-denial; less emphasis on your sexuality; exercise self-restraint.

Monkey: Mischievous; immaturity; trickery; demon-symbol; 'monkey on your back'; 'monkeying about'; 'make a monkey of yourself'; 'monkey see, monkey do' (See also: Ape)

Monsters: This is an archetypical symbol. They may represent destructive forces in your life or negative tendencies and characteristics. A task which seems over-whelming or some trait which is self-consuming e.g. bad temper; pessimism; hatred; prejudice; gossip; bigotry; jealousy (the green-eyed monster); drug-abuse or smoking habit.

Moon: The moon represents feminine energy. It is also associated with intuitive and irrational behaviour. It affects the tides, and has been linked to madness or lunacy. It can represent all these things and more. The moon could signify romance, passion and earthly impulses or inner peace, security and serenity. Think also of various related sayings: 'moon-struck'; 'shoot for the moon'; 'moonlighting'; 'mooning around'; 'reach for the moon.'

Mosque: Place of worship (See Church)

Motel: (See Hotel)

Moth: Being an insect of the night this could be a warning. Think of moths being attracted to a flame and coming too close, being destroyed. It may suggest that you are being led to a place where you will be hurt unless you recognize the danger.

Mother: This is an archetypical symbol. It represents the shaping side of us – procreative; nurturing; caring; comforting; compassionate; loving; tender. She symbolises the source and bringing to birth of something new, maybe a project or invention. If you're a woman, this may point to old attitude, or reflect on your relationship with your mother and ask, 'What in me is like her? What must I do about it?' Think also of related concepts: "mother nature'; 'mother earth'; 'mother country'; 'mother tongue'; 'Mother Church'; 'Mother Mary'; 'Eve, the mother of all humanity'; the Holy Spirit figure, bringing to birth and nurturing God's children to full maturity.

Motor Car: Movement towards a goal/mission in life or away from a situation/calling.

Fast car – Indicates that you are making speedy progress or excessive haste.

Low-powered car – Shows a low energy-level.

Luxury car – May reveal that you are self-indulgent, paying too high a price, high-powered or highly motivated.

Driving your own car – Shows that you are in control of your life.

Driving someone else's car – Points to you controlling or

trying to control others.

Reversing – May indicate that you are backsliding or going backwards.

As a passenger – being passive/controlled or driven by another/others, letting others take control of your life;

In the back seat – This could mean that you are taking a back seat or not taking responsibility for your life. A 'back-seat driver' – may indicate that you interfere.

Flat tyres – May mean that you are depressed or lacking spiritual empowerment.

Brakes – This could be a warning to slow down; that you need to be governed by your will rather than emotions.

Windshield wipers – This could indicate that you are trying to get clarity of vision.

Headlights – This reveals insight; clarity of direction; perception; seeing the way ahead; enlightenment.

Driving in the dark without headlights – Points to a loss of vision or unawareness of dangers.

Running out of petrol – This suggests a lack of motivation or being physically, mentally, emotionally or spiritually drained.

Mechanical problems – This indicates the need to have a physical examination, give yourself a spiritual check-up.

Motorboat: The driving force is from within yourself as you progress on your spiritual journey or as you investigate the unconscious mind. (See Water)

Mountain: This is an archetypical symbol. Climbing a mountain is challenging, and rewarding once we reach the top. The mountain may represent an obstacle or a goal in life. It may also be a symbol of the pinnacle of spirituality or experience. Think of Mount Moriah; Mount Zion; Mount Horeb; Mount Sinai; Mount Carmel; mount of the beatitudes; the mount of transfiguration; mount of ascension.[212]

Mouse: This is a symbol of timidity; insignificance; a timorous; hesitant; shy nature. Think of related concepts: 'mousey'; 'are you a man or a mouse?'; 'quiet as a mouse'; 'poor as a church-mouse'; 'mouse-coloured hair'; 'playing cat and mouse.'

---

212 Gen 22:2 Ex 3:1,12; 19:3,18; 1 Kings 18:19-39; Mat 4:8-10; 5:1; 14:23; 17:1; 28:16

Mouth: Related to speech – 'mouthing off'; 'he has a big mouth'; 'foot in mouth.' A closed mouth could be a warning to keep your mouth shut; 'tight lipped'; 'zip one's lip'; 'button your lip.'

Movie: This may indicate how you project yourself; a re-run of past events; more action and less observation; think also of: 'Picture this'; 'do you get the picture?'

Mud: This is often related to verbal abuse; being in a rut; inability to make progress. Think of being 'stuck in the mud'; 'being a stick-in-the-mud'; 'mud-slinging'; 'don't muddy the waters'; 'his name is mud.'

Mule: A symbol of obstinacy.

Murder: (See Killing)

Museum: Old, outmoded ideas; or review resources from the past; revisit previous methods; examine earlier applications.

Music: This is the art of the muses and symbolises harmony in life. Music is healing to the psyche and, as you are listening to it in your dream, you may be connected to the wonderful Spirit of Creativity or flow of life bringing peace and inner harmony to your soul. The song that you dream about may have a message for you. 'Music of the spheres' is being in balance with the universe, in harmony with creation. Think also of 'face the music' Consider the significance of the eighty-eight keys of a concert grand piano (See Chapter 9 - Numbers in Dreams)

ℵ N ℶ

Nail: Filing nails may indicate trimming the rough edges off a project. Painting nails could relate to enhancing yourself. Reflect on what painted nails means to you. Note also the colour. Think of related sayings: 'fighting tooth and nail'; 'hard as nails'; 'hit the nail on the head'; 'I nailed the liar'; 'a nail in his coffin'

Nakedness: You may be feeling exposed, vulnerable, or embarrassed as a result of a mistake, emotional reaction or being put on the spot. It reveals a state of innocence as newborn babies; uninhibited; having nothing to hide; freedom; openness; unassuming; non-judgemental; transparency; purity; sinlessness. Adam and Eve, created in the image of God, were 'naked and unashamed'[213]; 'naked truth'; 'bare facts'; 'to bare all.'

Names: To hear your name being called is thought of as a profound spiritual experience of being called to mission, service or a special ministry. The detail or nature of the calling will soon become clear.

Neighbour: This relates to some inner quality that you are not recognising in yourself. Reflect further on other elements in the dream, in particular the qualities in the neighbour that you admire – either in your dream or in waking life. 'Love your neighbour as yourself.'

Newspaper: This relates to information concerning recent events in life.

Night attire: An attitude of sleep or withdrawal. (see Clothes)

Night: Darkness represents a lack of awareness and illumination or it may suggest that you are hiding something or are unwilling to see things clearly.

Nightingale: A symbol of forlornness.

Nose: Think of: 'Nosey' = inquisitive; 'nose to the grindstone' = work hard; 'look down your nose' = being haughty; 'put someone's nose out of joint' = to thwart or humiliate them;

---
213 Genesis 2:25

'get up someone's nose' = irritate or annoy them; 'rub his nose in it' = hostile reminder of wrongdoing; 'cut off your nose to spite your face.' Which of these sayings strikes a chord for you?

Nudity: (See nakedness)

Numbers: (See Chapter 9 – Numbers in Dreams)

Nun: This is a symbol of the sacred vows of poverty, chastity and obedience. It may be a warning that you are too interested in money, sex or pleasure. It could also indicate a need for spiritual guidance or direction; a need to devote yourself more to spiritual matters; develop a higher spirituality; hear or make a confession; offer forgiveness; self-denial; less emphasis on your sexuality; exercise self-restraint.

Nurse: Something needs to be nursed back to health or some pain needs to be eased; a hurt healed. It may relate to a relationship or a project. Are you nursing a grievance?

Nut: Laying up stock for lean times or provision for the future. Think also of related sayings: 'Here we go gathering nuts in May'; 'I'm nuts about you'; 'he's a nut-case'; 'in a nutshell'; 'that's a tough nut to crack'

ಬ O ಲ

Oasis: This symbolises a haven of refuge, a place of renewal and the quenching of a spiritual or inner thirst; a quiet place of retreat from the dry, barren, desert patches in life; a sanctuary for the soul. It may indicate that you are being spiritually renewed or in need of a spiritual retreat to revitalise your life.

Oats: A symbol of fertility, prosperity and abundance. Think also of 'sowing wild oats.'

Observatory: A desire for a heavenly vision; revelation of the spiritual realm; eternal outlook.

Ocean: (See Water and Chapter 12 – The Four Basic Elements)

Octopus: This could indicate being clumsy; grasping; clinging.

Odour: Depending on whether the odour is pleasant or unpleasant, this could relate either to the fragrance of heaven or something stinking in your life. You will need to identify the smell and what it indicates to you, personally. Think of related sayings: 'I smell a rat'; 'it smells fishy'; 'wake up and smell the coffee'; 'come out smelling of roses.'

Office: Related to administration and work needing to be done. Preparation needed for achieving success; supervising or managing a task; much organisation needing to be done.

Oil: This can be interpreted as a symbol of wealth; spirituality; religious rite or sexual connotations. Oil is a symbol of the Holy Spirit and used in sacramental healing services.[214] What does it mean to you? Oil is also used in machinery to eliminate friction. Think of related sayings: 'grease my palm'; 'pour oil on troubled waters'; 'burning the midnight oil'; 'she's no oil-painting'; 'oil the wheels'; 'like greased lightning.'

Old Man: This could be seen as an archetype of God. (See also Old Person)

Old Person: This may represent outdated ideas/attitudes; wisdom; maturity; inflexible nature; senility; something ready to die and be reborn. It is an archetypical symbol.

---
214 James 5:14,15

Old Woman: An old woman may be seen as Mother Earth or Mother Nature. (See also Old Person)

Onion: Chopping onions may indicate something to cry about. If you are peeling an onion, it may suggest that you are, or need to, strip off the layers of something that causes you to weep so that you can get to the heart of the matter. (See Chapter 13 – Emotional Healing through Meditition and Lucid Dreams)

Orange: What do oranges and other citrus fruits mean to you? There are associations with Christmas; sunshine; breakfast; refreshment; half-time breaks in team sport. The fruit will no doubt have significant associations for you: explore these as you interpret what it symbolises in your dream. (As a colour, see Colours in Chapter 8)

Orphan: This relates to being deprived of nurture and guidance.

Ostrich: This is a flightless bird; a symbol of stupidity, or having your 'head in the sand.' (See: Birds in Chapter 12)

Outside: This indicates that something is exposed; out in the open; revealed; visible or excluded. Are you perhaps on the outside looking in?

Oven: The most obvious symbolism is that of a womb. A warm oven is said to be productive, but a cold one unrewarding. Reflect on the dream as a whole and relate this to your present situation, your hopes, joys or fears. It may represent cooking. (See Cook)

Owl: A symbol of wisdom and virtue. As a night bird it is a symbol of spiritual mystery. 'Wise old owl'; 'night-owl.'

Ox: A symbol of strength; hard work; patience; sacrifice.

Oyster: This is a common symbol having sexual connotations. It may represent the female genitalia. It is also considered symbolic of humility and wisdom. Their meaning is associated with that of pearls – 'pearls of wisdom.' The negative interpretation is that it may represent a recluse or well-guarded person, shut off from others – 'to clam up.' Reflect on how you would interpret this for yourself.

⊱ P ⊰

Packing: There could be several different interpretations depending on the motive. Are you packing for storage, in preparation for a move, going on holiday or tidying something away? Note also what you are packing and look that up. Perhaps you are storing information in your memory, or shelving issues that are not relevant for your present situation. You may also be dealing with some emotional baggage.

Palm: This is a symbol of victory, celebration; triumph and joy. On Palm Sunday Jesus rode into Jerusalem on a donkey and people threw palm branches on the road before him. Kings would ride into the city on a donkey to show their peaceful, gentle authority. A palm leaf may also be a play on the word and indicate the hand. Think of 'I have it in the palm of my hand'; 'cross my palm with silver'; 'he palmed it off onto me'; 'an itching palm'.

Panic: (See Fear)

Panther: (See Lion)

Pants: These cover the lower body, in particular the most private parts. Reflect on the style, colour and any other significant detail and why in particular this was a significant detail of your dream. (See also Trousers and Clothes)

Parakeet: (See Lovebird)

Paralysis: Being unable to flee from a pursuer or move is a common experience in dreams. It may indicate that you are longing to escape something challenging or frightening. The fear that paralyzes you in the dream could be symbolic of the fear that you are experiencing in waking life. You may feel unable to change a situation. Take note of the object of fear and think of what it symbolises for you.

Parents: (See Chapter 10 – Dream Characters)

Parking lot: (See Garage)

Parliament: Are you preparing to present an argument; weighing up the pro's and con's; making important decisions; expecting a confrontation; debating an issue; facing life-changing choices?

Parrot: A symbol of mockery; verbosity; repetition. 'Parrot fashion.'
Pastor: (See Minister)
Peacock: A symbol of pride; flaunting oneself; a show-off.
Pen/Pencil: Writing is a form of self-expression and a way to clarify and express our thoughts. This may indicate a desire or need to communicate with someone, or take note of something. A fountain pen is seen by many to be a phallic symbol.
Penguin: This is a flightless bird associated more with water than air. (See Birds, Water and Ice, and Chapter 12 – Animal Life & The Four Basic Elements)
Penis: (See Genitals)
Penny: This could symbolise an exchange: 'penny for your thoughts'; 'his two pence worth'; 'that's a pretty penny'; 'to turn an honest penny'; 'penny wise, pound foolish'; 'take care of the pennies and the pounds will take care of themselves'; 'in for a penny, in for a pound'; 'I need to spend a penny'; 'he turns up like a bad penny'; 'the penny dropped.'
People: (See Chapter 12 – Dream Characters)
Phoenix: This is a powerful symbol of resurrection life. In Greek legends, the phoenix is an exotic purple bird which lives a number of years, then makes a nest of spices, flaps its wings to create fire, burns itself to ashes then rises from death to new life again. 'Phoenix' means purple. (See purple in Chapter 8 – Colours in Dreams. See also Birds and Fire in Chapter 12 – Animal Life and the Four Basic Elements)
Photograph: If it is the photograph of a person, consider who it is and what that person represents to you. If the photograph or picture is of you, self-examination may be required. If it is a scenic picture see picture below.
Physician: (see Doctor)
Piano: (See Music)
Picture: These are reflections on your life or life experiences. Think about what the scene means for you. It may indicate that there is some unfinished business in your past, something that

needs to be revisited or something that needs healing. It may be a warning not to repeat mistakes, or giving encouragement concerning a past successful venture.

Pig: Symbolises gluttony; obstinacy; crudity; uncouthness; rudeness; uncleanness; coarse, loutish or ill-mannered behaviour.

Pigeon: A symbol of cowardice or betrayal – 'stool-pidgeon.'

Pink: A delicate, feminine colour; the pink ribbon of the breast cancer symbol; It says, 'Handle with care!' (See Colours - Chapter 8)

Pit: This may be a warning of a trap. Consider 'pitfalls'; 'it's the pits.'

Plants: (See under 'The Great Outdoors' in Chapter 11 – My World)

Pockets: These may represent those things that you keep for yourself – your valued possessions; memories; secrecy or inner resources. Hands in the pockets may suggest helplessness or guilt, hand in someone else's pocket – theft.

Point: A pointed object or pointing the way may indicate direction: Go back, forward etc. or 'get to the point'; 'that's beside the point'; 'to stretch a point'; 'make a point.'

Police officer: Something or some area of you life may need to be investigated, stopped, protected or disciplined.

Police Station: Need for protection from, or controlling that which is contrary to God's law; illegal; dishonest; deceitful; unlawful; counter-productive; destructive.

Pond/Pool: (See Water and Chapter 12 – The Four Basic Elements)

Porch: (see under House)

Porcupine: Defensive; sharp; prickly; bristling; barbed.

Port: This symbolises a safe haven, or a new experience. You may be harbouring feelings of guilt or resentment.

Portrait: (See: Picture and Photograph)

Preacher: (See Minister)

Pregnancy: This is a symbol of fruitfulness and ideas growing within you or some new project or responsibility coming your way.

Priest: (See Minister)

Primitive People: (See Chapter 12 – Dream Characters)

Prince Charming: Saviour; redeemer; restorer – The Christ figure.

Prison: This may indicate feelings of guilt; confinement; restriction; a desire for more freedom; the need to take captive disruptive thoughts or destructive intentions. Perhaps you believe that you are trapped or locked into your present condition. If you are the jailer, you may have a desire to dominate others or be in control of a current situation.

Prisoner: Anti-social tendencies that need to be restrained; attitudes that need to be put away; a warning about some harmful thoughts needing to be taken captive[215]; or, you are restricted by someone or something and your spirit is longing to be set free to discover your potential.

Professor: You may need to profess your faith; or are you professing to know it all? (See also Teacher)

Prostitute: Are you being solicited or are you doing the soliciting? A warning against getting involved in something reprehensible or offering your services in a humiliating way. Being used and abused; selling yourself shamefully. The positive aspect is the way of Tamar – being a channel of God's purpose in spite of general disapproval.[216]

Psychiatrist/Psychotherapist: (see Counsellor)

Pub: A Public House is a place where people connect with others in a relaxed and sociable atmosphere. Drinking alcoholic beverages also helps one to relax and lose inhibitions. To dream of a pub suggests a desire to escape responsibility or a need to socialise or relax and let yourself go.

Puppy: A symbol of immaturity; playfulness; carefree; dependency or fun-loving. (See Dog and also Chapter 12 – Animal Life and the Four Basic Elements)

Purple: (See Chapter 8 – Colours in Dreams)

Purse: (See Money)

Pyramid: It may represent the coming together of the world

---

215 2 Corinthians 10:5
216 Genesis 38:11-30, Mathhew 1:3

of man with the Kingdom of God – the temporal and spiritual. This may symbolise a sense of rising or striving to achieve wholeness in body mind and spirit.

෩ Q ଔ

Quadrangle: (See Square)

Quarrel: This may indicate some inner conflict; an inability to resolve important issues, ideas, or values; difficulty in making decisions, inability to accept authority; or, you may have carried an argument from your waking life into your dream.

Queen: This is a symbol of pomp and pageantry, wealth, power and prestige – 'queen bee.'

Quicksand: This may indicate feelings of helplessness and an inability to get out of a tricky situation in your life. (See Earth under 'The Four Basic Elements' – Chapter 12)

Quilt: As a covering for warmth. (See Blanket.) If it is a patchwork quilt it may indicate random memories or patchy, scattered thoughts; harmony in diversity.

ℜ

Rabbit: A symbol of fertility; productivity; sexual desires. Think of some associations: Alice in Wonderland's white rabbit = a whole new world opening before you; 'exploring inner mysteries'; 'pull a rabbit out of the hat' = surprises; 'jump to conclusions'; 'Easter' = new life or resurrection life; 'spring' = awakening; 'hare in the moon' (as seen in the Southern hemesphere) = a new or different perspective.

Race: Consider whether you are competing, running to or from something. If you are simply running, it may indicate that you need to slow down or speed up, depending on your situation in life – you will know which it is. If you are competing, you may need to consider your competitive drive and look at present challenges. If you are running in a race and win, it is an indication that things are going well for you.

Radio: This is to do with the transmission of an auditory message. Think of related sayings: 'He who has ears to hear let him hear'; 'listen up'; d'ye hear there.'

Railings: (See Fence)

Rain: Rain clears the air; refreshes; provides life-giving moisture to the earth, plant and animal life. This could suggest a period of renewal. Is it gentle rain or a storm? Think of some related sayings: 'I need to take a rain-check'; 'put something aside for a rainy day'; 'into each life a little rain must fall' (See Storm or Water under 'The Four Basic Elements' – Chapter 12)

Rainbow: It follows a storm or it appears when the atmosphere is laden with water vapour. White light is split into the full spectrum of seven colours and arches over the sky directly opposite the sun. The first rainbow followed the flood in Noah's time, and was a sign of God's covenant with the earth.[217] This is an archetypical symbol. (See also: Light, Water, Sun and Colours in Dreams)

Ram: Male sheep. (See Sheep)

Rape: This dream does not necessarily have sexual connotations. It has more to do with destruction, power and

---
217 Genesis 9:13-16

control. It may indicate an enforced and undesirable union or a warning against joining a cult or being accosted by members of a religious cult. Since it is a brutal and deeply personal violation, it may suggest that you could be feeling robbed of personal freedom or de-valued as a person. Think about the issues in your life that cause anxiety or fear. If you have been a victim of rape, this could be reliving that horrendous experience. (See Chapter 13 – Emotional Healing through Meditation and Lucid Dreams)

Rats: They are symbols of danger, poverty, filth, and illness. Think of associated name-calling: Scoundrel; rascal; rogue; good-for-nothing; sewer-rat. You may be apprehensive regarding a deal or venture. Consider your options and possible consequences of your decision.

Raven: A symbol of ill-luck. Alternatively, God's provision – Elijah was fed by a raven as he hid in the ravine.[218]

Rectangle: (See Square)

Red: Red is associated with intense human emotion; passion; sexuality; generative power; life-blood and birth as well as anger and warning signs. What does red mean to you? Think of associations: 'Red-letter day'; 'Mars, the red planet'; 'Paint the town red'; 'Hearts and Roses'; 'Valentine's Day'; 'Poppy Day' 'Communism'; 'red alert'; 'Seeing red!' (See Colours in Chapter 8)

Relative: (Aunt/Uncle/Cousin/Brother/Sister/Parent/Grandparent) = relating to you. Note what personality traits you associate with that person: how you relate to them could give you a clue into your own tendency in that personality trait. It could however relate to that person – a recent conversation or concern projected onto you. (See also under individual listing)

Restaurant: The dreamer feels the need to be spiritually fed; hungering for knowledge; nurturing the soul; craving nourishment for the spirit; more doctrinal teaching.

Ribbon: White ribbons may indicate a wedding in the offing; yellow ribbons may denote a welcome home; royalblue ribbons symbolise a winner; powder blue or pale pink

---
218 1 Kings 17:6

ribbons could mean a forthcoming birth.

Right: The right side of the body is governed by the left brain, which is logical, methodical, organised and orderly. It is associated with outgoing, masculine energy. Right also relates to being right; right-wing; conservative. Taking a right turn may indicate all or any of the above regarding your present circumstances. It may also symbolise making the right decisions. Think of various sayings: 'Being in your right mind'; 'put things right'; 'right up my street'

Ring: Is it the sound, a shape or a piece of jewellery? As a sound it may indicate a warning, a means of getting your attention or sending a message; as a shape see 'Circle'; as a piece of jewellery it may signify commitment as with a friendship; engagement or wedding ring. Think also of various related sayings: 'ring the changes'; 'ring of laughter'; 'that rings a bell'; 'she runs rings around me.'

River: This represents the course of life. Just as a river never stops flowing until it reaches the ocean, so our lives flow until we reach our end in God. It is an archetypical symbol. (See Water and 'The Four Basic Elements' in Chapter 12)

Road: A road usually symbolizes the journey we take through life, in particular the present journey. Reflect on the type of road and mode of transport. Is the road rough or smooth, straight or winding, flat, uphill or downhill, wide or narrow? Are there any other vehicles on the road or are you alone? All these factors will give you clearer insight for your interpretation. (See Vehicles in Chapter 11)

Robber: Intrusive element: anxieties that rob you of your confidence; faith; peace. You may be feeling that someone is taking credit for your idea – or are you taking recognition for what is not yours. A warning that you will lose the gifts that you are not using. Think also: 'Procrastination is the thief of time'; 'come as a thief in the night'; 'keep watch and pray'

Robin: A symbol of trust. (See Birds under Animal Life in Chapter 12)

Rocks: Reflect on the size, shape, roughness, smoothness and colour of the rock. Take note also where the rock is: is it an obstacle in your path, or is it a decorative feature? The interpretation of this symbol depends on the details and the mood of the dream. Rocks represent something worldly rather than spiritual, emotional or mental issues. It may possibly relate to earthiness; stability; durability; something immovable; a solid foundation or obstacles. It is also a Christ figure – 'Rock of Ages.' Think also of various sayings: 'rock solid'; 'on the rocks' = on ice or grounded; 'rock' = slang for diamond; 'rock bottom'; 'don't rock the boat.' (See Earth in 'The Four Basic Elements' – Chapter 12)

Roller-Coaster: This appears to symbolize emotional ups and downs that you may be experiencing. Are you enjoying it or does the ride seem to be out of control? It may also indicate the abuse of drugs.

Rooster: This may represent male energy or aggression. A rooster crowing could be a wake-up call. (See also Chicken)

Rope: This signifies restriction, bondage or lack of freedom. A tow-rope signifies pulling or hauling. Think of various sayings: 'I'm at the end of my rope'; 'give him plenty of rope and he'll hang himself'; 'he's tied up at the moment'; 'know the ropes.'

Rose: This is an archetypical symbol. It represents unfolding beauty, perfection and love. It could have many different interpretations depending on your associations. Write down the first thing that comes into your head. Note also the colour, number and fragrance of the rose. Flowers generally signify attraction, beauty, femininity. (See The Great Outdoors in Chapter 11)

Rowing-boat: There is a great deal of effort on your part because of the resistance of your unconscious mind or spiritual elements involved in your progress. (See Dream Vehicles – Chapter 11 and Water under The Four Basic Elements – Chapter 12)

Rubbish: (See Garbage)
Rug: (see Carpet or Blanket)

Ruin: This may signify a state of dilapidation through neglect. It could refer to neglect of one's body through poor diet or abuse; material ruin; spiritual destruction or the need to clear rubble from you life.

Running: Are you running in a race or running towards or away from something? What are you running to/away from? Is it a threat or a challenge? Are you moving with ease or difficulty? What are your emotions? Think of related sayings: 'Running around in circles'; 'he's out of the running'; 'running up debt'; 'running amok'; 'feeling run-down'; 'let it run its course'; 'take a running jump'; 'it's running like clockwork'; 'run rings around someone'; 'it runs in the blood.'

✽ S ✾

Sailor: Note the type of vessel and what the sailor is doing. Could you be rising above the flood? riding storms of life? tossed about on the waves of doubt or confusion? being carried along by the wind (Spirit of God)? Water symbolises both death and life. Noah safe in the ark while the wicked drowned in the flood; Baptism is a dying to sin and rising to newness of life – dying to the flesh and rising in the spirit. (See Water in 'The Four Basic Elements' – Chapter 12)

Saint: Dreaming about saints usually has spiritual implications. Your supra-conscious mind may be communicating a need for a more virtuous lifestyle or to get in touch with your spiritual side.

Salt: This is a valuable commodity, used as a preservative and flavour enhancer. It is a symbol of wisdom. Reflect on various common sayings: 'You are the salt of the earth'; 'pillar of salt'; 'take it with a pinch of salt'; 'he's worth his salt'; 'rub salt in the wound'; 'sitting above (or below) the salt' = place of distinction (or inferiority).

Satan: (See Devil)

Savages: Relating to behaviour that is uncivilised; bad-mannered; rude; coarse; impolite; foul-mouthed; crude – in thought, speech or behaviour. (See Chapter 12 – Dream Characters)

Scales: This symbolises justice; balance; weighing good against evil. Think of related concepts: 'Weighed and found wanting'; 'carry your weight'; 'don't throw your weight about'; 'pull your weight' This may also be a warning against eating disorders.

School: This is related to learning. It may be indicating that, to grow in spiritual and emotional maturity, there is something you need to learn; raise your thinking to a higher level; you have a degree of knowledge but don't know it all. Reflect on what you may still need to learn.

Scissors: The two blades coming together, in uniting divide the paper. Shears are a symbol of strength in unity and cooperation. It may be an indication of a need to work together or in partnership. Think also of various related sayings: 'That cuts both ways'; 'cut it out'; 'cut to the quick'; 'I'm cut up about it.'

Scorpion: This may be symbolic of something dangerous, or harmful. Reflect on the context of your dream to learn what it may be.

Sea: This is an archetypical symbol. (See Water and Chapter 12 – The Four Basic Elements)

Seasons: Spring is the season of birth and blossoming forth of new life; summer is the season of life at its peak of productivity; autumn the season of reaping the rewards and bringing in the harvest; winter is the season of rest. What is the season telling you about your present condition, and preparation for the next phase?

Seeds: These symbolise new life; new beginnings; new opportunities or increase. They generally relate to thoughts, ideas, concepts, knowledge or the Word of God.[219] Germinating in darkness in the soil, with the heat of the sun and nourished by water, they sprout and grow, bloom in the air. Follow those thoughts in relation to the Four Basic Elements (Chapter 12) to gain clarity as to their meaning for you.

Serpent: (See Snake)

Servant: It is the duty of the servant to clean, polish and keep things tidy. This could be indicating a need to clean, polish or tidy up something in your life, or a call to service; 'behold the servant of the Lord,' or to be of service to others. Think of related concepts: 'clean up your act'; 'get your house in order.'

Service Station/Body Shop/Garage: This could signify that you may need a physical check-up; a holiday; a break; to be spiritually renewed; revived; mentally rejuvenated; recharged.

Settee: (See Sofa)

Sewing: Sewing a garment may indicate the need to mend your ways; or, creating something new. Think also of the pun on the word: 'As you sow, so shall you reap'; 'sowing wild oats.'

---

[219] Luke 8:5-15

Sex: (See the section: Sexual Acts – Chapter 7)
Shapes: (See cross; square; circle; triangle; ring; star)
Shark: These have unpleasant associations for most people – snapping up food, alive or dead. Even in the womb, a shark will eat its weaker twin. A swindler; pilferer; extortionist.
Sheep: Symbolic of stupidity; timidity; a traditionalist; conformity; a conventional person; easily led; faithful; trusting; obedient; followers of Jesus, the Good Shepherd; spiritual virtue; guilt = 'sheepish'
Shell: The exo-skeletal home for some sea creatures, therefore a symbol of spiritual life; baptism; travel – as the travellers would use one as a drinking vessel. It may also symbolise a casing or protective covering.
Shellfish: (See Shell and Fish)
Shield: A symbol of protection; resistance against attack or injury. Faith shields us from the destructive false accusations of the devil.[220]
Ship: Being a large vessel having many levels, accommodating a large number of people and providing for all their basic needs and desires, a ship is a village or hotel on the seas transporting many beyond the horizon to distant shores. A ship then represents the Church universal giving passage to those on board to the Kingdom of Heaven, over the sea of spiritual depths and mysteries. Noah's ark symbolises just that.
Shirt: The shirt covers the upper body housing the heart and lungs. Shirts are generally more colourful and casual than jackets or suits. Reflect on the formality/informality, colour and style. Think of related concepts: 'Stuffed-shirt'; 'lose one's shirt'; 'give the shirt off one's back'; 'wear a hair-shirt'; 'getting shirty'; 'keep your shirt on!' (See Clothing)
Shoes: (See Footwear)
Shooting: This could symbolise feelings of hostility; aggression; power. For men in particular it is thought to have strong associations with sexual release. (See also: Guns)
Shopping: Reflect on what shopping means to you. For many people it is a pleasant pastime; for others it is a search

---
[220] Ephesians 6:16

for bargains; replenishing stocks; draining resources; quality time with family or friends; recreation; stressful; enjoyable... To interpret this dream you need to know yourself and your needs. What are you looking for in life – physically, emotionally, psychologically and spiritually?

Shops: *Bookshop* – relates to research; learning; study.

Chemist/Pharmacy – are you in need of physical, emotional, spiritual or inner healing? forgiveness and absolution? Think also of: 'take your own medicine.'

Clothing store – Looking for a new image; a new way of expressing yourself; a change in personality.

Department store – you may be presented with several choices.

Supermarket – Temptation could be set before you; relating to over-indulgence or building-up reserves.

Grocery store – Are you feeling spiritually or mentally malnourished?

Music shop – Indicating a search for inner harmony; rhythm of life; dancing psyche.

Pound store – making modest choices; taking the easy way out; not stretching yourself; lacking confidence; fear of failure; economic anxiety.

Shower: (See Bath)

Silver: Silver represents humanity and the price of redemption. Though precious, silver tarnishes and blackens if neglected. Mirrors are backed with silver and the spiritual symbolism of silver is humanity reflecting the image of God – clearly or dimly according to darkening by contamination. (See Metals in Chapter 8)

Singing: (See Music)

Sister: This relates to the supportive side of your nature. (See Brother/Sister)

Sitting-down: This may indicate that you are relaxed, retired or unemployed.

Skating: Whether it is roller-skating; ice-skating or skateboarding it requires balance and is done at some speed. This may indicate the need for balance in your life. Think too of: 'Skating on thin ice' = a warning of danger.

Skeleton: Something emerging that has been buried for a long time; a 'skeleton in the closet' = needing to be aired. (See also Bone/s)

Skiing: Whether on water or snow, it requires balance and speed. It could indicate you may be going downhill fast. (See Snow, also Water in Chapter 12 – The Four Basic Elements)

Skin: The outer covering which keeps the insides in and the outside out. It is mainly the colour and texture of the skin which identifies and classifies the individual by race; age; gender; status. 'Thick skinned' = insensitivity; 'thin-skinned' = oversensitive; 'that's no skin off my nose'; 'by the skin of your teeth'; 'skinned alive'; 'I've got you under my skin'; 'beauty is skin deep'; 'skin for skin.'

Skipping: This may be a sign of joy, a carefree nature, youthful energy, or it could indicate the avoidance of something.

Skull & Crossbones: A symbol for death or poison. Something or someone may be ill-intentioned; poisonous; evil; venomous; wicked or obnoxious in your life.

Slave: (See Servant)

Sliding or Gliding: On what part of your body are you sliding – on your bottom, back, tummy or feet? Do you feel insecure as slipping on ice, or are you enjoying it? Is it natural – as on skates, skis, a skateboard, down a banister? Or is it unnatural – feet along a rough surface? on water (without a ski)? Are you sliding down, up a slope or on the level? and how steep is the slope? Reflecting on these questions will give you greater understanding of the dream.

Slippers: (See Footwear)

Smell: A strong smell in your sleeping environment may come into your dream and influence the content, depending on the association – e.g.: a smell of smoke could cause you to dream of a smoker; or that your house is on fire; or you are enjoying a barbecue. If unrelated to your sleeping environment it may be enhancing the message of the dream. What are your associations and feelings about that particular smell?

Smile: This indicates approval and acceptance. Smiles are contagious. 'Smile and the world smiles with you'; think of a smile painted on the face of a clown with tear drops painted on his cheeks: 'smile, though your heart is breaking.'

Smoke: This may be a warning of impending trouble or evidence of the presence of an upheaval. Think of some related sayings: 'There's no smoke, without fire' = every rumour has some foundation; 'no fire without smoke' = no good without some drawback; 'a smoking gun'; 'put up a smoke-screen.' A cloud of smoke may signify God's guiding presence or God's glory.[221]

Snake/Serpent: This is an archetypical symbol. It is a symbol of both good and evil. The positive aspects are: flowing serpentine movement; wisdom/knowledge[222]; healing[223] and the medical emblem of healing; regeneration (shedding skins); Moses' rod[224]; Christ symbol[225]; 'Caduceus' for the expulsion of evil spirits[226]. The snake is also used as a phallic symbol and thus a procreative emblem of lust. As a symbol of evil, the serpent represents Satan the accuser; temptation[227]; subtlety; deviousness; cunning; deception[228]; forked tongue = deceit; secrecy = shhh as the hiss of a snake; swift strike of a cobra; venomous bite; slithering movement.

Snap/snapping: (see Bite/biting)

Snow: Being frozen water crystals, snow relates to the collective unconscious area of the psyche. It is white, soft and silent, indicating purity; tranquillity; truth; inner peace and harmony. Alternatively, it may suggest unresponsiveness; indifference; and emotional coldness. It could also represent new beginnings; fresh vision or a new way of seeing things. Dirty snow would possibly represent corruption or guilt. Think also of: 'snowed under'; pure as the driven snow'; 'snow-balling.'

221 Exodus 40:34-38 2 Chronicles 5:13,14
222 Matt 10:16, Genesis 3:1-4
223 Num 21:8,9
224 Exodus 4:4→"Rod of God" 4:20
225 John 3:14←Numbers 21:8,9
226 Mercury's Winged rod entwined with serpents
227 Genesis 3
228 Genesis 3:1-5, Revelation 12:10

Soap: This may indicate a need to clean up your life, your language, your thoughts or behaviour. Reflect on where, or to what the soap is being applied. Think of: 'soft soaping'; 'soap opera'; 'wash your mouth with soap.'

Socks: (See Footwear)

Sofa: Dreaming about a sofa could mean that you need to take it easy or be more relaxed. The settee also symbolises comfort; warmth; love; romance. Think also of the psychiatrist's couch.

Soiled clothing: Impure behaviour (see Clothes)

Soldier: This may be alerting you to be more disciplined in your life and work; or commending you on efficiency; warning you of pending conflict; bravery may be called for – 'soldier on' or doing battle with the enemy; fight for what's right; 'stand guard'; 'put on the whole armour of God'[229].

Spade: This symbolises the work of digging down into the earth; unearthing some hidden treasures or artefacts; preparing the ground for planting; digging a trench to lay foundations. Reflect on the purpose or use of the spade. Think also of: 'Dig up the dirt'; 'call a spade a spade'; 'shovelling it on.' (See also Earth, Digging)

Sparrow: A symbol of lasciviousness.

Spectacles: This could indicate enhanced vision. If the spectacles are the focal point in the dream it may indicate a need to see things more clearly; examine things closely; read the fine print; do a reality check. Reflect on the context. (See Eyes)

Speech: Inability to speak may indicate that you are not expressing yourself well or clearly. Making a speech could signify the need to tell it like it is or give expression to your thoughts or feelings. Listening to a speech might suggest you should listen to advice.

Sphere: 'Maximum concentration in a minimum space.' An orb is the shape of planets and suns. It is the shape of an egg and many seeds, symbolising wholeness, encapsulating life and energy.

---
[229] Ephesians 6:10-20

Sphinx: With human head and the body of a lion, the sphinx represents the dual nature of animal or worldliness and higher self or godly nature or calling. (See Lion and Man)

Spider: A symbol of wiliness, ingenuity or perseverence.

Spider-web: This is a symbol of wholeness, due to its structure, intricate framework and complexity of construction. It is considered to be a profoundly spiritual dream symbol that calls for greater understanding of yourself, encouraging you to find meaning and satisfaction from the interplay of intricacies in life. It could be calling for an assimilation of your personal traits and talents leading to deeper self-awareness resulting in fulfilment. It may also represent entanglement or some complex situation in your life. Think of a Native American dreamcatcher. (See also Mandala)

Spine: (See Back)

Spiral: A spiral seems to imply speed and intensity of motion, like a spinning top. It remains the same but ascends or descends at speed. Think of 'spin'; 'Spinning a yarn'; 'spinning out of control' (See Mandala)

Sponge: This may indicate that something needs to be absorbed, taken in or understood. Think also of related sayings: 'Sponging on someone'; 'throw in the sponge'; 'old soak' = drunkard.

Spoon: This symbolises giving or receiving nurture; food for the soul; primary or basic spiritual nourishment[230]; spoon-feeding a baby with soft food. 'Silver spoon' = born into wealth; 'spooning' = kissing and cuddling; 'wooden spoon' = booby prize.

Sport: Playing any type of sport may represent some aspects of the way that we run our lives, interact with others or relate to internal struggles where you are attempting to win in the battle with fear, temptation, weakness or substance abuse. Reflect on how you are playing the game – are you playing by the rules and keeping within the boundaries?

Sports Centre: (See Gym)

Spot: This may indicate a blemish; stain; blot on one's

---
230 1 Corinthians 3:1,2 Hebrews 5:11-14 & 1 Peter 2:2

character or reputation. Think also of: 'Being put on the spot' ; 'spot-cash'; 'Spot on'; 'spot-check'; 'under the spotlight.'

Square: A four-sided figure with four corners and four angles. Reflect on what this implies for you. Think of: 'See it from another angle'; 'You've got me cornered' (See Four in Chapter 9 – Numbers in Dreams. See also Cube.)

Squeeze: This could suggest that you are under pressure, crushed or making demands on someone.

Squirrel: Secretive; hoarding; collector; miser; saving; accumulating wisdom or spiritual treasures.

Stab: This might imply an act of hostility or a cutting remark that will or has injured you or others. 'Back-stabbing'; 'take a stab at it'

Stable: A place where farm animals are kept. Reflect on the state of the stable and the animals that are housed there. Think also as a play on the word 'Stable' - steady; constant; firm; unwavering; sure; secure; established; even…

Stag: A symbol of cuckoldry.

Stage Costumes: Signifies hidden identity; cover-up; pretence; sham; deception. Think of: 'a wolf in sheep's clothing'; 'mutton dressed as lamb'. Adam & Eve sewed fig leaves together and made for themselves aprons…and hid themselves from the presence of the Lord.[231] It might represent our persona and how we appear to others or the roles that we play in life such as parent, student, or worker. On the other hand, masks and costumes can symbolise pretentiousness. Look within and see if you are being sincere in the way that you present yourself, if you are hiding something or pretending to be something you are not. If other people are wearing masks, it suggests that you may be concerned about their genuineness.

Stage: This suggests that you or someone you know is putting on an act or you may be upstaging or being upstaged. Alternatively, it could relate to the stage of development or growth.

Stairs: (See Lift, but note that this ascent or descent is slower and uses more effort)

---
231 Genesis 3:7,8

Star: This is an archetypical symbol. It relates to high spiritual ideals. What do you associate with stars? Depending on your association it could mean insight, luck, fortune, rating or the mysteries of the universe. Think of: 'follow your star'; 'written in the stars'; 'you're a star!'; 'the star of the show'; 'five-star hotel'. If it is a star shape, note how many points it has and consult the number in Chapter 9 – Numbers in Dreams.

Starfish: (See Star and Fish)

Statue: Reflect on who or what the statue represents to you. It symbolises a memorial giving honour to an individual or what that person or object represents. It may also stand for something that is rigid; immovable; set in concrete; stone; bronze; unfeeling and unyielding; lacking of emotion or feeling. Something needs to be brought to life.

Stealing: There are three reasons for people to steal: they are poor and hungry and have no alternative but to take what they can lay their hands on to keep body and soul together; they are greedy and covet what takes their fancy without needing it; or it could be a psychological game of 'you lose, I win.' Reflect on your dream. Are you stealing something or has something been stolen from you? What is your spiritual, emotional or physical poverty or hunger? In what area (spiritual, emotional or physical) are you coveting what is not rightfully yours? Where do you feel that you are winning or losing in life?

Steam: This may indicate that more power needs to be put into a project. It could also relate to 'getting steamed-up'; 'letting-off steam.'

Steel: This is something unbending; firm; strengthened; tough; harden; fortified. Think of the play on the word steel/steal: This implies taking something for nothing; taking credit for something that you have not achieved.

Step-mother: This implies a destructive antagonist; an impostor; self-indulgence; vanity; cruelty; jealousy; lust; avarice; pride. (See Chapter 10 – Dream Characters)

Stockings: (See Footwear)

Stomach: A place that feels emotions – joy or fear. 'I can't stomach it'= no liking for it; 'His god is his belly' = gluttony; 'my gut feeling is...' = intuition; 'No guts' = cowardice; 'it takes guts' = courage.

Stone: This is an archetypical symbol. It is a symbol of permanence; stability; set ways; that which is unchanging and unchangeable; truth; law. 'Written in stone' = eternal; 'stonewalling' = being obstructive. (See also Rock/s)

Stork: A symbol of new birth. (See also Baby, and Birds in Chapter 12)

Storm: This usually suggests that you are going through sudden and unpleasant changes in your life. It indicates that there is an emotional upheaval on the horizon. If you are uncertain about doing something, don't do anything until you are sure. Consider where you took shelter and whether the storm passed quickly? Think about how you will weather the storms in your life.

Submarine: Vehicles symbolize the way that we travel on our journey through life. A submarine is a vessel that travels concealed by water. As water represent our collective unconscious this may relate to connecting with the depths of your being, bringing you to your destiny in life. You may never understand the dream, but be assured that it probably means you are growing to fulfilment. (See: Water)

Subway: As this is an underground passage it symbolises travel through your subliminal mind, in particular that which you want to bury. Reflect on other elements of your dream, in particular your mode of transport and what you encounter or observe in the subway. (See also under: Vehicles)

Sun: This is an archetypical symbol. The sun is a ball of fire, sustaining all life on Earth. It suggests that you are being sustained and invigorated. It may also represent a spiritual power or the light of God. Sunrise may indicate new beginnings or a new wave of energy, whilst sunsets suggest completion and closure. Light signifies consciousness; awareness; inspiration; enlightenment. Being a sphere, it is a symbol for unity; fullness; creativity; wholeness. (See: Sphere and Fire)

Super-Man: This is an archetypical symbol of human perfection. There is in all cultures a desire for the supreme pattern of human perfection, embodying the divine attributes of truth; power; wholeness; justice; love. The saviour of all, Jesus Christ both human and divine is the one true perfect human being.

Swan: A symbol of grace and beauty. 'Swan song' from the myth that swans sing sweetly as they die.

Swimming: Reflect on where you are swimming: in the ocean of memories; in the turbulent sea of emotions; in the pool of resources in a mountain stream or in the tranquillity of a pond. Or perhaps it is a race inwhich you are competing. Are you winning, struggling, out of your depth or in danger of drowning? Think also of related sayings: 'it's going swimmingly'; 'drown your sorrows'; 'keeping your head above water.'

Swimsuit: In a recreational mood (see Clothes)

Sword: A double-edged weapon of attack. Dividing truth from error; right from wrong; power used both constructively and destructively.[232] It symbolizes the Word of God.[233] Think also of 'sword of justice'; 'those who live by the sword, die by the sword'.

Synagogue: Place of worship (See Church)

---

232 Hebrews 4:12
233 Ephesians 6:17

⊱ T ⊰

Tavern: (see Pub)

Teacher: Is there something you need to study or learn? You or someone else may need to be taught a lesson.

Teeth: Teeth usually symbolize power; control; determination; wisdom; maturity. Think of some sayings: 'fight tooth and nail'; 'get your teeth into it'; 'kick him in the teeth'; 'long in the tooth'; 'sweet tooth'; 'tooth hunger'; 'set your teeth on edge'; 'by the skin of your teeth'; 'showing one's teeth'; 'eating with long teeth' = distaste for the food.

Telephone: This symbolises communication or the need to communicate. The ringing of a telephone may be calling you to attention.

Television: Communicating by sight and sound, implying a fuller use of the senses. It may be saying to you: 'Do you get the picture?'

Temper: Could this be a warning to control your temper?

Tempest: (See Storm)

Temple: Place of worship (See Church)

Theatre: Just as dreams are acted out in the theatre of the soul, so all of life is a performance. To quote Shakespeare 'All the world's a stage, and all the men and women merely players.' This dream may indicate that you are putting on pretences; exaggerating; dramatising; being pretentious/false; wearing a mask; shewing false modesty or bravado; not taking life or a particular situation seriously.

Therapist: (see Counsellor)

Thief: (See Robber)

Thorns: Protective barbs growing on the stems of plants may point to some thorny issue in your life; a prickly situation; hurtful remark, or irritating habit. A crown of thorns was placed on Jesus' head at his pre-crucifixion trial. Think of: 'a thorn in the flesh.'

Thumb: Being a vital digit on the hand for grasping or picking up things, it relates to control. Think of various related sayings: 'I'm all thumbs'; 'thumbs up'; 'thumb a lift'; 'rule of thumb'; 'he's got me under his thumb'; 'a thumb-nail sketch'; 'a thumb-suck' = guess.

Thunder: Associated with storms. The thunder clap follows a flash of lightning. It may be a warning of coming trouble. Think of the saying 'to steal one's thunder' = pre-empting someone else's special effort or catchphrase. Thunder may also be interpreted as the awesome voice of God.[234]

Tiger: Cats symbolise femininity, this large cat may represent exaggerated feminine traits or cat-like qualities. Reflect on your feline nature, or the characteristics of a tiger in you. (See also Lion and Chapter 12 – Animal Life)

Toad: A symbol of inspiration.

Tombstone: It may be important to take note of whose tombstone it is, and interesting to see how it is inscribed. It can be an enlightening and enriching spiritual exercise to compose what you would like to see inscribed on your tombstone. This dream may be suggesting you reflect on how you would like to be remembered.

Tongue: The tongue is used in speech, for tasting, to manoeuvre food for chewing and directing it towards the gullet. Mostly we associate the tongue with speech. In the Bible, James Chapter 3 describes many ways the tongue is used to enrich and devastate. Reflect on how your tongue has been used recently. Some suggestions from James 3 (expanded) are to: teach; direct; guide; gossip; accuse; humiliate; lie; swear; curse; encourage; affirm; praise; pray...

Tools: Always related to work or hobbies, this may be encouraging you to complete the present project or to get on with the job in hand. The type of tool can give you an indication of what it is suggesting needs fixing or doing.

Tornado: (See Storm)

Tortoise: A symbol of instinctive withdrawal and introversion: reflective; longevity; eternal life; resilience; slow; thorough; leisurely; easy-going; restful; tranquil.

Tower: As it rises above all other structures it relates to the supra-conscious. What type of tower is it? The aim for

---
234 Exodus 20:18-20, 2 Samuel 22:14, John 12:28-29

building the Tower of Babel was to reach up to heaven. Church towers point heavenwards. Reflect: are you trying to reach God through your own efforts/ or is your life pointing others towards God? What is your dream tower telling you? Think of: 'you are a tower of strength'; 'living in an ivory tower.'

Toys: These are miniature imitations of the real thing. Reflect on what toys represent for you: playthings; immaturity;avoiding reality; evading serious issues; pastime; idling away time.

Tragedy: (see Disaster)

Train/Bus Station: This could symbolise anticipation of change or a new venture.

Train: All modes of transport symbolise our journey in life. A train runs on rails, so its course is set. Powered by steam or electricity indicates Holy Spirit power. Once on you cannot stop when or where you choose, so there is neither alighting nor deviating from the set route. It may be a warning to keep on track or not to be side-tracked; follow your train of thought. If you normally travel to work by train every day, it would be better to reflect on other details of the dream. Freud believed that a train is a phallic symbol and that a train going into a tunnel relates to sexual intercourse.

Tramcar: As train but slower, smaller and involving less people on the journey.

Travel: There are many modes of travel – by car; train; bus; bicycle; boat; ship; plane and more. Take note of the type vehicle; the starting point and desired destination; who is in control; the surface on which you are travelling and possibly the weather conditions for greater clarity. (See Vehicles – Chapter 11 and Four Basic Elements – Chapter 12)

Treasure Chest: To find or open a treasure chest indicates that you are in the process of discovering hidden talents or spiritual gifts.

Tree: This is an archetypical symbol. From earliest times trees have been associated with encapsulating all of nature. "Tree of life'; 'tree of knowledge' or people are also likened to trees: 'He shall be like a tree'.[235] In what ways are you like

---
[235] Psalm 1

a tree and to what kind of tree would you liken yourself. Is this the tree in your dream? Is it a healthy tree in need of pruning or feeding? fruitful or barren? The cross on which Jesus was crucified was often referred to as 'a tree'; a gallows is also referred to as 'the tree' or 'the fatal tree.' Think also of the sayings: 'Can't see the wood for the trees'; 'up a gum-tree'; 'barking up the wrong tree'; 'great oaks from little acorns…'; 'out on a limb'; 'the tree is known by it's fruit'; 'family-tree.' A fallen or uprooted tree may indicate that you are going through a period of being uprooted or unsettled. Roots symbolise foundations or ancestry. Branches may indicate expansion; growth; branching-out in life. Blossom relates to being in full bloom; blooming; flourishing. Fruit symbolises a period of fruitfulness. Leaves indicate healthy growth. Autumn leaves symbolise a colourful outlook on life.

Triangle: A three-sided figure with three angles (See Three in Chapter 9 – Numbers in Dreams. See also Pyramid)

Troll: Distorted facts; warped thinking; perversions undermining…

Trousers: These are usually associated with men to cover the lower body and legs. Short trousers indicate immaturity, long trousers maturity. Reflect on the style, colour and any other significant detail and why in particular this seemed a significant detail in your dream. (See also Clothes)

Truck: carrying a heavy load; weighty undertaking; associated with work. Pick-up truck – energy needed in the project. Refuse truck – get rid of the garbage in your life.

Tunnel: These usually pass through hills and mountains. Are there any mountainous obstacles in your path of progress? Note the mood and your feelings in the dream. Is the tunnel dark and frightening? Does there appear to be no way out or do you see light at the end of the tunnel? Depending on the context, it may indicate transition to a new level of understanding or a different venture. Freud thought that any tunnel-like object represented the vagina. What does the tunnel represent to you? Think also of 'tunnel vision.'

Turkey: A symbol of insolence. It is also usually associated with Christmas.

Turtle-dove: A symbol of marital fidelity.

Turtle: Living both on land and in the water, the turtle reveals spiritual and worldly facets to the interpretation of this symbol. Having a hard shell, it indicates resilience. With the head in, it indicates withdrawal.

ಬು U ೞ

Umbrella: This is a protective barrier from rain or the heat of the sun. It may symbolise our unwillingness to deal with adversity in life. If the umbrella is closed it could indicate a measure of caution on your part in facing difficulties. Is your umbrella keeping rain or sun off you? (See Sun or Rain, and Chapter 12 – The Four Basic Elements)

Underground: One of earth's four basic elements, ground is related to the subliminal area – below the threshold of consciousness of the psyche or mind. (See Earth in Chapter 12 – The Four Basic Elements)

Underwear: This relate to things that are close to us and personal. It may relate to secret thoughts, undisclosed prejudices, attitudes, private ideas, personal habits.

Unicorn: A mythological animal. It is pure white with a single horn, the face and feet of a goat, the body of a horse and the tail of a lion. It is a symbol of chastity; single-mindedness; spiritual purity; blessings; gentleness; peace; goodness.

Uniform: Take note of what type of uniform it is and the occupation of the person who usually wears it. How do you identify with that occupation and what does it convey to you about your role in life? Perhaps your uniqueness is being ignored as you function as a member of a group rather than as an individual.

University: (see School)

Urinating: To dream of the release of any bodily wastes may indicate the need to let go of some bottled-up emotion, like anger, resentment, jealousy…etc. Or maybe you simply need to wake up and go to the lavarory.

༄ V ༅

Vagina: (See Genitals)

Vase: A vase is usually made of glass, pottery, china and clay. All are earth symbols. God created 'man' from the dust of the earth and breathed life into him.[236] In God's hands we are compared to clay in the Potter's hands.[237] The vase may represent you! Reflect on the vase, where it is placed, whether treasured or not, and what it is being used for. Is it filled with flowers? and what do they represent to you? For the flowers to remain fresh, the vase needs to be topped-up with water. (See the symbolism of Earth, Water and Flowers) Perhaps the vase has some other symbolic significance for you. With what do you associate it?

Vegetables: To interpret the meaning of vegetables in your dream depends on how you feel about that specific vegetable in your diet. Do you enjoy it, turn-up your nose at it or eat it simply for its nutritional value? What is this dream telling you about the physical, psychological, emotional or spiritual needs and preferences required to nurture your body, mind or spirit? Note also if it is a root or tuber (underground), flower (blooming), fruit or seed (fruitfulness) or leaf (healthy growth) vegetable.

Violence: A dream with violence in it may possibly imply that you are harbouring emotions of anger. The dream may be a way of releasing the feelings that you cannot or will not express in waking life.

Violet: For the colour, see Colours in Chapter 8, for the flower, see Chapter 11 – The Great Outdoors.

Violin: This, together with all stringed instruments, relates to rapid vibrations and may indicate spiritual sensitivity. Alternatively it could imply avoidance of responsibility: Nero fiddled while Rome burned. Think of 'fiddling-about.'

Virgin: A symbol of purity; virtue; goodness.

Volcano: Molten rock and fire spew out of the earth in

---

236 Genesis 2:7
237 Jeremiah 18:5 Romans 9:20-21

volcanic eruptions. In dreams this usually indicates the release of bottled-up emotions. Reflect on your feelings and what needs to be brought into the open.

Vomit: This possibly indicates the need for a purging of the soul. Something swallowed needs to be got rid of. Think of: 'You make me sick.'

Vulture: A carrion-crow, feeding on dead flesh. A predator, scavanger and symbol of greed, preying on others.

ಐ W ಲ

Walking: This possibly relates to your walk in life. Is it easy or hard? are you carrying burdens or walking with a spring in your step? Is it with determination, with purpose or in a relaxed or casual manner? Do you know where you are going? or simply enjoying whatever you encounter along the way? Are you seeking direction? What is the surface under your feet? Is it rough or smooth, easy or hard going? Going up-hill or down? How steep is it? What is my mood? Am I eager or reluctant, enjoying it or anxious?

Wall: (See Fence)

Wallet: (See Money)

War: Dreaming about a battle may indicate inner conflict. Your emotions may be doing battle with your will, or your reason with your instinct. If you have been through a war the dream may be based on memory of the trauma you experienced. You will then need to seek counselling and emotional healing. (See Chapter 13 – Emotional Healing through Meditation and Lucid Dreams)

Washing: This signifies that you are in the process of inner cleansing, or need to clean up something in your life. Think also of various related sayings: 'I washed my hands of him'; 'don't wash your dirty linen in public'; 'I feel washed out'; 'it was a washout'; 'it will all come out in the wash'; 'it just won't wash with me.'

Water: One of earth's four basic elements; it is associated with our primeval life – from creation through to life in the womb. This is an archetypical symbol. (See Water in Chapter 12 – The Four Basic Elements)

Waves: Waves disturb the natural tranquility of water. The turblence brings to the surface what is in the lower depths. Moving water and crashing waves could represent the ebb and flow of the collective unconscious mind. Tidal waves or tsunamis suggest emotional upheaval. Issues stored in the unconscious may be coming to the surface causing confusion and affecting moods which you do not understand. If this is not the case, and you are in a tranquil frame of mind, the saline seawater of your dream waves may be gently washing through your unconscious with the therapeutic flow, like profoundly mystifying healing tears.

Weasel: Lacking commitment; not dependable; shirking responsibility; deceptive; avoids obligations; shrewd.

Web: A spider weaves a web to trap insects to devour. The web symbolises the weaving of a scheme in order to trap something or someone. It indicates traps, snares; pitfalls. It may also relate to the web of a dream-catcher and relate to your practice of analysing your dreams. Think also of the sayings: 'Web of intrigue'; 'oh what a tangled web we weave, when first we practice to deceive.'

Wedding: This is an archetypical symbol. It represents unity; harmony; the coming together of opposites to bring about balance; completion; fulfilment. If you dream that you are getting married it is a symbol of the integration of the masculine and feminine traits within your being. It may signify the balancing of intellect and emotions; logic and instinct; sensing and perceiving. If you are a wedding guest, it has the same symbolism but in a less dynamic and immediate sense. For those who are planning a wedding it may be related to your waking preoccupation and therefore a Common Dream. (See also Marriage)

Weeds: These are symbols that represent neglect. They are unwanted growth that has the potential for choking or inhibiting healthy growth. It could suggest that you have not been tending to your physical, psychological or spiritual needs. There may be a need to identify those things that are preventing you from realising your full potential and eliminating them. Note the parables of the weeds and wheat[238] and the farmer sowing seeds.[228]

Well: Sunk deep into the earth to draw pure, clear water, the well symbolises depths of thought; going down into the hidden corners of the psyche; of discovering your innermost being; exploration of the collective unconscious of the mind.

---
238 Matthew 13:24-30, 36-43

Think of related terms: 'well-being'; 'well-bred'; 'well-known'; 'leave well enough alone'; 'well-off'; 'well-balanced'; 'wishing-well.'

Whale: These are large water dwelling mammals. Water represents the subliminal area of the psyche. They are generally thought to be docile. In our dream they may represent our passive movement between the conscious and the subliminal depths of our being. (See Chapter 12 – Animal Life & The Four Basic Elements)

Wheat: A symbol of fertility, prosperity and abundance.

Whirlwind: (See Storm)

Whistle: A whistle is blown to call attention to something or as a signal to stop. We whistle to express happiness or admiration. Think of some related sayings: 'Whistle while you work'; 'whistle in the dark'; 'if you want me, just whistle'; 'wet your whistle.'

White: (See Colours in Chapter 8)

Widow: This may mean that your feelings are lacking wisdom and logic – your heart is ruling your head.

Widower: This may indicate that your thinking is lacking sensitivity, love and tenderness.

Wife: The feminine side of our nature relating to our heart; soul; emotions; feelings; intuition; sensing; instinct. It can also relate to our receptive; creative; nurturing; gentle; caring; supportive; submissive; communicative side. Review your relationship with your spouse. (See Woman)

Wilderness: (See Desert)

Wind: Wind is turbulent air. It related to the supra-conscious area of the mind that is in tune with the infinite or the omnipotent and omniscient God. Reflect on the force of the wind, whether it is a gentle breeze or a raging hurricane – either could be a symbol of the Holy Spirit.[239] (See also Breath, and Air in Chapter 12 – The Four Basic Elements)

Window: (See under House)

Wings: Wings are associated with flying and freedom from physical restraints. Dreaming about wings suggests that you

---
[239] John 3:6-8 Acts 2:2-4

may have a desire to be freer or rise to new heights physically, emotionally, psychologically or spiritually. (See Birds, and Air in Chapter 12 – Animal Life and The Four Basic Elements. See also Flying)

Witch: This is an archetypical symbol. It symbolises someone who is mean and heartless. She is a menacing person appearing in fairy tales and perhaps in the theatre of your dreams. A white witch could also represent supernatural power, enchantment and goodness. It describes something sinister; 'witch's brew' – a hotchpotch of ideas; or confusion – 'which' way to go? Witchdoctor – 'which' doctor should I see? Witch-hunt – search for the antagonist. Reflect on your current situation. Could it be revealing negative characteristics? or perhaps, about solving your problems or using shortcuts to get what you want out of life?

Wizard: He may symbolise a tendency in the lower self to be attracted to false ideas or taking the easy way out.

Wolf: In western culture this is an archetypical symbol of cruelty; ferocity; hostility; aggression; sneakiness; gluttony; avarice; covetousness; insatiable appetite; voracious, sexual aggression.

Woman: If she is unknown to you it would relate to the feminine side of your nature, even if you are a man. This is the feeling, sensing, sensitive, emotional, gentle, compassionate, affectionate, sympathetic, submissive, spiritual, passive, receptive, creative, inspirational, intuitive side of our being. Reflect on what she is doing or saying in order to interpret this dream for yourself. (See Man for the masculine side of all of us)

Wooden structures: These are associated with the higher identity. Wood comes from trees which are or once were living, growing and fruitful; therefore wood, grass, bamboo or thatch structures are organic and hold more energy than a stone structure.

Woods: (See Forest)

Working clothes: This indicates that you are ready for

action (see Clothes)

Worm: A symbol of self-abasement. (See Insects in Chapter 12 – Animal Life)

Writing: This is a means of communication. It may indicate your desire to make an announcement or send a message to others; it could point out the need to be in touch with yourself – your innermost being; or it may signify a message for your enlightenment or warning – 'The writing on the wall'

ℰ X ℬ

X-Ray: Unless you have recently been or will be getting x-rayed it probably has nothing to do with your health. If you dream of being x-rayed or are looking at an x-ray negative it suggests that you should look beneath the surface of your present condition, situation, issues or problem facing you right now, especially the negative issues.

ℰ Y ℬ

Yacht: A sailboat is propelled by the wind, which is an image of the Holy Spirit.[240] It indicates a spirit-controlled and directed journey into spiritual matters or to explore the unconscious; God is therefore the driving force.

Yellow: (See Chapter 8 – Colours in Dreams)

Young Boy: This could indicate that your actions or thought processes concerning logic, intellect or reasoning tend to be immature. Alternatively, a new, fresh approach or flexibility.

Young Girl: This may indicate that you are being emotionally immature, over sensitive or sentimental.

Young Man: He could represent strength; bravery; fearlessness; or being open to some challenges that are facing you.

Young Woman: She may represent feelings of love, sentimentality, freshness, strong emotions or tender feelings.

ℰ Z ℬ

Zebra: Black/white; diversity; mixed emotions; mixed feelings; indecisive; non-committal; evasive; ambiguous; vague; elusive.

Zero: Generally a zero has the same meaning as a circle. The circle is a symbol of eternity; infinity; wholeness; completeness and the life cycle. It may indicate a greater degree of spiritual awareness. (See: Circle and Chapter 9 – Numbers in Dreams)

---

240 Genesis 1:2; John 3:8; Acts 2:1-4

*The day thou gavest, Lord, is ended,
The darkness falls at thy behest;
To thee our morning hymns ascended,
Thy praise shall sanctify our rest.*

John Ellerton (1826-1893)

Dream Worksheet #1 – The Dream

Sketch of the Dream:

Dream Content: (Relate the Story) _____

_____

_____

_____

_____

Dream Setting & Atmosphere: _____

_____

_____

Dream People: Who/what they Symbolise: _____

_____

_____

Dream Objects: Symbols: _____

_____

_____

Any Other Details: (e.g. Numbers, colours)_____

_____

_____

Emotions in the Dream: _____

Feeling on Waking: _____

_____

Context: (Events or Dominant Thoughts of the Previous Day/s)

_____

_____

_____

What type of dream is this? _____

What is it telling me about myself/what I need to do?

_____

Dream Title: _____

Date: _____

Dream Worksheet #2 – Action Dream

What was the first thing that came to mind on waking?

_____

_____

Atmosphere: _____

_____

Emotions: _____

_____

_____

_____

Actions _____

_____

_____

Speech _____

_____

Objects _____

_____

Colours _____

Numbers _____

_____

How does all this relate to the previous day, past week or significant events in my life? _____

_____

What is the dream Telling Me? _____

_____

What Type of Dream is it? _____

Dream Title: _____

Date: _____

Dream Worksheet #3 – Remembered Fragments

What was the first thing that came to mind on waking?

_____

_____

What fragments of my dream do I remember?

_____

_____

_____

_____

_____

Draw the dream fragments or symbols:

Expand on or link the fragments to get the whole story:

_____

_____

_____

_____

What in the dream is related to the previous day, week or event in my life:

_____

_____

_____

_____

_____

_____

What Type of Dream is it? _____

Dream Title: _____

Date: _____

Dream Worksheet # 4 – Interview with My Dream

What did I feel when I awoke from the dream? _____

What is the mood of this dream? _____

What was my prevailing emotion in the dream? _____

_____

Who are the Characters in the Dream?

_____

_____

_____

What are these Characters Doing? _____

_____

_____

What personality facet does each characters display?

_____

_____

What are the emotions of the various characters in the dream?

_____

What are the characters personalities, attitudes & actions telling me about myself?
_____
_____

What symbols are important in this dream?
_____
_____

Where are the warnings in this dream?
_____
_____

Is there a helping or a hindering force in the dream?
_____
_____

How am I being encouraged through this dream?
_____
_____

How am I being challenged through this dream?
_____
_____

Who or what is the adversary in this dream?
_____
_____

If so, where is it coming from ?_____

What or who is being harmed? _____
_____

Who or what is being helped or healed? _____

_____

_____

What am I avoiding or what would I like to evade?

_____

_____

What actions are being carried out and by whom?

_____

_____

What relation does this dream have to recent events or concerns I have had lately?

_____

_____

Does this dream clarify events in my waking life?

_____

_____

Is this dream telling me that there is something I need to deal with in my life?

_____

_____

Is this dream giving me some guidance in how to deal with those concerns?
_____

_____

What choices should I make as a result of working with this dream?
_____

_____

_____

_____

_____

_____

What Type of Dream is it? _____

Dream Title: _____

Date_____

Bibliography:

Bishop, Jim, *The Day Christ Died*, New Youk 1965

Boushahla, Jo Jean & Reidel-Geubtner, Virginia, *The Dream Dictionary*, New York 1983

Bradner, John, *Symbols of Church Seasons and Days*, London 1977

Brewer's Dictionary of Phrase and Fable, London 1995

de Mello, Anthony (S.J.) *Wellsprings*, Gujarat 1996

Epp, Theodore H., *Portraits of Christ in the Tabernacle*, Nebrasca 1976

Foster, Richard, *Celebration of Discipline*, London 1989

Freud, Sigmund, (Translation by A.A. Brill), *The Interpretation of Dreams*, Hertfordshire 1997

Larousse, *Dictionary of Science and Technology*, Edinburgh 1995

Payne, F.C. *Seal of God*, Australia 1980

Roget's Thesaurus of English Words and Phrases, London 2000

Seamands, David, *Healing for Damaged Emotions*, Wheaton 1987

Shorter Oxford English Dictionary, London 1964

Slemming, C.W. *These are the Garments - The High Priest's Garments*, Pennsylvania 1974

Smith, William George, *The Oxford Dictionary of English Proverbs*, Oxford 1970

Stapleton, Ruth Carter, *The Gift of Inner Healing*, Waco, Texas 1977

Tapscott, Betty, *Inner Healing Through Healing of Memories*, Taxas 1982

The Bible – New International Version, Cape Town 1985

The Bible – New Revised Standard Version, Iowa 1990

The Interpreter's Bible, Nashville 1989

Whittemore, Carroll E. & Duncan, William, *Symbols of the Church*, Nashville 1981

Internet Sources:

Britannica Online Encyclopaedia
Gray, Henry, *Anatomy of the Human Body*, 1918
Spirit Community, *The Dream Dictionary*
Wald, August H. (PhD), *The Dream Dictionary*